Zénó Vernyik and Sándor Klapcsik (Eds.)

Brutal Aspects of Migratory Esthetics
Migration and Violence in Modern and Contemporary Culture

Zénó Vernyik and Sándor Klapcsik (eds.)

BRUTAL ASPECTS OF MIGRATORY ESTHETICS

Migration and Violence in Modern and
Contemporary Culture

Bibliografische Information der Deutschen Nationalbibliothek

Die Deutsche Nationalbibliothek verzeichnet diese Publikation in der Deutschen Nationalbibliografie; detaillierte bibliografische Daten sind im Internet über http://dnb.d-nb.de abrufbar.

Bibliographic information published by the Deutsche Nationalbibliothek

The Deutsche Nationalbibliothek lists this publication in the Deutsche Nationalbibliografie; detailed bibliographic data are available on the Internet at http://dnb.d-nb.de.

Cover Picture taken by Zénó Vernyik on August 6, 2020 on the island of Vir in Croatia.

ISBN (Print): 978-3-8382-1731-4
ISBN (E-Book [PDF]): 978-3-8382-7731-8
© *ibidem*-Verlag, Hannover • Stuttgart 2025

Alle Rechte vorbehalten

Leuschnerstraße 40
30457 Hannover
info@ibidem.eu

Das Werk einschließlich aller seiner Teile ist urheberrechtlich geschützt. Jede Verwertung außerhalb der engen Grenzen des Urheberrechtsgesetzes ist ohne Zustimmung des Verlages unzulässig und strafbar. Dies gilt insbesondere für Vervielfältigungen, Übersetzungen, Mikroverfilmungen und elektronische Speicherformen sowie die Einspeicherung und Verarbeitung in elektronischen Systemen.

All rights reserved. No part of this publication may be reproduced, stored in or introduced into a retrieval system, or transmitted, in any form, or by any means (electronic, mechanical, photocopying, recording or otherwise) without the prior written permission of the publisher. Any person who commits any unauthorized act in relation to this publication may be liable to criminal prosecution and civil claims for damages.

Printed in the EU

Table of Contents

Acknowledgments 9

Introduction: Deep Structural Reasons behind Migratory Violence through the Medium of Cultural Representations
(Sándor Klapcsik and Zénó Vernyik) 13

PART I: The Violence of Walls and Borders

Brutal Borders: *Walls* Preventing *Human Flow*
(Ana Belén Martínez García) 41
    Introduction: Migrations, Violence, Auto/Biographical Documentary 41
    The Visual Impact of *Walls* 45
    Pervasive Movement in *Human Flow* 48
    Conclusion 51

Reversing the Logic of the Border: Violence and Migration in Contemporary Hispanic Dramatic Literature
(Irene Alcubilla Troughton) 57
    Narratives of the Immigrant 57
    Conceptualizing Strangers 59
    Tolerance and Hospitality 60
    The Reverse Logic on the Border 63
    Autonomy and Vulnerability 66
    Fictive Pacts and the Failure of Language 69
    Spectator as Third-Party 72
    Conclusion 75

PART II: Violence in the Lives of Immigrants

Children of *Brexit*: Violence Against Immigrants as Nativist Practice in *Night of the Party* and *We Come Apart*
(Cornel Borit) 81
    Nativism, Populism, and Violence 85
    On the "Playground" of *Brexit*: Exploring the Path of Violence from Culture to Practice in *Night of the Party* and *We Come Apart* 90
    Final Considerations and Conclusion 104

Indefinite Detention in Britain: A Literary and Philosophical Understanding of Detainee Lives in the Twenty-First Century
(Rebecca Deluce) 111
    Introduction: The Media Image of Migration vs the Emerging Genre of Refugee Literature 111
    Sovereignty, Power, and the Precarity of the Other in a State of Exception 114
    Literature of/in Detention Camps 118
    Conclusion: Literature as Phonopolitics 130

The Representation of the Immigrant Population in Leïla Slimani's *Chanson Douce*: A Sociological Perspective
(Vedran Ćatović) 135
    Introduction 135
    Representation of Migrants in the Novel 136
    Chanson douce in a Contemporary Context 140
    Migration and Different Models of Integration 142
    The Case of France: The French Model of Assimilation 145
    Conclusion 151

Turkish for Advanced: Domestic and Ethnically Motivated Violence in Turkish-German Cinema
(Sándor Klapcsik and Zénó Vernyik) 155
    Introduction 155
    The Conventions of Art Cinema 159
    Romantic Comedies 166
    Gangster Films 171
    Conclusion 174

Active Submission as a Form of Defense against Gender-Based Violence: Threats for Women Migrants in Amy Bloom's *Away*
(Michaela Weiss) 181
    Introducing the Concept of Active Submission 181
    The Psychological Abuse of an Immigrant Woman 184
    Scars of Physical Violence 187
    Abuse on the Move: Handling the Female (Im)migrant 191
    Surviving the Wilderness 195
    Concluding Remarks 199

PART III: Migration and Terrorism

Terrorism and Transnational Identity: Islamic State Recruiting among Second-Generation Migrants and Kamila Shamsie's *Home Fire*
(Cassandra Falke) 205
    Introduction: Cross-cultural Experience as a Catalyst for Recruiting 205
    Terrorism and Second-Generation Immigrants 209
    Constructing a Homeland 212
    National Identity and Terrorist Recruiting in *Home Fire* 218
    Conclusion 225

Terrorism as Communication in Arthur Koestler's *Thieves in the Night*
(Zénó Vernyik and Sándor Klapcsik) 231
    Introduction: Koestler's Novel on the Terrorist's Journey ... 231
    Beating Around the Bush: Reasons to Avoid Discussing the Terrorist Motif 233
    Controversial Then, Controversial Now: The Critical Reception 238
    Terrorism as a Means of Communication 254
    From Pacifist Youth to Terrorist Adult: *Thieves in the Night* as a *Bildungsroman* 257
    Addendum: Reading Koestler's *Thieves in the Night* Following October 7, 2023 260

Contributors 269

Acknowledgments

This volume could not have been made without the generous support of several agencies, institutions, as well as individuals. This applies both to the whole collection and the various events that have led to its creation, but also to some of the specific contributions.

The international multidisciplinary conference, Interpreting Migration, held in Liberec between April 28 and April 30, 2017, where the idea of a follow-up volume emerged, was held with the generous support of the Czech-Norwegian Research Program of the Norway Grants, as a part of the project CZ09 7F16020, Migration: Sociopsychological and Cultural Factors. This book, at the same time, is not a publication of conference proceedings, nor is it a planned output of that original project. In fact, only a fraction of the papers presented at that conference has found its way into the present volume: Cassandra Falke's chapter on terrorism and transnational identity, Zénó Vernyik's and Sándor Klapcsik's contribution on terrorism as a form of communication, and Vedran Ćatović's text on the representation of immigrants.

Yet, the former two chapters are hardly the original conference contributions, since they have both been significantly reworked during the numerous workshops held in Liberec and Tromsø in the period between August 2019 and August 2022. The second contribution of the authorial team of Sándor Klapcsik and Zénó Vernyik, the chapter on domestic and ethnically motivated violence in Turkish-German cinema, emerged and organically developed during this four-year cooperation of the Borders and Migration Research Group of the Technical University of Liberec and the Border Poetics/Border Culture Research Group of the University of Tromsø, the Arctic University of Norway. Cornel Borit's chapter on violence against immigrants as a form of nativist practice is also a result of this fruitful cooperation. While the first contact with the Tromsø group was established in early 2017, with the help of the already mentioned project, CZ09 7F16020, Migration: Sociopsychological and Cultural Factors, what made the later, much more intense and long-term work possible were two projects sponsored by EEA Grants, in the 2014–2021 project period of their Education Program: EHP-CZ-MOP-1-008, Borders and Migration: Approaches and Methods in Research and Teaching, running between August 2019 and August 2021, and EHP-CZ-MOP-2-022, Sites and Channels of Contact Within and Across Borders: Languages, Narratives and Representations, running from August 2020 to August 2022.

The already mentioned chapter on terrorism as a form of communication would have also not been possible to write without Zénó Vernyik's multiple stays in the Center for Research Collections of the University of Edinburgh, sponsored three times by the Mobility Fund of the Technical University of Liberec (in 2012, 2014 and 2018) and once also by a research bursary provided by the European Society for the Study of English (in 2018). Just as crucial was his stay at the University of Kassel in 2015, during which he could discuss his ideas with fellow Koestler-scholar, Matthias Weßel, once again generously funded by the Mobility Fund of the Technical University of Liberec. Last, but certainly not least, his sabbatical in Vienna, between October 2018 and February 2019, which was funded by CZ.02.2.69/0.0/0.0/16_027/0008493, International Mobility of Researchers at the Technical University of Liberec, a project sponsored by the Operational Program Research, Development and Education, itself funded by European Structural and Investment Funds under the administration of the Ministry of Education, Youth and Sport of the Czech Republic.

Likewise, Sándor Klapcsik's research on the representation of migration and minorities, showcased in this volume in the introductory essay, as well as in the two other chapters Klapcsik has co-authored, has been strongly influenced by two research stays, both at the University of Łódź. The first one of them, held between October 2017 and February 2018, was funded by a Czech-Polish Bilateral Scholarship administered by the Academic Information Agency of the Czech National Agency for International Education and Research. The second one, in March and April 2024, by a faculty mobility sponsored by the Central European Exchange Program for University Studies.

Other contributors have also received funding for the research that has led to their chapters in the present volume. Cornel Borit would like to acknowledge the support of the Marie Skłodowska-Curie (MSC) project ITN-EJD-MOVES—Migration and Modernity: Historical and Cultural Challenges under grant agreement No 812764. Michaela Weiss's contribution is a result of the project SGS/10/2022, Silesian University in Opava internal grant Text from Current Linguistic and Literary Perspectives.

Further, the editors of the volume would like to express their gratitude to the Publication Fund of the Faculty of Science, Humanities and Education of the Technical University of Liberec, which helped cover the costs of proofreading and manuscript preparation.

As far as individuals are concerned, our heartfelt thanks go to deans Jan Picek and Aleš Suchomel and vice-dean Martin Plešinger of the Faculty of Science, Humanities and Education of the Technical University of Liberec, as well as to vice-head and timetable guru of the English Department, Petra Peldová, at the same institution, for their support and for their flexibility and willingness to accommodate our needs in terms of sabbaticals, research stays and research-compatible timetables. Nandi Weder, our competent, fast, yet meticulous proofreader and copy editor has contributed immensely to the volume by not merely correcting our mistakes, but also making the final text easier to read. Finally, but most crucially, we are grateful to our editors, Jakob Horstmann and Jana Dävers at ibidem for their belief in this project and their patience during the long years it took us to finalize the manuscript.

Introduction: Deep Structural Reasons behind Migratory Violence through the Medium of Cultural Representations

Sándor Klapcsik and Zénó Vernyik

Migration is a phenomenon older than civilization itself, and it has had many fundamental effects on human society and economy. It has eventually led to the formation of multiculturalism in the 20th century, a social phenomenon which has been hailed, or at least meticulously discussed, by postmodern cultural studies (Hall 2001; McNeil, Meerzon, and Dean 2020, 1–2), whilst it has been, often intentionally, misinterpreted and strongly criticized by nationalist political discourses. Despite certain beneficial outcomes, migration is rarely discussed in scholarly and journalistic forums as a solely, or even primarily, problem-free social phenomenon; historically, after all, it has been connected to transatlantic slavery, colonialism, forced displacement, pogroms, xenophobia, anti-immigration laws, genocide, racism and eugenics.

At least since the Second World War and the subsequent Cold War, refugees as well as those migrating for better work and study opportunities, or a more democratic life have been making headline news. Especially recent events such as the ongoing Syrian Civil War, the 2015 European Refugee Crisis, Brexit, the 2021–2022 Belarus–EU Border Crisis, the Russian–Ukrainian War and the 2023 events of the Israeli–Palestinian conflict, alongside the increasingly dramatic threat of Global Warming, turn migration into one of the most topical, and frequently the most violent, issues of the present day. As van Heuckelom says, "if the European constellation can become a hospitable 'home' for some people, it may be equally perceived as an inaccessible 'fortress' that should keep its doors and gates shut for unwanted intruders" (2014, 73-74). Racism and ethnic violence, which form some of the underlying philosophies of

"Fortress Europe" and similarly restrictive policies towards refugees in affluent regimes in North America and Australia (FitzGerald 2019, 160), come to the foreground in the re-emergence of the extreme right and in "the discourse of refugees, immigrants, asylum seekers and the Muslim population of Europe" (Sardar 2008, xix). Thus, refugees, border walls, terrorism, the integration of cultural minorities, as well as violence within and across ethnic and religious groups are hot topics of journalism, political debates, as well as national elections and referenda.

Ethnographic, political, criminological and anthropologic research keeps close track of the violent events of migration in the 21st century. For example, a few recent publications of the enormous contemporary sociological literature on the topic include books that have been published on violence against powerless migrants in Central and South America (Halstead 2018; Speed 2019) or against asylum seekers (Pickering 2010). Scholarly attention has been paid to state violence and criminal behavior in the migration process (Bhatia and Canning, 2021), as well as tensions on the external borders of the EU via the combination of photographic and sociological projects (Domanski and Ferenc 2019). Just as importantly, such current issues provide source material for documentaries, films, television series, novels and plays, and the criticism which discusses these works of art.

The connection between migration and literary works has received increased scholarly attention since the postcolonial turn in literary criticism, that is, the theoretical writings of, for example, Frantz Fanon, Homi Bhabha, Edward Said, and Gayatri Chakravorty Spivak. Fanon's *Black Skin, White Mask* (2008) describes the destructive effects of colonialism on the human psyche through analyses that often focus on migration between "metropolitan France" (10) and his native Martinique. In a similar fashion, Bhabha's paradigm-shaping book, *The Location of Culture* (1994), owes a debt to Bhabha's experiences of "the gathering of people in the diaspora: indentured, migrant, interned" (139). Said observes in his well-known essay, "Reflections on Exile," that those who experience exile live in "the perilous territory of not belonging" (2000,

177), which derives from a sense of homelessness, depression, eccentricity and estrangement, as well as "the loss of something left behind forever"; hence, it is "terrible to experience" (Said 2000, 173).

These and similar arguments have helped critics and the general public to understand racism and ethnic violence in the works of "émigré" and migrant writers such as Mayotte Capécia, Joseph Conrad, Salman Rushdie and Mahmoud Darwish. Since then, several generations of migrant and hyphenated writers have entered the postcolonial and Western canons. Their works often subvert the traditional stereotypes of the marginal East or underprivileged South and the quintessentially normative West or affluent North; for example, Rushdie's "Good Advice is Rarer than Rubies" (1987; reprinted in 1994) describes a seemingly naïve and feeble female character who deliberately sabotages her application at the embassy to migrate to Britain, simply because she prefers her independent life at home to the household of an arranged marriage in England.

The theories and approaches of postcolonialism have also been modified to apply to other situations and cultural products of migration, in various disciplines. For example, they have been utilized in research on post-socialist Eastern Europeans (Owczarzak 2009) or the recent waves of immigrants (De Genova 2016) and refugees (Davies and Isakjee 2019; Bromley 2021) from the Global South to Europe and elsewhere.

As Ponzanesi (2018) observes, at least in comparison to literature, "postcolonial theory has hardly been a defining paradigm in the field of film studies." Here, the turning point in criticism on migrant cinema can be traced back to Hamid Naficy's 2001 book on "accented cinema." Naficy discusses "exilic, diasporic or ethnic" filmmakers who are in a liminal position, as they often need to face an "extraordinary burden of representation," insofar as they "must continually wrestle with the problem of multiple reception communities" (2001, 11, 82, 89). Following this, there have been countless publications on migrant cinema, especially on productions of the last four decades in various countries (see, for example: Bayraktar 2016; Berghahn and Sternberg 2010; Engelen and van Heuckelom

2014; Hake and Mennel 2012; van Heuckelom 2019; Higbee 2013; Trifonova 2022).

Recent film criticism often focuses on productions which describe migration from the Global South to the Global North, or from Eastern Europe, and further East, to "Fortress Europe." Several films display the destructive effects of migration, visualizing the harmful psychological impacts in the process of migration and the following attempted upward mobility. Such films revolve around ethnic violence against the immigrants, "Fortress Europe" (Hackett 2022, 102), human trafficking (Brown, Iordanova, and Torchin 2010), "brain waste" (van Heuckelom 2019, 166)[1] and alienation, bearing a "social realist strain," in addition to "engagement with socioeconomic inequalities and unbalanced power relations in the era of postcolonial and postcommunist globalization" (Engelen and van Heuckelom 2014, x). In some films, following in the tradition of gangster movies (Berghahn 2014) and "banlieue cinema" (Higbee 2013), immigrants react to their hard situation with violence, initiating fistfights and street riots or partaking in organized crime.

Nevertheless, in a way similar to postcolonial literature, many of the films of migrant cinema intend to subvert stereotypes and deconstruct the traditional narratives of migration between the peripherally underprivileged East or old-fashioned South and the affluent West or modern North. They try to find "ways in which notions of East and West... central and marginal, are being rethought and reframed" (Gott and Herzog 2013, 6). Such works refuse to portray diasporas as marginalized and peripheral communities, by showcasing migrants as empowered agents and reversing traditional power dynamics. For example, *Cover Boy* (2006; dir. Carmine Amoroso) describes the homosexual connection between Ioan (Eduard Gabia), a Romanian immigrant and Michele (Luca Lionello), who moved to Rome from Abruzzo (a region associated with the impoverished South). Although initially Michele is in a superior financial and authoritative position, this gradually changes as he is

---

[1] Van Heuckelom defines brain waste as a situation when immigrants "are highly qualified and skilled [but] they will typically end up in low-paid (and typically clandestine) blue-collar employment" (2019, 166).

forced to do menial jobs and pretend to be a foreign immigrant, whilst Ioan becomes the model of an advertising campaign (Bardan and O'Healy 2013).

Documentary filmmaking, since its beginning, has been interested in nomadism and migration. As recent criticism indicates, documentaries form a bridge between areas of anthropological, ethnographic or sociological enquiry and arthouse cinema (Köhn 2016, 11; Demos 2013, 62). One of the earliest examples of documentary filmmaking, *Nanook of the North* (1922), is a good example of this, simultaneously recording and staging the encounters between nomadic native groups of ethnic Inuk people and the "civilized" Canadians. Although it was criticized for staging sequences and thus mixing documentary with docudrama (Aufderheide 2007, 2), the film clearly had an agenda of "warm humanism" to describe "the purity of native cultures" (Aufderheide 2007, 28), in addition to bringing attention to the destructive effects of Western migration to the native lands of Canada. After this, a visible tradition of such filmmaking started, one that is on the borderline between documentary and fiction, racist and empathic, degrading and understanding approaches to migration; it is enough to mention here landmark films of "docufiction," such as *Les maîtres fous*, a 1955 short film directed by Jean Rouch about West African migrant workers in Ghana and his *Moi, un Noir* (1957), a documentary about a week of Nigerian migrant workers living in Ivory Coast (Aufderheide 2007, 111–112). While *Moi, un Noir* occasionally depicts a romanticized and exotic picture of the lives and surroundings of African migrant workers, its emphatically masculine characters react to their hopeless economic situations with aggression, getting into fistfights which lead to the arrest and short prison sentence of one of them.

As Köhn (2016, 4) observes, recent documentary filmmakers use more revolutionary and subversive perspectives, insofar as they "seek for new, transformative forms of visibility that do not merely reproduce the visual discourse of the government or the corporate mass media [...] articulating what has not yet been said and picturing viable alternatives to the status quo." What has not changed is that, in several cases, the distinctions between documentary-style feature films or television dramas, such as Michael Winterbottom's *In this World* (2002), Lukas Moodysson's *Lilya 4-Ever* (2002), Gerardo Olivares' *14 kilómetros / 14 kilometers* or Peter Kosminsky's *Britz* (2007), and documentaries which evoke popular genres like thrillers (*Missing in Brooks County* [2020]) or road movies (*On the Bride's Side* [2014]) become extremely hazy (Bromley 2021, 43, 51; Köhn 2016, 48; Lacey and Paget 2015, 7).[2]

Violence against migrants frequently appears in such documentaries. While its depiction varies, it ranges from highly metaphorical descriptions, for example in *Gravesend* (2007) or *Liquid Traces: The Left-to Die-Boat Case* (2014; see Demos 2013, 25; Köhn 2016, 50–51), to more direct representations of violence against migrants, for example in *Missing in Brooks County*, *The Facility* (2021) and the Netflix docuseries *Immigration Nation* (2020). Some of these films acquire a high visibility and so they are used by organizations to influence politicians and generate activist support, utilized "as resources to publicise and politicise specific [migration] issues" (Bromley 2021, 30).

Dance, theater and performance art frequently foreground migration, also because, historically, theatrical troupes were often nomadic themselves, going through experiences similar to those of migrants. Dramaturgy inspired by these phenomena displays "traveling and migrating bodies," which are "in crisis or in unstable conditions… or they are controlled by an authority, regulated and limited in their trajectories and decisions" (Brandstetter, Egert, and Hartung 2018, 5). Recent theatrical productions bring together activism and art, as they subvert stereotypes about migrants and turn their tragedies from mere numbers or news events to tangible images and stories. They accomplish this with experimental and provocative techniques, and radicalized performances which help to

---

[2] In the case of feature films, this may stem from a deliberate attempt by the director to evoke a documentary style, as it happens in *In this World* and *14 Kilometers* (Ghorbankarimi 2008; Köhn 2016, 48). The technique usually serves to describe, with a strong moralistic overtone, an extremely relevant topic, such as human trafficking in *Lilya 4-Ever* or the radicalization of second-generation immigrants, as a result of the hostile attitude of society, in *Britz*.

"seize the attention of audiences that may be desensitized to statistics about the deaths of anonymous refugees and migrants" (McNeil, Meerzon, and Dean 2020, 4).

Scholarship on such literary, filmic and performative productions provides detailed analyses on the reflections of the brutal aspects of migration. Nevertheless, volumes which focus solely on the violence of migration in the context of artistic narratives are rare. Perhaps the closest publication to our endeavor is Roger Bromley's excellent survey (2021) on the representation of forced migration in cinematic, testimonial and literary narratives. Bromley discusses, from a perspective heavily influenced by Cultural Studies, "the attempted erasure of the agency, experience, voice and tactics of resistance from the displaced", focusing on "human suffering, the excluded, the silenced, the undocumented and marginalised […] but also […] a range of forms of resistance" (Bromley 2021, 14, 23). He deals with forced migration in a broader sense, insofar as, he is aware of the traditional distinctions between asylum seeker, refugee and migrant, although he questions the contemporary strict differentiation between these terms, which are primarily based on the 1951 UN Refugee Convention. He explains this choice with "the effects of neoliberal regimes [which] deplete biodiversity, create unemployment and conditions of immiseration which force people to migrate 'voluntarily' in search of a better life" (3). Bromley's book is also influenced by "decoloniality" and "border thinking," which are philosophical approaches emphasizing that "violence […] shapes lives and relations that are played out across borders worldwide" (16).

There are a few other similar works, but they all have a relatively limited, and more specific, scope compared to ours and that of Bromley. Oswaldo Estrada's Spanish-language volume (2021) describes in detail the representation of violence in the U.S.–Mexico border zone, especially in literature and film (see Erazo 2022). The essay collection of Tolan et al (2013) features a section entitled "Migration and Terrorism," with articles that discuss cultural productions that draw "attention to the informing conceptual overlap [of the] notions of terrorism and migration—how the two disparate acts become increasingly entangled in contemporary representation, as immigration control becomes central to the 'war on terror,' and immigrants become conflated in the media and in the popular imagination with terrorists" (Tolan 2013, xi). Rellstab and Schlote's interdisciplinary collection (2015) revolves around the representability of war, specifically those conflicts which have repercussions involving refugees, migrants and exiles.

Perhaps the reason for this scarcity is that it may seem offensive and unempathetic to directly approach migration via the lens of violence. We believe, however, that it is time to outline an overview of this phenomenon in order to clearly see the present-day representations of violent migratory processes. Our volume thus brings together articles from various disciplines within the humanities to discuss the phenomenon of migration, in its complexity, focusing on its challenges, violent consequences, and potential dangers to migrants and society.

The writers of this volume focus on literature primarily, but documentaries, feature films and theatre productions are also discussed. A common goal of our articles is to find deep structural, mainly societal, reasons of migratory violence in the analyzed cultural artifacts. One of the main results is a renewed interest in Johan Galtung's theory on violence from the perspective of humanities, which explicitly or implicitly appears in several articles. Galtung's definition of violence is relatively broad, insofar as it is described as a force which is *"present when human beings are being influenced so that their actual somatic and mental realizations are below their potential realizations"* (Galtung 1969, 168; emphasis in original). His abstract sociological model hypothesizes a triangle of three major types of violence: direct, structural and cultural violence. Whilst personal or direct violence describes the most obvious acts of aggression and destruction, structural violence can be seen as an "image of a violent structure," which has "exploitation as a center-piece;" this means that the neoliberal ruling class or "top dogs" receive most of the benefits of the violent interactions (Galtung 1990, 293). Structural violence indicates potential for direct violence, as it is a massive controlling force used by economic, political and cultural entities, which results in the situation whereby "those lower down are really hurt or harmed, meaning that their basic needs are molested/left unsatisfied by a structure of exclusion" (Galtung 2007, 18, 30). Cultural violence, in the form of populist, Orientalist and religious discourses, national symbols, and propagandistic cultural artifacts, "can be used to justify or legitimize direct or structural violence" (Galtung 1990, 291). As one of our contributors, Borit observes, the latter two types of violence form the invisible part of an imaginary iceberg, being less conspicuous but more destructive than the first (see also Sarachon 2023, 6).

The articles in this volume shed light on instances whereby scholarly work can subvert or deconstruct structural and cultural violence against migrants. The former, i.e. structural violence is pinpointed in the state's demonization and dehumanization of migrants, brutal patrolling actions at the borders, internment policies, war on terror and immigrants, reducing the death toll of migration to numbers and statistics, legislations which disregard the human rights of irregular immigrants, and housing discrimination. The latter, i.e. cultural violence, is detected in cultural appropriation, exclusion, silencing migrants, marginalization or segregation, and other techniques of nationalist and racist discourses.

Thematically, the main areas of focus in this volume can be grouped into the following three categories:

- The representations of violence around the borders, policing via walls, patrols, rerouting and other aggressive methods, which often result in the abuse of migrants by smugglers and criminals as well as a high death toll.
- Violence and aggression in, and against, migrant households, including Neo-Nazi street riots, domestic violence, rape, and trafficking.
- War, terrorism and other conflicts of ethnic hostility caused by migration, which is encapsulated in the recent "war on terror" events, a clear expression of structural and cultural violence which often becomes a "war on immigrants."

As Bromley (2021, 16) observes, "border thinking" is an influential philosophical approach, which is often traced back to Gloria E. Anzaldúa's *Borderlands/La Frontera: The New Mestiza* (1987).

Anzaldúa's essayistic, semi-autobiographical work emphasizes that the author grew up as "a border woman," amidst multiple cultures, and that this is "not a comfortable territory to live in, this place of contradictions. Hatred, anger and exploitation are the prominent features of this landscape." On the other hand, there are always "compensations" for this liminal existence, in addition to "certain joys" (Anzaldúa 1987).

The two articles in our first section highlight that, although borders and walls are not intrinsically violent, they often become utilized for structural or cultural violence. Ana Belén Martínez García applies the auto/biography theories of Leah Anderst (2017), Elsa Lechner (2019), Sidonie Smith and Julia Watson (2010), to shed light on the self-presentation strategies featured in two auto/biographical documentaries: *Muros / Walls* (2015) and *Human Flow* (2017). She points out that autobiographical approaches dominate documentaries about migration. These two productions are discussed because they deal with very similar topics, but with radically different methods. The former makes its narrator entirely absent from the film, so much so that many times the participants talk to each other in dialogues instead of speaking to the camera or an interviewer; in contrast, the second documentary, produced and directed by Ai Weiwei, places the filmmaker as a somewhat obscure, and yet vital, witness in the midst of the refugees' plight, an interviewer who not only shares their journey but accompanies them in their grief and joins the extremely tragic tone that permeates the storytelling process.

In Martínez García's reading, the two works complement each other to portray analytical information, media coverage and mediated pieces of news, but, first and foremost, they foreground interviews conducted in the first person to give voice to migrants and let them tell their own stories. The first documentary, a predominantly Spanish co-production, intersperses several auto/biographical interviews from different places where a border is being delineated by a physical "wall," which symbolizes the violence that the physical barrier entails. The film uses crosscutting and split screen to alternate between border walls dividing the U.S. and Mexico,

Morocco and Spain (Melilla), as well as South-Africa and Zimbabwe. The film shows people on both sides of the borders, including refugees, former migrants who enact their border crossing as an amateur theatrical show to educate children, cross-border commuters, border guards, and a Vietnam veteran who leaves water bottles in the desert to save migrants from dehydration. Although they have different views on migration and some of them even support isolationism to a certain degree, they all agree that the walls create an absurd situation instead of solving the problem.

In the second documentary, Ai Weiwei, who is an exiled Chinese artist living in Europe and so a migrant himself, is trying to come to terms with the reality of migratory violence. The interviewer turns to people who find it hard to claim refugee status and who are left without any choice but to keep moving, while he himself occasionally joins their wanderings or everyday activities such as cooking food or haircutting. He always remains in the background, and yet via subtle ways, including captions of poetry, he manages to clearly express his compassion towards the sufferings of the migrants.

According to Martínez García, the participants' stories in both cases testify to Lechner's assertion that migration often becomes "a biographical disruption" (2019, 5) and, thus, a trauma. Yet, the borders and walls also represent hope, which helps the migrants to refuse the role of the victim, and so the films balance between evoking pity in the viewer and becoming activist works which avoid the potential commodification of suffering.

In the second article of this section, Irene Alcubilla Troughton discusses how violence and migratory practices are portrayed in three Hispanic plays: *Alguien silbó (y despertó a un centenar de pájaros dormidos)* (2007) by Antonio de Paco, *Cazador de Gringos* (2005) by Daniel Serrano and *Ternura Suite* (2013) by Edgar Chías. Troughton uses a complex philosophical approach to discuss the dichotomies of the stranger and the citizen, and that of master and slave, leading to a Derridean-Žižekian re-interpretation of tolerance and hospitality. In this theoretical framework, which highlights the conceptualization of the immigrant as a stranger and the ensuing tolerance and hospitality, the author addresses the "reverse logic" that the characters of these plays exhibit on the border: an exchange of the roles of the victim and the aggressor, the vulnerable and the dominant. As poststructuralist thinking observes, such a reversal of dichotomies easily turns into "an arbitrary, open system in which the attributes [...] can be deceptively exchanged, substituted for each other at will. As a consequence, our confidence in the original, binary model that was used as a starting point is bound to be shaken" (De Man 1979, 108). Accordingly, Troughton's analysis leads to "a circle of endless and pointless violence."

Troughton's poststructuralist arguments lead to distinguishing between three kinds of violence: instrumental, structural, and symbolic. The first one indicates direct violence, which points at a primary force behind it, a system that precedes brutal situations and that is structural or symbolic. Her structural violence (a term identically named to that of Galtung but understood here somewhat differently) comes from identity construction, which constitutes lawful subjects and good citizens, linked to a definition of "home", as well as who has the right to dwell in that space, in opposition to "illegal" migrants. Symbolic violence, which is understood here in a way similar to Galtung's cultural violence, is "embedded in a logic of signs and names," treated in relation to the power of language and naming. Finally, Troughton emphasizes that the spectator of these plays also partakes in structural violence, taking the role of an active witness of violence; thus, the performances remind us of our ethical obligation to detach ourselves from the position of passive bystanders and become active participants in these situations.

Our second section starts with Cornel Borit's analysis of two contemporary young adult novels which feature migration from CEE countries (specifically Romania) to Britain: Tracey Mathias' *Night of the Party* (2018) and Sarah Crossan and Brian Conaghan's *We Come Apart* (2017). The former depicts the experiences of disenfranchised Romanian teenage migrants, living in a society which is similar to the one in Alfonso Cuarón's 2006 science fiction film *Children of Men*, insofar as the characters are exposed to the constant threat of forced repatriation in a dystopian Britain governed by the

"British Born policy." In the latter novel, *We Come Apart*, the protagonist undergoes the routine of alienation, bullying and brutality in a school system imbued by pervasive anti-migrant mentalities, racism and stereotypes.

The novels reflect on the Brexit referendum and the following political events, whereby the British society has been highly polarized, with migration being one of the main topics of contention. As Borit observes, this atmosphere is highlighted, for example, by the full recitation of Enoch Powell's infamous "rivers of blood" speech on Radio 4, voiced by an actor in 2018. In contemporary British society and in these novels, migrants often become victims of violent acts, either carried out by state authorities, groups, or individual agents. Various forms of violence, from discrimination, exploitation, social exclusion and marginalization, to bullying, expulsion, incarceration or forced repatriation, have accompanied the growing anti-migrant rhetoric, which permeates British society.

Borit focuses on the representations of Galtung's cultural and structural violence in the novels. Galtung considers these forms of violence to be the most dangerous, as they are the most widespread, harder to identify, and difficult to oppose. Borit thus examines nativist discourse as a form of cultural violence that creates the premises of structural violence against immigrants by reinforcing stereotypes, constructing a demonizing image of migrants, and disseminating detrimental migration myths. He traces the origins of nativism and populism in contemporary Britain to explain the socio-historical background of violence against migrants and then turns to the texts to analyze the specific tropes they employ to negotiate cultural and structural violence. In Borit's reading, cultural violence is present in billboards, advertising, and stereotyping newspaper articles, which construct demonizing images of migrants and disseminate detrimental migration myths. Structural violence appears in drastic legislations against immigrants, which many members of the society are happy to adhere to, acting as voluntary nativist agents of the state. Borit describes in detail and with compassion the tangible impacts of these forces on the emotional, social, cultural, and economic aspects of the lives of immigrant characters, finding a ray of hope in "intercultural dialogue" and "cosmopolitan visions," which can become small but visible aspects of reality in these novels.

Vedran Ćatović's chapter is a case study of Leïla Slimani's Goncourt Award-winning novel *Chanson Douce* (2016; published in 2018 as *The Perfect Nanny* in the U.S. and as *Lullaby* in the UK). The novel is a fictionalized account of the murder of the Krim siblings in New York, committed by their nanny, Yoselin Ortega, in 2012 (see Davis 2018, 11). Ortega, an immigrant from the Dominican Republic, was sentenced to life imprisonment and condemned as "pure evil" by Judge Carro (Ransom 2018, 20). Slimani's account provides a completely different story: by presenting a gallery of characters originating from former French colonies (Senegal, Ivory Coast, Morocco), the novel offers a particularly clear-eyed and sharp take on the condition of the migrant population in France.

Like the plays analyzed by Troughton in this volume, the novel somewhat reverses the conventional ethnic power structures, insofar as Louise, the nanny, is white, while her employer, Myriam, is a young lawyer of Arabic origin. Slimani also describes the social milieu of immigrant nannies, a "trade union" of some sort; thus, in Ćatović's reading, the novel, following the classical French realisms of Honore de Balzac, Émile Zola or Edmond and Jules Goncourt, provides an unapologetic testimony of the ongoing struggle and oppression experienced by female subaltern migrants from former French colonies.

Ćatović uses human geographical research and sociological theories about assimilation and acculturation to detect structurally deep reasons behind the murder. Based on such research, he emphasizes that immigrants in Western societies are rarely given a chance at upward mobility, which is reflected in their housing, as the likelihood of migrating away from dilapidated settlement areas is extremely small for a wide range of immigrants. Housing discrimination, legal or illegal, over or covert, still exists worldwide, and it is often inflicted on immigrants in the form of Galtung's structural violence (Sheehan 2018).[3]

---

[3] As Sheehan (2018, 152) observes, due to "neoliberal policies" and "bureaucratic articulations that are simultaneously enacted by a range of state and nonstate

Accordingly, the main character of the novel commutes from her banlieue to reach her workplace in the central Parisian flat, which is interpreted by Ćatović as a symbol of a futile attempted migration process from the impoverished world of the working-class suburb to the well-off milieu of the bourgeoisie.

Rebecca Deluce analyzes similar literary works, which also focus on the vulnerability of migrant lives. The texts that she explores, mainly poems and short stories, portray the detainment of refugees in 21st-century Britain, and the distorted public perceptions of these people. Based on the violent events that occurred in Yarl's Wood Detention Centre, and the unjust threat of removal as a result, she builds on the concept of "indefinite detention," meaning deprivation of freedom, systematic abuse, and distortion of identity between migrants, asylum seekers and refugees in the public sector. As Sarachon (2023) observes, the state's "instrumentalization of migration through policy, the state's functions and migration management," which disregard human rights, can be understood as instances of Galtung's invisible structural violence, which "fuel direct violence" (6). Deluce, however, approaches these incidents with poststructuralist theories. She uses, specifically, Foucault's concept of "sovereignty (2003), Agamben's "state of exception," "bare life" and his "homo sacer" (1998), in addition to Judith Butler's "precarious life" (2006), to show the state's ongoing ability to exploit and abuse immigrants, by making detainees politically irrelevant, situating them outside the legal sphere of citizenry and criminalizing their public image.

Based on this comprehensive theoretical framework, Deluce's chapter explores precarity, grievability and temporality as imposed on migrant lives. These issues are investigated in refugee literature, that is, texts authored or co-authored by those with direct experience of refugees' lives, with a special focus on the collections *Refugee Tales* (2016) and *Refugee Tales II* (2017). These volumes were edited by an organization which aims to inform the public about the

---

actors," migrants often need to "find housing through informal networks and live in the shadows of the housing market."

indefinite detention through its solidarity walks and published narratives. The texts depict the experiences of being indefinitely incarcerated and/or living precariously in Britain, exposing a wide range of discriminations suffered.

These topics are also considered through Lucy Popescu's edited anthology, *A Country of Refuge* (2016), a collection compiled with the help of human rights activists. The violence often faced by refugees during migration, detention and removal to and from countries are explored directly through Ruth Padel's essay and poetry in this collection, whilst A.L. Kennedy's short story, "Inappropriate Staring," shows the lack of empathy and the unquestionable belief in authority in the twenty-first century. Marina Lewycka's short story in *Refugee Tales* examines the absurdity and injustices of detention produced by the apathy and lack of supervision in the administration of the immigration sector. These texts highlight the significance of direct communication between citizens and detainees, contributing to discussions by providing a platform for previously hushed voices.

Klapcsik and Vernyik's contribution on Turkish-German migrant cinema discusses the process whereby migrant cinema, formerly dominated by "the cinema of duty" (Malik 1996; Malik 2010), turns into a more light-hearted and commercialized migrant-themed cinema.[4] These more recent works are commercially successful, also amongst non-minority audiences, and are occasionally produced by non-minority directors who are inspired by migrant filmmakers and create similar films without relying on a biographical background.[5] Thus, the chapter raises the question whether

---

[4] The "cinema of duty" is defined by Malik as films that are "preoccupied with the task of telling forgotten or buried stories, writing unwritten histories and 'correcting' the misrepresentations of mainstream production" (2010, 135), while Berghahn and Sternberg characterize it "as a social issue-based cinema with a documentary–realist aesthetics […] that presents social dramas of disadvantaged individuals and/or communities, articulating a perspective from within migrant and diasporic culture and providing a critique of hegemonic structures and dominant ideologies" (2010, 34).

[5] To further complicate this question, certain Turkish-German filmmakers, such as Thomas Arslan, gradually distance themselves from the themes and stylistic methods of ethnic cinema, striving for, and utilizing, more universal cultural expressions (see, for example, Abel 2013).

such films potentially become instances of cultural appropriation (Jackson 2021, 84–86), "consumer cannibalism" or "the commodification of Otherness" (Hooks 2006), eventually contributing to "cultural violence" (Galtung 1990). The critics eventually deny this, primarily because Hooks' concept of cultural appropriation or "getting a bit of the Other" would entail superficial sexual encounters that mainly serve as "rites of passage" for white males (2006, 368). In many of the analyzed films, however, the—primarily female—Turkish-German characters are still empowered, and they remain in the center of the narratives. As Benjamin Nickl observes, such individuals are "more than just a token character [...] no damsel in distress and [someone who] needs no saving" (2020, 76). Furthermore, as critics observe, although migrant cinema is an expressive form of minority cultures, migration is also, arguably, a key aspect of European identity (Trifonova 2022, 8) and European cinema as such. As Berghahn and Sternberg note,

> a considerable number of nonmigrant and non-diasporic screenwriters and directors have produced films that are centrally concerned with questions of migratory and diasporic existence. [...] Such inclusion is not meant to diminish the role migrant and diasporic *film-makers* have played in challenging invisibility and misrepresentation by introducing specific themes, characters, points of view and styles to European cinema [...] [but] to acknowledge that migration, diaspora and cultural diversity are so central to the European imaginary of the present moment that they occupy a prominent position in the work of film-makers of very different backgrounds (2010, 16–17; emphasis in original).

Accordingly, Klapcsik and Vernyik's analysis reveals that Turkish-German films produced in the period between 1998 and 2017 negotiate the conventions of art cinema and those of popular entertainment in their portrayal of domestic violence. The social-realist depictions of domestic violence can still be detected in certain cases, but they are often combined with the modality of romantic comedies or the narrative elements of the gangster film. Thus, although certain female protagonists still occasionally appear as victims of domestic violence and their lives are influenced by their patriarchal fathers and brothers, the films use humor, international soundtracks, and the aestheticization of urban violence, to show the protagonists as strong, multiculturally conscious and active characters.

Michaela Weiss' chapter introduces the concept of "active submission" into literary studies, exploring its potential to serve as a defense mechanism against various forms of direct violence (pogroms, patronizing behavior and sexual abuse), in addition to structural violence (anti-immigrant laws and xenophobic public sentiments). Weiss' notion is somewhat similar to Luce Irigaray's feminine mimicry (1991, 124–25) and Bhabha's colonial mimicry (1994, 85–92), insofar as the term originates from zoology (see, for example, Caillois and Shepley 1984), but it is primarily concerned with the social, psychological and cultural behavior of subaltern, female immigrant subjects, who seemingly utilize an opportunistic mentality in order to survive in a hostile environment. In Weiss' study, the term is specifically used to describe submissive attention-seeking behavior which vulnerable and traumatized women expect patriarchal men to appreciate. Weiss emphasizes that this is how Lillian Leyb, the female migrant protagonist, reacts to gender-based violence in Amy Bloom's historical novel *Away* (2007).

Set in the 1920s, but still highly relevant today, Bloom's recent novel narrates the journey of a Jewish immigrant woman who travels from Turov (in today's Belarus) to America, and then subsequently decides to walk to Siberia, depicting the struggles of a minority woman on the move and her survival strategies. The novel is inspired by early 20th century Jewish immigrant narratives and follows historical sources about an Eastern European immigrant, Lillian Alling, who felt homesick in New York and, in 1926, decided to walk home to Siberia via the Yukon and the Bering Strait. Due to the invisibility and social inferiority of migrant women, the method of active submission is adopted by the protagonist as a tool to cope with oppression, violence, and other forms of maltreatment.

Finally, the third unit of our book revolves around the contradictory relationship between migration and terrorism. Based on recent scholarship on these topics, both articles intend to question whether it is sudden, abrupt and unforeseen incidents that lead to becoming a terrorist; instead, in both cases, deep structural reasons are detected and explored.

Cassandra Falke analyzes Islamic terrorist recruitment discourses in Kamila Shamsie's critically-acclaimed novel *Home Fire* (2017), which—in a way similar to the TV drama *Britz*—investigates what turns second generation immigrants into terrorists. In Falke's reading, the structural reasons why one of the protagonists, Parvaiz, starts to support radical Islamic groups are threefold.

First, it may be a reaction to state violence, especially state terrorism, which indicates events like, for example, the Forest Gate raid by the Metropolitan Police in 2006. State terrorism is a seemingly contradictory term which has been denied by many, as the conventional definition of terrorism indicates that the violent acts are committed by non-state actors. However, Falke and numerous other critics use this term (Galtung 2007, 28, 29; Thomas 2011, 1824–25). Noam Chomsky, for example, defines state terrorism as "low intensity conflicts" which are state sponsored (1991, 14); accordingly, Alexander George (1991, 1) observes that "the United States and its friends are the major supporters, sponsors, and perpetrators of terrorist incidents in the world today." In the novel, Parvaiz's father was reported to have died on the way to Guantánamo, perhaps the most infamous facility in the world where abducted persons become the victims of state condoned torture.

Second, Falke explains that second generation residents are extremely vulnerable to radicalization because of our present-day "transcendental homelessness," a term borrowed from György Lukács (Lukacs and Bostock 1971), but used here for our contemporary experience of living without a unified framework. Falke claims that individuals who grow up in immigrant households find this state especially taxing and contradictory; hence, their minds can open up to Islamic terrorist propaganda, which constructs a transnational homeland, an Islamic identity regardless of European borders and origins, and a stability that they long for.

Third, in a way similar to the novels analyzed by Borit in our volume, the immigrant characters constantly feel pressured by their friends and the general public to maintain and show their Britishness. This is triggered here by the fact that Parvaiz's family lives in the shadow of the deceased father's former terrorist activities; his death, which is a "shameful secret," can potentially turn their British neighbors into vigilantes and voluntary nationalist agents of the state.

Similarly to Falke, Vernyik and Klapcsik explore the representation of terrorist acts by immigrants. Specifically, their chapter focuses on such acts committed by the early Zionist Jewish immigrants of the 1930s in Arthur Koestler's novel *Thieves in the Night* (1946). Based on the close reading of the novel and 21st-century theoretical discussions on terrorism, and especially on observations in John Horgan's *The Psychology of Terrorism* (2005), their interpretation emphasizes that terrorism is rarely triggered by a single traumatic event, as the previous critical consensus—both on the novel and terrorism in general—argues. On the contrary, it is usually caused by, as Horgan (2005) notes, progressive "communal identification" (88) with (other) victims of oppression and should be interpreted as a "form of communication" (2) between minorities and other members of the society.

In addition, Vernyik and Klapcsik point out that besides the complex historical background portrayed in the novel, events which led to the present-day political turmoil and the catastrophic Israeli-Palestinian conflict, the structurally deeper reason why terrorism has not been fully explored in the novel is that terrorism invites strategies of silence, avoidance, or euphemism (Mitchell 2005, 298). Thus, terrorism is not only, and not even primarily, a battle of arms, but one of narratives, a struggle for signification. It is a reaction to Galtung's structural violence, a form of violence which, in Koestler's novel, is the result of the British authorities' deliberate attempts to maintain and intensify unequal power structures in a multiethnic society. This included the strategy of limiting, or even eliminating, Jewish immigration and deporting migrants at a time when staying in, or returning to, Nazi-controlled Europe meant that the refugees were in great danger of fatal direct violence.

To sum up, the articles in our book explore the deep structural reasons behind migratory violence through the medium of cultural artifacts, while utilizing structuralist or poststructuralist theories. Keeping these reasons in mind, they also show how migrants react to such violence psychologically or culturally. The articles warn us that structural and cultural violence is frequently covert, forming a hidden, imaginary and ideological, yet highly influential and destructive, dichotomy between "us" and "them," self and the Other, the safe home behind the wall and threatening strangers (Galtung 1990, 298). As Galtung observes, such violence "is silent, it does not show — it is essentially static, it is the *tranquil* waters" (Galtung 1969, 173; emphasis in original). Cultural artifacts about, and especially by, migrants, in addition to scholarship on this topic, break this silence and remind the public of the concealed powers of violence targeting these people and communities.

Ostensibly, it would seem logical that we intend to blend cultural scholarship with activist intentions here. However, we are aware of the difficulties of this, since "cultural violence is the hardest to change, [as] it is the deep-rooted constant which legitimates structural and direct violence" (Galtung 2007, 131). We also understand the dangers of turning this endeavor into a dogmatic counterculture. As Galtung observes, it is questionable to form "peace culture" as an antithesis to cultural violence, as it also evokes "inculcation [which] is an act of violence." Rather, what can potentially help is to aim for "peaceful education, including socialization [which] would probably imply exposure to multiple cultures and then a dialogue" (Galtung 1990, 303). What we can — and sincerely do — hope, then, is that our volume will contribute to an extensively pluralistic dialogue about migratory issues.

Bibliography

Agamben, Giorgio. 1998. *Homo Sacer: Sovereign Power and Bare Life*. Redwood City, CA: Stanford UP.

Anderst, Leah. 2017. "The Self as Evidence and Collaborative Identity in Contemporary Autobiographical Documentary." *A/b: Auto/Biography Studies* 32 (2): 255–57. https://doi.org/10.1080/08989575.2017.1288030.

Anzaldúa, Gloria E. 1987. *Borderlands/La Frontera: The New Mestiza*. San Francisco: Aunt Lute.

Aufderheide, Patricia. 2008. *Documentary Film: A Very Short Introduction*. Oxford: Oxford UP.

Bardan, Alice, and Áine O'Healy. 2013. "Transnational Mobility and Precarious Labor in Post-Cold War Europe: The Spectral Disruptions of Carmine Amoroso's Cover Boy. In *The Cinemas of Italian Migration: European and Transatlantic Narratives"*, edited by Sabine Schrader and Daniel Winkler, 69–90. Newcastle: Cambridge Scholars Publishing.

Bayraktar, Nilgun. 2016. *Mobility and Migration in Film and Moving Image Art: Cinema Beyond Europe*. New York: Routledge.

Berghahn, Daniela. 2014. *Far-Flung Families in Film: The Diasporic Family in Contemporary European Cinema*. Edinburgh: Edinburgh UP.

Berghahn, Daniela, and Claudia Sternberg, eds. 2010. "Introduction." In *European Cinema in Motion: Migrant and Diasporic Film in Contemporary Europe*, edited by Daniela Berghahn and Claudia Sternberg, 1–11. Basingstoke: Palgrave Macmillan.

Bhatia, Monish, and Victoria Canning, eds. 2021. *Stealing Time: Migration, Temporalities and State Violence*. Berlin: Springer Nature.

Bhabha, Homi K. 1994. *The Location of Culture*. New York: Routledge.

Brandstetter, Gabriele, Gerko Egert, and Holger Hartung. 2018. "Movements of Interweaving: An Introduction." In *Movements of Interweaving: Dance and Corporeality in Times of Travel and Migration*, edited by Gabriela Brandstetter, Gerko Egert and Holger Hartung, 1–22. Abingdon: Routledge.

Bromley, Roger. 2021. *Narratives of Forced Mobility and Displacement in Contemporary Literature and Culture*. Cham: Springer Nature.

Brown, William, Dina Iordanova, and Leshu Torchin. 2010. *Moving People, Moving Images: Cinema and Trafficking in the New Europe*. St Andrews: St Andrews Film Studies.

Butler, Judith. 2006. *Precarious Life: The Powers of Mourning and Violence*. London: Verso.

Caillois, Roger, and John Shepley. 1984. "Mimicry and Legendary Psychasthenia." *October* 31: 17–32. https://doi.org/10.2307/778354.

Chomsky, Noam. 1991. "International Terrorism: Image and Reality." In *Western State Terrorism*, edited by Alexander George, 12–38. Abingdon: Routledge.

Davies, Thom, and Arshad Isakjee. 2019. "Ruins of Empire: Refugees, Race and the Postcolonial Geographies of European Migrant Camps." *Geoforum* 102 (June): 214–17. https://doi.org/10.1016/j.geoforum.2018.09.031.

Davis, J. Madison. 2018. "The Nightmare Tropes of Three Women Writers." *World Literature Today* 92 (4): 10–12.

De Genova, Nicholas. 2016. "The European Question: Migration, Race, and Postcoloniality in Europe." *Social Text* 34 (3): 75–102. https://doi.org/10.1215/01642472-3607588.

De Man, Paul. 1979. *Allegories of Reading: Figural Language in Rousseau, Nietzsche, Rilke, and Proust*. New Haven, CT: Yale UP.

Demos, T. J. 2013. *The Migrant Image: The Art and Politics of Documentary during Global Crisis*. Durham, NC: Duke UP.

Domański, Marek, and Tomasz Ferenc. 2019. *Borderlands: Tensions on the External Borders of the European Union*. Łódź: Akademia Sztuk Pięknych im. Władysława Strzemińskiego w Łodzi.

Engelen, Leen, and Kris van Heuckelom. 2014. *European Cinema after the Wall: Screening East-West Mobility*. Film and History. Lanham, MD: Rowman and Littlefield.

Erazo, Adrienne. 2022. "Book Review: Fronteras de Violencia En México y Estados Unidos. Edited by Oswaldo Estrada. Valencia: Albatros, 2021." *Chasqui* 51 (1): R5–7.

Estrada, Oswaldo. 2021. *Fronteras de violencia en México y Estados Unidos*. Valencia: Albatros.

Fanon, Frantz. 2008. *Black Skin, White Masks*. Translated by Charles Lam Markmann. London: Pluto Press.

FitzGerald, David Scott. 2019. *Refuge beyond Reach: How Rich Democracies Repel Asylum Seekers*. Oxford: Oxford UP.

Foucault, Michel. 2003. *"'Society Must Be Defended.' Lectures at the Collège de France 1975–1976."* New York: Picador.

Galtung, Johan. 1969. "Violence, Peace, and Peace Research." *Journal of Peace Research* 6 (3): 167–91.

———. 1990. "Cultural Violence." *Journal of Peace Research* 27 (3): 291–305.

———. 2007. "Introduction: Peace by Peaceful Conflict Transformation—the TRANSCEND Approach." In *Handbook of Peace and Conflict Studies*, edited by Charles Webel and Johan Galtung, 14–34. New York: Routledge.

George, Alexander. 1991. "Introduction." In *Western State Terrorism*, edited by Alexander George, 1–11. New York: Routledge.

Ghorbankarimi, Maryam. 2008. "*14 Kilometres* (2007) Movie Review from Eye for Film." Eye for Film. Last modified May 18, 2008. https://www.eyeforfilm.co.uk/review/14-kilometres-film-review-by-maryam-ghorbankarimi.

Gott, Michael, and Todd Herzog. 2014. "Introduction: Mapping Post-1989 European Cinema." In *East, West and Centre: Reframing Post-1989 European Cinema*, edited by Michael Gott and Todd Herzog, 1–20. Edinburg: Edinburgh UP.

Hackett, Jon. 2022. "Trafficking on Film: A Critical Survey." In *Modern Slavery and Human Trafficking: The Victim Journey*, edited by Carole Murphy and Runa Lazzarino, 95–112. Bristol: Bristol UP.

Hake, Sabine, and Barbara Mennel. 2012. *Turkish German Cinema in the New Millennium: Sites, Sounds, and Screens*. New York: Berghahn Books.

Hall, Stuart. 2001. *The Multicultural Question*. Milton Keynes: The Open University.

Halstead, Narmala. 2018. *Competing Power: Landscapes of Migration, Violence and the State*. New York: Berghahn Books.

Higbee, Will. 2013. *Post-Beur Cinema: North African Emigre and Maghrebi-French Filmmaking in France since 2000*. Edinburgh: Edinburgh UP.

Hooks, Bell. 2006. "Eating the Other: Desire and Resistance." In *Media and Cultural Studies: Keyworks*, edited by Meenakshi Gigi Durham and Douglas Kellner. rev. ed, 366–80. Malden, MA: Blackwell.

Horgan, John. 2005. *The Psychology of Terrorism*. New York: Routledge.

Irigaray, Luce. 1991. "The Power of Discourse and the Subordination of the Feminine." In *The Irigaray Reader*, edited by Luce Irigaray and Margaret Whitford, 118–32. Cambridge, MA: Basil Blackwell.

Jackson, Jason Baird. 2021. "On Cultural Appropriation." *Journal of Folklore Research* 58 (1): 77–122.

Köhn, Steffen. 2016. *Mediating Mobility: Visual Anthropology in the Age of Migration*. New York: Columbia UP.

Lacey, Stephen, and Derek Paget, eds. 2015. "Introduction." In *The "War on Terror": Post-9/11 Television Drama, Docudrama and Documentary*, edited by Stephen Lacey and Derek Paget, 1–10. Cardiff: U of Wales P.

Lechner, Elsa. 2019. "Migrants' Lives Matter: Biographical Research, Recognition and Social Participation." *Contemporary Social Science* 14 (3–4): 500–514. https://doi.org/10.1080/21582041.2018.1463449.

Lukacs, Georg, and Anna Bostock. 1971. *The Theory of the Novel: A Historico-Philosophical Essay on the Forms of Great Epic Literature*. London: The Merlin Press.

Malik, Sarita. 1996. "Beyond 'the Cinema of Duty'? The Pleasures of Hybridity: Black British Film of the 1980s and 1990s." In *Dissolving Views: Key Writings on British Cinema*, edited by Andrew Higson, 202–15. London: Bloomsbury Academic.

— — —. 2010. "The Dark Side of Hybridity: Contemporary Black and Asian British Cinema." In European Cinema in Motion: Migrant and Diasporic Film in Contemporary Europe, edited by Daniela Berghahn and Claudia Sternberg, 132–151. Basingstoke: Palgrave Macmillan.

McNeil, Daniel, Yana Meerzon, and David Dean. 2020a. "Introduction." In *Migration and Stereotypes in Performance and Culture*, edited by Daniel McNeil, Yana Meerzon, and David Dean, 1–17. Cham: Palgrave Macmillan.

— — —. 2020b. *Migration and Stereotypes in Performance and Culture*. Cham: Palgrave Macmillan.

Mitchell, William John Thomas. 2005. "The Unspeakable and the Unimaginable: Word and Image in a Time of Terror." *ELH* 72 (June): 291–308.

Naficy, Hamid. 2001. *An Accented Cinema: Exilic and Diasporic Filmmaking*. Princeton, NJ: Princeton UP.

Nickl, Benjamin. 2020. *Turkish German Muslims and Comedy Entertainment*. Leuven: Leuven UP.

Owczarzak, Jill. 2009. "Introduction: Postcolonial Studies and Postsocialism in Eastern Europe." *Focaal* 2009 (53): 3–19. https://doi.org/10.3167/fcl.2009.530101.

Pickering, Sharon. 2010. *Women, Borders, and Violence: Current Issues in Asylum, Forced Migration, and Trafficking*. New York: Springer Science & Business Media.

Ponzanesi, Sandra. 2018. "Postcolonial Theory in Film." *Obo*. Last modified February 22, 2018. https://www.oxfordbibliographies.com/display/document/obo-9780199791286/obo-9780199791286-0284.xml.

Ransom, Jan. 2018. "Nanny Who Killed 2 Children Is Sentenced to Life in Prison." *New York Times, Late Edition (East Coast)*, May 15, 2018.

Rellstab, Daniel H., and Christiane Schlote. 2014. *Representations of War, Migration, and Refugeehood: Interdisciplinary Perspectives*. New York: Routledge.

Rushdie, Salman. 1994. "Good Advice Is Rarer than Rubies." In *East, West*, edited by Salman Rushdie, 3–16. New York: Random House.

Said, Edward W. 2000a. "Reflections on Exile." In *Reflections on Exile and Other Essays*, edited by Edward Said, 173–86. Cambridge, MA: Harvard UP.

— — —. 2000b. *Reflections on Exile and Other Essays*. Cambridge, MA: Harvard UP.

Sarachon, Thunyanun. 2023. "Availability of Human Rights and the Case Study of Irregular Economic Migrants in Thailand and Hungary." *Prosperitas* 10 (2): 1–12. https://doi.org/10.31570/prosp_2022_0031.

Sardar, Ziauddin. 2008. "Foreword to the 2008 Edition." In *Black Skin, White Masks*, edited by Frantz Fanon, translated by Charles Lam Markmann, vi–xx. London: Pluto Press.

Sheehan, Megan. 2018. "Migrant Residents in Search of Residences: Locating Structural Violence at the Interstices of Bureaucracies." *Conflict and Society* 4 (1): 151–66. https://doi.org/10.3167/arcs.2018.040112.

Smith, Sidonie, and Julia Watson. 2010. *Reading Autobiography: A Guide for Interpreting Life Narratives*. 2nd ed. Minneapolis, MN: U of Minnesota P.

Speed, Shannon. 2019. *Incarcerated Stories: Indigenous Women Migrants and Violence in the Settler-Capitalist State*. Chapel Hill, NC: U of North Carolina P.

Thomas, Claire. 2011. "Why Don't We Talk about 'Violence' in International Relations?" *Review of International Studies* 37 (4): 1815–36. https://doi.org/10.1017/S0260210510001154.

Tolan, Fiona. 2013. "Introduction." In *Literature, Migration and the "War on Terror"*, edited by Fiona Tolan, Stephen Morton, Anastasia Valassopoulos, and Robert Spencer, x–xii. London: Routledge.

Tolan, Fiona, Stephen Morton, Anastasia Valassopoulos, and Robert Spencer, eds. 2013. *Literature, Migration and the 'War on Terror'*. London: Routledge.

Trifonova, Temenuga. 2022. *The Figure of the Migrant in Contemporary European Cinema*. New York: Bloomsbury.

van Heuckelom, Kris. 2014. "From Dysfunction to Restoration." In *European Cinema After the Wall: Screening East-West Mobility*, edited by Leen Engelen and Kris van Heuckelom, 71–93. Lanham: Rowman & Littlefield.

———. 2019. *Polish Migrants in European Film 1918–2017*. Cham: Palgrave Macmillan

The Violence of Walls
and Borders

Brutal Borders:
Walls Preventing *Human Flow*

Ana Belén Martínez García

Introduction:
Migrations, Violence, Auto/Biographical Documentary

In her introduction to *International Migration into Europe*, Gabriella Lazaridis reminds readers that "Migration is not a new phenomenon" (2015, 1). Not even the numbers—over 200 million people—so often magnified in the media, exceed those of previous historical periods of unrest and upheaval such as World War I and the Great Famine in Ireland, in comparison with the extant global population at the time, as other authors have remarked (Sandoval-García 2017, 1–2). Lazaridis goes on to highlight, however, that "a paradigm shift has taken place since 2001" (2015, 1), by which migration is no longer considered to be a question of low, but of "high politics" (Lahav 2004), meaning that national security is seen to be at stake:

> migration has been securitized, because the underlying socio-political discourses conceive it as an issue that can undermine the capacity of the state to maintain sovereignty (mainly in the areas of border control and national identity, which are understood as basic responsibilities of the state in matters of security). (Lazaridis 2015, 2)

Among the manifold expressions of state violence constraining migration, one should address the role of the state in controlling, shaping, and re-creating migratory policies. Furthermore, some migrants are neither under the protection of the state they are leaving nor the state they are trying to enter: "There continues to be an unstable connection between human rights and national rights as the refugee has a painfully uncertain legal status" (Stevenson 2017, 32). Clashing with such statelessness is Hannah Arendt's famous reflection that, for a person to be granted human rights, they should previously have "the right to have rights" (1951, 247). A stateless person may lack the entitlement to claim refugee status, for example, when it is difficult to ascertain whether there exists risk of persecution in staying or returning to their country of origin as stated in the definition set forth in Article 1 of the Refugee Convention (UNHCR 2010: 14). Similarly, protection under the banner of the Universal Declaration of Human Rights (UN 1948) is hard to assess, since it is not legally binding: "Human rights in this sense become meaningless without an authority to enforce them" (Stevenson 2017, 32). This inherent contradiction at the root of human rights legislation is what drives some skeptics to complain of their futility (DeGooyer et al. 2018). Whenever a new border is set up, the state may be depriving migrants of their rights and thus part of their identity.

The aim of this chapter is to analyze in depth two examples of human rights auto/biographical documentaries that deal with both the issue of migration as well as violence, the overarching topic of this volume. I will apply auto/biography theory to shed light on the self-presentation strategies featured in these auto/biographical documentaries for activism and advocacy purposes. Sidonie Smith and Julia Watson have written extensively on the link between ethics and witnessing:

> Narratives of witness […] make an urgent, immediate, and direct bid for attention and call the reader/listener to an ethical response through their affective appeals for recognition. While there can be many unpredictable responses to the publication, circulation, and reception of personal narratives of suffering and loss, their scenes of witness entwine the narrator, the story, and the listener/reader in an ethical call to empathic identification and accountability, recognition, and oftentimes action. (2010, 133–134)

The "I" in auto/biographical documentaries is the "I" of the witness, but the audience is also compelled to become a "witness" in a way conducive to testifying against human rights transgressions present (and endemic) in western societies, namely the fact that "others" are not particularly welcome in the "land of opportunities"—be that the USA or Europe. The "I" enters into a dynamic relationship—and tension—with the audience. The speaking, testifying agent needs the presence of a witness so that their text is imbued with significant meaning. As Gillian Whitlock has famously argued, "in the absence of its witness, testimony fails: the sound of one hand clapping" (2015, 68).

Contemporary autobiographical documentary, Leah Anderst suggests, is part of the so-called memoir boom, raising

> new questions for autobiography, about identity and authenticity, and about the individual and the collective. How can the self and one's life story represented cinematically serve to bring about social change? [...] How do you find the "true" story among all of the many threads woven together by the distinct voices that come into play in the collaborative process of filmmaking? (2017, 255)

Anderst reflects on the self as constructed individually and collectively via the film medium (2017, 256–257). The "I" will therefore at times reveal the innermost thoughts and preoccupations while at other times standing for the collective suffering of migrants. As with other testimonial biographical and autobiographical texts, one voice may be raised to speak for others "either silent or silenced" (Martínez García 2017a, 2). While *Walls* (Iraburu and Molina 2015) and *Human Flow* (Ai 2017) are not advertised or commercialized as autobiographical practices per se, they are indeed activist films and so belong in the wide category of what Kay Schaffer and Sidonie Smith call "human rights life narratives" (2004), narratives that are personal as well as collective with the aim to expose rights violations that affect oneself and a group of people. A condition of such a text to function as advocacy work is that it invokes humanitarian emotions which, by mobilizing empathy on its recipient, may provoke an "ethical response" (Wilson and Brown 2009, 2).

Documentary working hand in hand with activism has its roots in the 1960s, when it emerged as a tool to give voice to the voiceless:

> Video activism as political advocacy for social justice is a field of scholarship that emerged during the 1960s alongside a wider social activist movement that was characterized by the desire to bring marginalized thought and practice to public awareness. [...] Through such means video has demonstrated efficacy in mobilizing political consciousness and, by association, advocating and promoting greater awareness about important contemporary social issues. (Gaffney and White 2018, 1–2)

That such activist documentaries include biographical and autobiographical elements should not come as a surprise. Rather, it is a major trend nowadays: "Autobiographical documentaries abound in our contemporary cinematic landscape" (Anderst 2015, 255). Yet, other experts in media culture and documentary filmmaking caution against these ethics of humanitarianism, in particular Rangan in her work *Immediations* (2017), where she criticizes the "documentary tropes that generate a sense of emergency around endangered humanity–a sensation that makes us feel like 'nothing else matters,' especially when these tropes are employed directly by disenfranchises subjects" (Rangan, Story and Sarlin 2018, 199). Though up for debate, the complex nature of these activist biographical and autobiographical documentaries that are so common in the current contemporary cinematic scene needs to be further addressed.

The reason why I focus on only these two documentaries is to tease out their common ground as well as their differences, trying to address the popular acclaim they have received not only at a national but at an international level in shaping public awareness of the migrant crisis. *Walls* (Iraburu and Molina 2015) was nominated for Best Documentary Film at the 2016 Goya prize ceremony, with Goya awards being the Spanish film industry counterpart to the American Oscars. It did not win on that occasion, but did later, for Best National Documentary at the 2016 Film Festival in Zaragoza. The public also made their opinions heard in the 2016 International Film Festival in Murcia IBAFF, where it received the Audience Award for Best Feature Documentary. At a supranational level, it won the Jury Prize for Best Feature Film at 2015 Ajyal Youth Film Festival hosted by the Doha Film Institute. More importantly, it won the Oxfam Global Justice Award for Best Feature Documentary at 2016 IDFA (International Documentary Film festival Amsterdam). As for *Human Flow* (Ai 2017), it won in four categories at the 2017 Venice Film Festival and the 2017 Bambi award for courage. As is clear, its impact has been greater outside of the US, which makes sense considering Ai's positionality with respect to President Trump and his walls rhetoric.

The main focus of my study is how violence and migration is represented in these documentaries. I undertake a close reading of the two documentaries with several research questions in mind. What specific discursive strategies are deployed by filmmakers to encourage empathetic engagement? What kinds of shots are prevalent, e.g. close-ups vs aerial shots, and why? How is the face of the migrant shown as the core of the narrative while the victim-turned-survivor speaks? Is a 1st-person or a 3rd-person narrator more prevalent? How does that change its potential emotional impact? Are common human traits emphasized or is ethnic identity manifested? How is the border conceptualized?

The Visual Impact of *Walls*

A close reading of the documentary titled *Walls* (Iraburu and Molina 2015) must start by addressing the symbolic power of its namesake—"walls" as barriers, both in a physical and in a metaphorical sense of the word. As Bernardo Saldaña has recently pointed out, when describing the border between the United States and Mexico, "It is a stage for a daily three-act performance: migration, deportation and abuse of human rights" (2017, 258). Indeed, it is a kind of "stage" of recent creation, as Reece Jones cautions:

> The surge in interest in border walls and fences is not simply a media creation but rather represents a very recent historical trend, arising in response to the growth in spontaneous international migration. Although we often imagine that there was a past era in which most borders were secured with physical barriers, in fact the construction of border barriers is a relatively new phenomenon. (2016)

Though borders are not intrinsically violent, they epitomize the structural violence (Galtung 1990) at the heart of western institutions. Thus, the migrant who is fleeing from actual violence such as war, conflict, etc. is faced with a different kind of violence on arriving in the west, but violence, nonetheless.

Also deserving of attention is the documentary's distinct strategies for presenting the "victims." *Walls* (Iraburu and Molina 2015) features interviews where the camera does not reveal the (certain) presence of a mediator (filmmaker, translator or interviewer) nor are the questions or prompts heard in any case. In fact, the narrator is absent from the film, leaving the characters to speak for themselves. This might well be a purposeful authorial "strategic empathizing" technique (Keen 2008) to present migrants' voices as the legitimate bearers of their own personal true story. This is in line with recent sociological endeavors to highlight biographical research and extend agency to migrants, following Elsa Lechner's clever assertion that "Migrants' lives matter": "The goal was to hear the migrants themselves, to hear their truth, to cultivate dialogue between different people, to have access to their concrete life experiences, different from commonsensical discourses that reify identities and stereotypes" (2018, 4–5). Besides defying such processes of commodification, granting migrants their right to tell their stories may allow them to deal with their so often traumatic experience which, hidden and silenced, could otherwise never heal. As Lechner goes on to assert, "Most migrants actually experience migration as a biographical disruption, a source of solitary pain and suffering" (5). The fact that border people are struggling to cope with the reality that surrounds them is vital for their role as an authoritative witness to injustice: "it is the witness to suffering who is seen to occupy a position of particular importance in public and popular history and who has a unique relationship to the concept of authenticity" (Jones 2019, 136). Their first-person audio-visual testimony enhances audience responses to their plight.

Provided with a means to tell their stories to the whole world, the migrants featured in *Walls* are enacting a personal—self-reflective—as well as a collective—awareness-raising—role. These individual voices are meant to stand for the collective of border inhabitants and migrants whose stories are rarely heard in an unmediated format. As with other testimonial forms of life-writing advocacy, each voice represents some collective suffering worth of public attention (Martínez García 2017b, 596). However, in the absence of a third-person narrator that would facilitate some details and/or the migrant's own explanation about their exact place of origin, or their ethnic, socio-cultural or religious background, spectators are encouraged to use their imagination to fill that lacuna of information. A set of assumptions about shared human emotions, responding to known cases of extreme deprivation and violence, enable what Keen has called "broadcast strategic empathy" (2016, 22), which calls upon every audience (in the present day or later on) to experience emotional fusion by emphasizing our common human experiences, feelings, hopes, and vulnerabilities. Narrative empathy in the form of an author's broadcast strategic empathizing employs universals that will reach everyone, including distant others, connecting faraway subjects to sensitive readers and viewers. (22)

At the same time, these people's lives are quite peculiar to the place they inhabit. This need to portray their specific local differences is part of a different technique — that of "ambassadorial strategic empathy" (20), which "addresses targeted audiences with the aim of cultivating their empathy for the needy, the disenfranchised, or the misunderstood, often with a specific appeal for recognition, assistance or justice" (20). The combination of different strategic empathizing appeals, far from being uncommon, is what makes for the durability of these testimonial texts.

The scenes are shot as if they were happening right then and there. The camera moves slowly from close-ups to background and back to these border inhabitants' faces. The result of this realistic technique is that the film is not very elegant, but looks like a collage of stories, with the camera gaze at times focused on one character, at times on another, as if in real time. This focus on people's faces is a common strategy in documentary, as noted by Carl Plantinga (1999, 239), and creates affective engagements with the viewer, as one is made to wonder whether this circle of activity will ever be disrupted or whether, on the contrary, each of the main characters will carry on their strife for a better life without ever achieving their goal. A marked feature is the use of voiceover to relay information seemingly derived from some of the protagonists' deepest thoughts. Two particular instances stand out: first, two old American men are heard saying that children are "symbols of innocence" (Iraburu and Molina 2015) while they are conducting their humanitarian work of leaving water bottles at odd places in the desert separating Mexico from the US, where many die of dehydration; second, someone is watching TV while there is news on the Palestinian-Israeli wall, and the voiceover adds: "Arabs may not be so different from us as the media projects" (Iraburu and Molina 2015). While it is unclear exactly which person is saying these statements, they are meant to move consciousness on a global scale, so it is strategic that the narrating voice is anonymized.

Interestingly, the border represents a threat, but also a lifeline. Whereas it implies danger—of being shot, as in the case of Zimbabweans crossing into South Africa; of being detained, as Mexicans if caught by US border patrols; or of being beaten, as Moroccan women crossing merchandise into Spain on a daily basis, each "wall" featured in the documentary (Iraburu and Molina 2015) offers hope—of a better life on the other side, waiting for those who succeed in crossing and staying there. As the Moroccan young mother tells the camera with sad eyes, she will carry on this way of life as long as it is possible for the sake of her daughter—there is no alternative. But her determination and strength of will also show that she has become a survivor. By voicing her story, she is no longer a victim. The ambivalence of borders, summarized in her testimony, suggests migratory movements, though heavily restricted and potentially dangerous, will likely continue to exist.

Pervasive Movement in *Human Flow*

The human need to move toward a better life is the subject of the second documentary analyzed in this chapter—*Human Flow* (Ai 2017). Drone aerial shots are here strategically devised to capture the vastness of the space covered, both by the filmmaker and the migrants who are forced to stop at places as varied as Lesbos, the Bangladesh-Myanmar border, the Greece-Macedonia border, the Serbia-Hungary border, the Syria-Jordan border, South Italy, East Turkey, Lebanon, Gaza, Kenya, Pakistan, Afghanistan, Berlin, Calais, Iraq, the Mediterranean, and the Mexican-US border. Deserts seem never-ending, but refugee camps seen from above look indescribably large. Images take the place of words to reflect on human rights and the impact that geographical barriers may have on people's lives.

At this point, a hurdle in praising the affective power of images would be the notion that the image may function as part of a "regime of pity" (Chouliaraki 2006, 74). When Lilie Chouliaraki addresses the issue of pity in television news, she stresses the semiotic processes that collaborate toward the creation of, in her own words, "a coherent regime for the representation of suffering—a regime of pity that construes the event of suffering as the spectator's most immediate reality" (74). She problematizes spectators' feelings of powerlessness and compassion fatigue (113). Nevertheless, some amount of "pity" may indeed be a significant driver that motivates social change, effectively demonstrating the power of what Luc Boltanski calls the "politics of pity" (1999, 33): "when confronted with suffering all moral demands converge on the single imperative of action" (xv). The spectator plays an important role, Boltanski continues: "having knowledge of suffering points to an obligation to give assistance. Why else present a spectacle of suffering human beings to unconcerned people if not to draw their attention to it and so direct them to action?" (20). As long as spectators become actively engaged in the cause, even in the form of speech acts, Boltanski believes political constituencies may be mobilized (73). Instead of an emotional response, what activists seek is an ethical response to injustice.

Human Flow (Ai 2017) takes a radical departure from the observational praxis of *Walls* (Iraburu and Molina 2015) as it leads the viewer carefully from one place to another, with captions explaining history as well as context. These non-obtrusive bits and pieces of news information have a cumulative effect, building up the drama of migratory patterns today and slowly but consistently leading western viewers to empathize with these people in remote (like an African desert) or familiar (like the US-Mexican border) places. What *Human Flow* (Ai 2017) shares with *Walls* (Iraburu and Molina 2015) is this usage of both ambassadorial empathy—presenting a reality far away from viewers—and strategic empathy—presenting a nearby reality (Keen 2016, 20, 22), even if each documentary resorts to various other discursive mechanisms.

Intriguingly, Ai is part of the auto/biographical enterprise. He is narrating his own self coming to terms with this new reality which, as he has expressed in public appearances and other media, has deeply affected him and his perception of who he is (Loos 2017; Pogrebin 2018). Thus, Ai constructs a narrative that helps visualize the so frequently called "migrant crisis" but imbues it with human emotions — those of the people he encounters on his journey across the globe and those of the audience as they ethically engage with the subject of the film they are watching.

The face of the interviewee is of utmost importance. It becomes the emblem of an identity at stake — that of the vulnerable subject who, fleeing war, fighting poverty and destitution, needs to overcome fear and hardship in order to find a better life. This is what film theorist Carl Plantinga has called "the scene of empathy" (1999, 239), where

> the pace of the narrative momentarily slows and the interior emotional experience of a favored character becomes the locus of attention [...] we see a character's face, typically in closeup, either for a single shot of long duration or as an element of point of view structure [...] In either case, the prolonged concentration on the character's face is not warranted by the simple communication of information about character emotion. Such scenes are also intended to elicit empathetic emotions in the spectator. (239)

This kind of scene features prominently in Ai's documentary, for example when he interviews a woman about her journey and she starts crying, unable to explain with words what she has experienced, in effect reliving her trauma. The scene is devoid of background sound or music, and spectators are forced to contemplate this woman's face and extreme suffering, with just the presence of Ai's back to the camera as the interviewer. She testifies to the nonsense of agreements like repatriation from refugee camps: "No one asked where I wanted to go. I can't stay but..." (Ai 2017). Her "I" condensates the plight of millions forcibly returned without any explanation or kindness. Her words are filled with a mixture of anger and bereavement, and she starts crying. In seconds that feel like hours, Ai compels the spectator to acknowledge her trauma and her silence. Then, he gets up and consoles her, thus ending the highly emotional close-up on her face.

A similar denouncing voice is that of a male refugee in what was The Jungle, the camp on the outskirts of Calais that populated the news for months on end. This man, when asked why he had decided to come to Europe, voices his disappointment with European policymakers and society: "when we were in our countries, we heard Europe had democracy, we'd have freedom, respect..."

(Ai 2017). After living through The Jungle and its dismantlement, this man does not sound so optimistic about what the future holds. These two examples of first-person testimonial witnessing, directly witnessed by Ai, and secondarily by viewers, epitomize the ethical engagement which is one of the expected outcomes of this text.

In *Human Flow* (Ai 2017), Ai Weiwei consistently—and carefully—guides the whole process of the audience becoming a witness by constructing appropriate settings, shooting landscapes, doing close-ups on protagonists' faces, allowing for emotion-laden silences, and, first and foremost, being present before the camera at almost all times. In a way, it is as if he was reclaiming his own status of refugee and political exile, however not revealing his intention to do so. Yet, given his prominent public figure, he is in a privileged position to bring the hardship endured by stateless people to light, as he mentioned in an interview to *The New York Times*:

> It's really a challenge when you see these people—it's too big, too many—like an open wound. It's not a problem that can be easily solved. You have generations of people who have no education and who see how the world has treated them. (Pogrebin 2016)

Ai's careful choice of words—"an open wound"—harks back to a long-standing tradition of trauma literature. The audience is undoubtedly asked to question the ethics of migration and its obstruction policies, and to seek answers for the problematics of who actually gets to reach a destination or not, and why.

Conclusion

Mediation plays a vital role in shaping people's life stories so that they can be effective means of communicating a social, collective fight. Migrants may both benefit from such collective identifications and suffer from the stereotypes associated with them. On the one hand, media and mediation offers the possibility of reaching wider publics at an unprecedented scale. On the other hand, this may produce further movements against them, causing new legislation to be passed that, instead of working in their favor, is highly detrimental—proof of which has been the agreement signed between Europe and Turkey to send back refugees, and President

Trump's insistence on an improved, harder-to-cross wall between Mexico and the US.

Visualizing the border as a wall or a fence is not only symbolic but also a powerful metaphor of the forces limiting freedom. Ai's interview about his ironically titled project "Good Fences Make Good Neighbors" illustrates a feeling most viewers of documentaries such as *Walls* (Iraburu and Molina 2015) and *Human Flow* (Ai 2017) are left with: "Of course I hate fences, any kind of fences. You know, it stops people, they separate people, and they make so many lives so different" (Swift, Chainon, and Mullin 2017). As opposed to freedom of movement, border control exacts violence upon migrants' lives. In contrast to the right to one's own sustenance, stateless people cannot claim justice. Hunger, rape and destitution may not fit the description according to which one is granted refugee status, but those are key drivers for people on the move escaping violent contexts.

Amid current political debates on migration, there remains a noticeable silence: "the voices of migrants with irregular status themselves are rarely heard. This silence is rarely questioned, because migrants with irregular status are usually in no position to give voice to their treatment and experiences" (Lazaridis 2015, 14). What the documentaries in this chapter provide are precisely those missing voices, aiming to let the migrants tell their own story in their own words, rather than being subject to the objectification of the media. Despite the precarious nature of this voicing of the other in documentary cinema, studied among others by Hongisto (2018), it is an important chance for passive victims to become active agents. In that sense, these documentaries are survivors' life-writing texts, attempts by which migrants strive to inscribe themselves in History while constructing an identity at odds with their sociopolitical status.

In a culture dominated by the visual, human rights may benefit from narratives that make them—and their absence—visible. This is what documentary practitioners engaged in activism already know. They thus resort to distinct but complementary strategic empathizing techniques, levelling the tension between pointing out the plight of individuals as well as groups of people who are at risk of exclusion and emphasizing that which is shared by all humankind—humanity. Human dignity and human rights should not depend on the place where one is born, effectively depriving the person of their rights. This tension is not easily released, nor is an answer—political or otherwise—ready for viewers. Still, hope remains in the ethical engagement of viewers. As examples of auto/biographical testimonial practices, *Walls* (Iraburu and Molina 2015) and *Human Flow* (Ai 2017) serve an awareness-raising agenda. Though perhaps unable to affect politics, by making "potent ethical claims" (Martínez García 2017a, 13), they may change people's minds—the first step in a chain of potential social change. Migrants, facing brutal borders and experiencing violence on a regular basis, are in need of an urgent change of people's mindsets.

Bibliography

Ai Weiwei, dir. 2017. *Human Flow*. USA: AC Films.

Anderst, Leah. 2017. "The Self as Evidence and Collaborative Identity in Contemporary Autobiographical Documentary." *a/b: Auto/Biography Studies* 32 (2): 255–257. doi:10.1080/08989575.2017.1288030.

Arendt, Hannah. 1951. *The Origins of Totalitarianism*. New York: Harcourt, Brace.

Boltanski, Luc. 1999. *Distant Suffering: Morality, Media and Politics*. Translated by Graham Burchell. Cambridge: Cambridge UP.

Chouliaraki, Lilie. 2006. *The Spectatorship of Suffering*. London: SAGE.

DeGooyer, Stephanie, Alastair Hunt, Lida Maxwell, and Samuel Moyn. 2018. *The Right to Have Rights*. London: Verso.

Gaffney, Michael, and E. Jayne White. 2018. "Video Activism as Political Advocacy for Social Justice: The Legacy of Professor Anne Smith in Education." *Video Journal of Education and Pedagogy* 3 (5): 1–8. doi: https://doi.org/10.1186/s40990-018-0017-z.

Galtung, Johan. 1990. "Cultural Violence." *Journal of Peace Research* 27 (3): 291–305.

Hongisto, Ilona. 2018. "Realities in the Making: The Ethics of Fabulation in Observational Documentary Cinema." In *Storytelling and Ethics: Literature, Visual Arts and the Power of Narrative*, edited by Hanna Meretoja and Colin Davis, 190–199. New York: Routledge.

Iraburu, Pablo, and Migueltxo Molina, dirs. 2015. *Walls*. Spain: Arena Comunicación.

Jones, Reece. 2016. "Borders and Walls: Do Barriers Deter Unauthorized Migration?" *Migration Information Source*, Migration Policy Institute. Last modified October 5, 2016. https://www.migrationpolicy.org/article/borders-and-walls-do-barriers-deter-unauthorized-migration

Jones, Sara. 2017. "Mediated Immediacy: Constructing Authentic Testimony in Audio-Visual Media." *Rethinking History* 21 (2): 135–153. doi: 10.1080/13642529.2017.1305726.

Keen, Suzanne. 2008. "Strategic Empathizing: Techniques of Bounded, Ambassadorial, and Broadcast Narrative Empathy." *Deutsche Vierteljahrsschrift für Literaturwissenchaft und Geistesgeschichte* 82 (3): 477–493.

— — —. 2016. "Life Writing and the Empathetic Circle." *Concentric: Literary and Cultural Studies* 42 (2): 9–26.

Lahav, Gallya. 2004. *Immigration and Politics in the New Europe: Reinventing Borders*. New York: Cambridge UP.

Lazaridis, Gabriella. 2015. *International Migration into Europe: From Subjects to Abjects*. Basingstoke: Palgrave Macmillan.

Lechner, Elsa. 2018. "Migrants' Lives Matter: Biographical Research, Recognition and Social Participation." *Contemporary Social Science*, 500–514. doi: 10.1080/21582041.2018.1463449.

Loos, Ted. 2017. "Ai Weiwei, Once and Future New Yorker, Barnstorms through the Boroughs." *The New York Times*, October 5, 2017. https://www.nytimes.com/2017/10/05/arts/ai-weiwei-good-fences-make-good-neighbors-new-york.html?_r=0

Martínez García, Ana Belén. 2017a. "TED Talks as Life Writing: Online and Offline Activism." *Life Writing*, November 28, 2017. doi:10.1080/14484528.2017.1405317.

— — —. 2017b. "Unearthing the Past: Bringing Ideological Indoctrination to Light in North Korean Girls' Memoirs." *a/b: Auto/Biography Studies* 32 (3): 587–602.

Office of the United Nations High Commissioner for Refugees (UNHCR). 2010. *Convention and Protocol Relating to the Status of Refugees*. Geneva: UNHCR. http://www.unhcr.org/protection/basic/3b66c2aa10/convention-protocol-relating-status-refugees.html

Plantinga, Carl. 1999. "The Scene of Empathy and the Human Face on Film." In *Passionate Views: Film, Cognition, and Emotion*, edited by Carl Plantinga and Greg M. Smith, 239–255. Baltimore, MD: Johns Hopkins UP.

Pogrebin, Robin. 2016. "Ai Weiwei Melds Art and Activism in Shows About Displacement." *The New York Times*, October 20, 2016. https://www.nytimes.com/2016/10/21/arts/design/ai-weiwei-melds-art-and-activism-in-shows-about-displacement.html.

———. 2018. "Ai Weiwei's Little Blue Book on the Refugee Crisis." *The New York Times*, April 23, 2018. https://nyti.ms/2Hlfayy.

Rangan, Pooja, Brett Story, and Paige Sarlin. 2018. "Humanitarian Ethics and Documentary Politics." *Camera Obscura* 98, 33 (2): 197–207. doi: 10.1215/02705346-6923166.

Saldaña, Bernardo. 2017. "Tijuana: Walls and Borderlines." In *Human Dignity: Establishing Worth and Seeking Solutions*, edited by Edward Sieh and Judy McGregor, 247–262. London: Palgrave Macmillan. doi: 10.1057/978-1-137-56005-6_15.

Sandoval-García, Carlos. 2017. *Exclusion and Forced Migration in Central America, Mobility & Politics: No More Walls*. Cham: Palgrave Macmillan. doi: 10.1007/978-3-319-51923-4_1.

Schaffer, Kay, and Sidonie Smith. 2004. *Human Rights and Narrated Lives: The Ethics of Recognition*. New York: Palgrave Macmillan.

Smith, Sidonie, and Julia Watson. 2010. *Reading Autobiography: A Guide for Interpreting Life Narratives*. 2nd ed. Minneapolis, MN: Minnesota UP.

Stevenson, Nick. 2017. *Human Rights and the Reinvention of Freedom*. Abingdon: Routledge.

Swift, Hilary, Jean Yves Chainon, and Kaitlyn Mullin. 2017. "Ai Weiwei Puts up Fences to Promote Freedom." *The New York Times*, October 13, 2017. https://nyti.ms/2z47g41.

United Nations, General Assembly. 1948. Universal Declaration of Human Rights (UDHR). Resolution 217 A, December 10, 1948. Paris. http://www.un.org/en/universal-declaration-human-rights/index.html.

Whitlock, Gillian. 2015. *Postcolonial Life Narratives: Testimonial Transactions*. Oxford: Oxford UP.

Wilson, Richard Ashby, and Richard D. Brown, eds. 2009. *Humanitarianism and Suffering: The Mobilization of Empathy*. Cambridge: Cambridge UP.

Reversing the Logic of the Border: Violence and Migration in Contemporary Hispanic Dramatic Literature

Irene Alcubilla Troughton

Narratives of the Immigrant

This chapter addresses how violence is conceived and structured within the logic of the border and migratory practices in three Hispanic theatre plays. The first one, *Alguien silbó (y despertó a un centenar de pájaros dormidos)* by Antonio de Paco narrates the encounter of two characters on the border between Morocco and Spain: an illegal immigrant from Senegal (Cocodrilo) who tries to cross the border to get to Spanish ground and a Moroccan officer (Hombre). After having been hit in the head, Hombre loses his consciousness and wakes up to Cocodrilo who, in a mysterious attitude, makes him believe that he recognizes Hombre as a fellow immigrant. Hombre, in a futile attempt to save his life, plays along, adopting as his own the story of one of the immigrants he himself captured once. After several unclear exchanges of words, when we still do not know exactly who Hombre is, Cocodrilo discloses both his knowledge of Hombre being a migration officer and his intention of forcing him to cross the border as well.

In *Cazador de Gringos*, Daniel Serrano situates the action in the division between Mexico and the USA. In this play, another direct confrontation between two agents takes place: Heberto, a Mexican citizen ridiculously obsessed with protecting Mexico by impeding US citizens to go there, and Tony, an Americanised Mexican that works as a migration officer. This time, the border crossing happens only in role play, when Tony, after a casual visit to Heberto, is forced by him to pretend that he is trying to get into Mexico. Heberto, playing the role of the officer, calls into question Tony's claim of being Mexican, ordering him to perform humiliating tasks, such as eating a chili pepper while singing the Mexican national anthem. Either in reality, or within a fictional macabre game, both Hombre and Tony will suffer the same deadly fate.

As has been shown, the conflict does not arise between people from the two countries separated by the border, as would seem logical at first, but between someone conceptualized as an immigrant and a man who, even if he does not belong to the country of destiny, does retain certain privileges and reinforces the *status quo* of the border exchange. As Domennech de la Lastra (2017) highlights, the creation of contemporary borders does not correspond to the military enterprises of the past, as governments today do not try to protect themselves against an adjoining country but, on the contrary, collaborate with them in the creation of those frontiers. This is what, by the selection of characters, Daniel Serrano and Antonio de Paco are able to portray. The fact that these migration officers are not from Spain or the USA, but behave as if they were or are at ease with the immigration policies of the countries of destiny, creates bigger resentments and tensions between the two agents and points at the systemic, global pacts that are taking place in order to reinforce these divisions.

In the third play, *Ternura Suite* by Edgar Chías, we encounter a more metaphorical approach to the issue of migration, where a person (*el vistante*, the visitor) enters someone's house (*el anfitrión*[1], the host) uninvited. After a few failed attempts to establish a dialogue, marked by fear and frustration, the two agents engage in an extremely violent exchange of power where physical damage is constantly inflicted, and which serves as a way of feeling secure in what they both consider their right to dwell at home.

To analyze how violence is portrayed in these plays and the consequences of it, I shall offer a theoretical framework for the figure of the immigrant that will aid us in comprehending the key concept of being a stranger, as well as those of tolerance and hospitality. Furthermore, I will align Derrida's distinction of two kinds of

---

[1] It is important to note how the name of the character "anfitrión" is masculine, although it must be, according to the author, portrayed by a woman. The importance of gendering the two agents of this play shall be pointed out in the upcoming sections.

hospitality with two distinct instances of violence: instrumental violence, embedded in the logics of retributive justice in advance capitalism, and structural violence, which is generated by the same system that seems to protect us from it. This shall provide the basis for reading these three plays in a new light, thus opening new paths in discussing migration and violence.

Conceptualizing Strangers

A useful starting point for thinking about the situation of the immigrant is through the dichotomy of the stranger and the citizen. Sarah Ahmed, in her book *Strange Encounters: Embodied Others in Post-Coloniality* (2000), highlights how the creation of the "stranger" strengthens identity formations that do not accept, and indeed fear, alterity, at the same time that it helps in constructing myths about the good citizen. For her, a "stranger" is not someone who we fail to recognize but someone that we recognize as such, as already "not belonging". This differentiation of others (the safe and familiar one versus the stranger) occurs in "inter-subjective encounters in public life [where we] continually reinterpellate subjects into differentiated economies of names and signs" (21). Therefore, and expanding on Althusser's theory of interpellation through a performative misrecognition in hailing[2], Ahmed considers a previous sphere where bodies are marked and to which we can later on assign the labels of the "lawful subject, the one who has the right to dwell" (21) and the stranger.

In this way, Ahmed subverts the Hegelian model of the master-slave dialectic by asserting that it is not the recognition by others that constitutes the subject but, instead, the recognition of others as strangers that creates the lawful subject as such. These strangers are considered to be the carriers of danger; thus, their recognition is embedded in a discourse of both survival and of caring. The good citizen will be, on the one hand, streetwise inasmuch he or she is able to distinguish where the dangerous strangers are and, on the

---

[2] Interpellation, imagined as everyday police hailing on the streets, equivalent to a "hey, you", is considered by Althusser as a misrecognition that constitutes the subject that it names in the present.

other hand, shall be willing to protect their own kind from that peril.

From there emerges the neighborhood watch, which can be understood either literally or metaphorically as a post-Foucauldian panopticon that transposes the logic of the neighborhood and the stranger to the nation and the immigrant. As Ahmed herself asserts, the immigrant is the ultimate stranger and poses a danger to the purified nation, the purified community, the purified life of the good citizen. In contrast to this concept, an image of the safe home materializes, presenting violence as exceptional and always coming from outside the protective walls of the home. This violence, however, turns out to be two-fold: in the same way that it comes from outside, it is also considered to be justifiable when the danger has dared to come too close (Ahmed 2000, 25). This brings us to the problem of tolerance and hospitality in migration.

Tolerance and Hospitality

Jacques Derrida, in his famous treatise on hospitality, analyzed how the word play "pas d'hospitalité" — meaning both "step of hospitality" and "no hospitality" — marked the impossibility and the paradoxical structure of such a concept. According to the author, two types of hospitality can be distinguished: "the law of absolute, unconditional, hyperbolical hospitality" (2000, 75) and the laws, in plural, of hospitality, where the rights and duties of everyone involved in this process are determined. In a double movement, the unconditional hospitality demands that we transgress every individual law of hospitality and, equally, by ascribing ourselves to the laws of hospitality, to its delimited frames of action in everyday life, we surpass the conditions for the hyperbolical welcome. Both laws are contradictory and yet need each other: conditional laws require guidance by the law of unconditional hospitality and the latter, in order to be what it is and not turn into its opposite — in order to not become utopian and abstract — needs the laws that nonetheless deny unconditional hospitality. Such a situation creates a system that is self-perpetuated and that, at the same time, constitutes an impossibility.

As Carlos Thiebaut (2010) notes, in contemporary society we have witnessed a conflation of the logics of tolerance and hospitality. Tolerance, according to him, is an internal claim made by a familiar other, by a neighbor, that asks us to accept their differences. Tolerance is considered to be a transitory state until those differences are accepted by the rule of law. Hospitality, also transitory, is directed nonetheless toward the exterior, to a visitor that makes a claim of acceptance during their visit. Our mode of recognition through hospitality will then be valid as long as that person remains a mere visitor. Nowadays, however, we are confronted with experiences of migrants that cannot or do not want to follow the requirements that the country of destiny establishes for them to assimilate to that culture and abandon their status of "visitors". Therefore, a claim for tolerance within the frame of hospitality occurs.

This new type of tolerance-hospitality, however, is configured, as Žižek (2008) points out, not as real acceptance of difference but as fear of harassment. Žižek highlights how harassment works as the supposedly threatening presence of the stranger that trespasses and destabilizes the borders that conform the citizen's identity. Therefore, the other is allowed to share space with us as long he or she does not come too close, as long as he or she is not really "other". Regarding the author, ours is an era characterized by a post-political bio-politics where harassment occupies a central role. On the one hand, bio-politics are structured around a politics of fear that aims at defending itself from potential harm. On the other hand, post-politics try to mobilize and manipulate a paranoid crowd: a communion of terrified people. By bringing those two terms together, Žižek is able to analyze how, in contemporary society, the drive of protecting a supposedly safe home from potential harm is achieved by a politics of terror where the danger is conceptualized as an always lurking harassment that comes from outside. Liberal tolerance, then, is strictly linked to a fear of harassment which finally makes tolerance equivalent to its contrary: "in other words, I should respect his *intolerance* of my over-proximity. What increasingly emerges as the central human right in late-capitalist society is *the right not to be harassed*, which is a right to remain at a safe distance from others" [emphasis in the original] (2008, 41).

With this in mind, it is possible to distinguish the two types of violence that I would like to consider in these plays. Within the discourse of the stranger and the citizen, the logics of tolerance-hospitality situate violence as an external force that threatens to trespass the safe walls of the home. Once the immigrant-stranger has crossed this previously stablished border and it has consequently proved the necessity and even existence of that real or imagined border[3], violence is justifiable "in the name of safety, safety for the citizens of the Nation States that allow for these atrocities" (Dzodan 2011). Violence, then, is understood as instrumental, as a means to an end: protecting the home. This instrumental violence is applied when, in Derridean terms, the laws of hospitality are imperiled.

As will be shown in the next subsections, nonetheless, these plays allow for a second reading of violence as structural, as constitutive of the same system that claims to give protection to it and as symbolic; that is, embedded in a logic of signs and names that precedes and conditions the subjects of migration. In this sense, a parallel between the structural violence and the constitutive violence of the unconditional Law of Hospitality can be drawn. According to Derrida, the predominant structure of hospitality (the conjugal phallogocentric model) implies that it is the master of the house who lays down the laws for it: "he represents them and submits to them to submit the others to them" (2000, 149), usually sending women to the visitors in the name of hospitality. In the same way, the system that allows for hospitality (and instrumental violence in cases of exception) to happen, is grounded in a previous violence based on the conceptions of home, belonging and identity, as will be shown in the forthcoming sections.

---

[3] It is essential to take into account the performative power of the border, which creates the possibilities of its own existence, in the same way that a cut is previous to a division of parts. By the act of establishing a border "in the name of safety", those agents that try to cross it can be immediately conceptualized as potential dangers, as illegal threats that consequently support the necessity of having such a border.

The Reverse Logic on the Border

As has been discussed, in those cases where the stranger does get "too close", instrumental violence comes in. In these situations, the immigrant defies the unwritten rule of this new tolerance claim within the frame of hospitality: that of harassment. Thus, violence is accepted as a force employed in a state of exception (Agamben 2017) where those rules have been defied[4]. In the plays analyzed, nonetheless, a reverse logic takes place whereby the immigrant himself is allowed to initiate that violence. This dramaturgical strategy takes place in the three case studies: in all of them the immigrant-stranger enacts an active position, not a passive reception, towards violence, therefore subverting the roles of strangers and citizens.

Through a close reading of the characters' intentions, it will become evident how they portray the frustration towards a law that seems to neglect them within the narrative of redistributive justice: "the logics of claims and compensations which is central to advanced capitalism" (Braidotti 2010, 202). As a consequence of this mode of thinking, several assumptions regarding the subject and its relation to autonomy and vulnerability shall be indicated. This is achieved by the exposure of the underlying principles of that instrumental violence (namely, a particular conception of autonomy/vulnerability and the ideas of retributive justice), as well as by exposing how subverting the roles only reinforces a circle of endless harm, hint at the existence of a primordial violence that comes before the instrumental one: a structural violence, which has been already mentioned, and symbolic violence, which will be the topic of the next section.

The confrontations observed in the plays between the agents at the border all come from a perceived failure of the law: the

---

[4] Giorgo Agamben largely theorized the "state of exception" as a situation where laws can be suspended in relation to individuals deprived of their rights: *homini sacri* who can be killed but not sacrificed. Furthermore, in the same way that the bare life of the *homini sacri* relates to the system through an inclusive exclusion, the sovereign law gets confirmed by its suspension in the state of exception.

stranger feels the frustration of an unjust jurisdiction that never benefits him. Heberto illustrates such a position when he asserts:

> HEBERTO: pero fíjate bien, Gringoprieto, fíjate bien la diferencia: mientras ellos vienen a echar desmadres y nosotros ni siquiera les preguntamos a qué chingados vienen, nosotros vamos allá a gastar, a trabajar, a pagar impuestos, y ustedes arman un pedotote (2005, 48).[5]

The anger does not only come from the position of inequality that subjects at both sides of the border experience but also from the fact that no one takes responsibility for such a situation. In that line of thought, Cocodrilo and Hombre interchange this dialogue:

> HOMBRE: Yo no soy culpable de lo que le pasa a usted. No tengo nada que ver. ¿Es que no lo entiende? Está usted loco y lleno de rencor […]
>
> COCODRILO: (soltándole del cuello) Nada… no vamos a solucionar nada, porque nadie es culpable. Nadie, nadie es culpable de lo que pasa aquí. ¿Verdad? (2007, 56).[6]

In those circumstances where the law seems unreasonable and noone takes responsibility, the strangers feel entitled to create their own sense of justice. As Visitante asserts:

> Un día, nomás porque me sale de los huevos, así, casi gratuitamente, decida servirme yo solo con la cuchara grande. Porque ya me toca, ¿no? ¿O cuándo? ¿Cuándo me va a tocar si no es ahora? ¿Cuándo mierdas, cuándo remierdas me tocaría si no? ¿Cuándo? (2013, 25).[7]

---

[5] "But pay attention, Gringoprieto, pay attention to the difference: while they come here to party and we don't even fricking ask them why, we go there to spend money, to work, to pay taxes and you all make a big fuss about it." (All translations provided are mine.)

[6] "MAN: I am not guilty of what is happening to you. I have nothing to do with it. Don't you understand? You are crazy and full of resentment […]
COCODRILO: (letting go of his neck) Nothing… we are going to solve nothing, because no one is guilty. No one, nobody is guilty of what is happening here. Right?"

[7] "One day, just because I fucking want to, just like that, I might decide to serve myself with the big spoon. Because it's my turn now, isn't it? Or not? When then? When it's going to be my turn if not now? When the fuck, when the flying fuck would otherwise be my turn? When?"

In the case of *Ternura Suite*, that justice consists of the visitor's supposed right to dwell in a house and demand tenderness, attention and sex from their host, constantly using the threat of rape as a way to compensate for his position of subalternity. In *El Cazador de Gringos* and *Alguien silbó*, the sense of justice rests in the migration officer crossing the border themselves. In the latter play, we as spectators are not aware of the identity of either of them until the plot progresses, but Cocodrilo is, which serves to prove his point about the power of stories. The stories that the two characters tell and that we overhear as an audience have the ability to conceal the truth, to re-shape the past but also to conform our identity. Ultimately, stories offer the possibility of the ethical decision:

> COCODRILO: Y usted dijo que era un hombre bueno... Si usted hubiera sido quien decía ser, ahora estaría en esta situación justificadamente... intentando saltar, tendría razones para saltar, ¿verdad? Pues entonces, imagine que es usted ese estudiante que dijo ser y todo arreglado. Será más fácil así... ¿Cómo prefiere pasar al otro lado? ¿Como quien es o como quien decía ser? (2007, 59).[8]

This reversal of roles is understood in the play as a political pact in lieu of an efficient law:

> COCODRILO: Llegaremos a un acuerdo, usted y yo, como hacen los gobiernos [...] Usted, como representante del gobierno de su país y yo del mío, alcanzando un acuerdo para solucionar el problema de la inmigración y poniéndolo en práctica esta misma noche de manera efectiva (2007, 54).[9]

But such a pact that ends in the double meaning of "going to the other side" (as in crossing the border and dying) is necessarily fictive and absurd. Consequently, the drive to achieve justice turns

---

[8] COCODRILO: And you said you were a good man... if you had been who you said you were, you would have justifiably been in this situation... trying to jump, you would have had reasons to jump, right? Well then, imagine that you are that student you said you were and all sorted. It will be easier that way... how would you rather go to the other side? As you are or as you said you were?"

[9] "COCODRILO: We will come to an agreement, you and me, like governments do [...] You, like a representative of your county's government and me like one from mine, reaching an agreement to solve the problem of immigration and putting it to practice this same night in an effective manner".

into a drive for vengeance, continuing a circle of endless and pointless violence.

In *El cazador de gringos*, the crossing of borders does not happen in reality, but through roleplay, a roleplay that at first is understood by the rest of the characters as a sort of game and by the audience as a comic situation. Heberto is a Mexican that lives in Tijuana, right in front of the border between Mexico and the US, where he has created a trench to prevent Americans from crossing. The fact that, unlike in *Alguien silbó*, from the very beginning, the audience is aware of Heberto's nonsensical enterprise and his futile attempts at being a hero in a distorted neighborhood watch, gives this play a grotesque and comic tone. After roleplaying being a migration officer that does not allow US citizens (exemplified by Toni) to come to Mexico, he proceeds to torture and kill him in an attempt to restore his power, which takes us to the next step: the conceptualization of autonomy and vulnerability within these frames.

Autonomy and Vulnerability

Building on psychoanalytic discourses on how masculine positions are built on a denial of their vulnerability, Butler, Gambetti and Sabsay (2016) point out how, within the scene of power, this denial of vulnerability can take place by either disavowing it or exacerbating it. When the exacerbation route is taken, the recourse to vulnerability serves as a way of excluding minorities, like when nation-states proclaim their hypervulnerability to the arrival of immigrants. This strategy can work both ways then: "'others' might be exposed to vulnerability as a way of shoring up power, but vulnerability can also be claimed by those who seek to rationalize the subjugation of minorities. Such strategies of claiming vulnerability on the part of the powerful become all the more complicated, and paradoxical" (2016, 5). This at first contradictory position can be explained through the lens of the previously addressed fear of harassment, as the liberal respect for the vulnerable other can be taken to such an extreme that there would arise "an attitude of narcissistic subjectivity which experiences the self as vulnerable, constantly exposed to a multitude of potential 'harassments'" (Žižek 2008, 42).

The appearance of vulnerable figures in this panorama, as Ahmed (2000) highlights, serves as a moral justification of both the constant self-policing of strangers and the eventual violence it takes to preserve the safe space of the home. As she poses it, "the discourse of vulnerability allows self-policing to be readable as the protection of others: the risk posed by suspects and strangers is a risk posed to the vulnerable bodies of children, the elderly and women" (2000, 27–28). The good citizen would be someone who can protect the weaker ones. In the plays analyzed, however, a shift of roles takes place, and the immigrant stranger is the one that attains power understood as a form of domination.

In *Ternura Suite*, this constant search for domination is addressed through a conflict of gender and class. The host, who is described from the very beginning as in need of being portrayed by an attractive woman, lives alone in her house, where, as we are told by the visitor, she tends to bring different men. This is a decisive factor for the visitor, a lower-class male, to feel entitled to demand non-consensual sex from her. Yet she, as the privileged owner of a well-off house, has the right, supported by the authorities, to protect her property and deny entry to whoever she pleases. The limits of hospitality, due to a fear of harassment, become clear in the next passage:

> VISITANTE: Créame. Yo sé que es difícil, pero tengo un problema. Un problema muy serio. Estoy desesperado. Nadie quiere ayudarme. A nadie le importa que la gente tenga problemas. Tú me puedes ayudar. Ayúdame. Por favor.
> ANFITRIÓN: No. Mira, no. Entiéndeme. Te metiste en mi casa sin el menor respeto por mi espacio. Aunque fuera cierto que tienes un problema, no te voy a ayudar. Estás abusando. Quiero que te vayas. Perdóname. (2013, 29).[10]

After her refusal, both actors engage in a physically violent war where they constantly interchange the roles of the victim and

---

[10] "VISITOR: Believe me. I know that it is difficult, but I have a problem. A very serious problem. I am desperate. No one wants to help me. No one cares about people having problems. You can help me. Help me. Please.
HOST: No. Look, no. Understand me. You have entered my house without respecting my space. Even if it is true that you have a problem, I am not going to help you. You are being abusive. I want you to leave. Sorry."

perpetrator, of the vulnerable and the dominant. Under this light, autonomy is in strict opposition to vulnerability which needs to be either subjugated or under a paternalistic protection. The understanding of the autonomous subject as one who avoids frailty, who is self-determined and exercises power, can be observed in the words of the Visitante in *Ternura Suite*:

> VISITANTE: Elijo ser yo mismo la medida del orden y la autoridad. Yo soy el poder. Yo. Elijo mandarme yo y no obedecer a otro. Yo. Elijo ser el patrón de mis impulsos. Yo. Yo elijo. Yo (2013, 38).[11]

In *El cazador de gringos*, such an autonomy is searched for in the control over the vulnerable figures: women and children, who, due to the grotesque character of the play, are completely outside of his control. Clara, his wife, does not accept his attempts at patriarchal authority and tends to stay outside of Heberto's fruitless plans:

> HEBERTO: *(A Clara)* ¡Tú tampoco te vas a ninguna parte!
> *Clara que está de espaldas a Heberto, se para en seco. Y lentamente se da la vuelta, transformada. Nico se queda pasmado, viendo la escena.*
> CLARA: *(Se acerca a Heberto, enfurecida)* ¿Qué dijiste, loco cabrón?
> HEBERTO: *(Ya no tan autoritario)* Que tú te quedas...
> CLARA: ¡Nomás eso me faltaba! ¡Que un cabrón paranoico como tú me ande preguntando qué hice hace treinta años! *(Clara lo empieza a golpear. Heberto suelta el rifle para cubrirse con los brazos)* Como si te interesara. Si no te interesa lo que hice hace diez minutos, ¡menos te importa lo que hice en Tubutama!
> HEBERTO: ¡Pérate Bárbara!
> CLARA: ¡Y ahorita mismo te metes y te cenas lo que te hice, que no voy a estar tirando la comida! *Clara lo va metiendo a golpes* (2005, 19).[12]

---

[11] "VISITOR: I choose to be myself the measure of order and authority. I am the power. Me. I choose to be in command of myself and not to obey any other. Me. I choose to be the master of my impulses. Me. I choose. Me."

[12] "HEBERTO: *(To Clara)* You won't go anywhere either!
Clara, who has her back towards Heberto, suddenly stops. And slowly turns around, transformed. Nico stays bewildered, watching the scene.
CLARA: *(approaching Heberto, furious)* What did you say, crazy bastard?
HEBERTO: *(Not as authoritarian as before)* that you shall stay...
CLARA: that's what I needed! That a paranoid bastard like you would ask me what I was doing thirty years back! *(Clara starts hitting him. Heberto drops the rifle to cover himself with his arms)* As if you were interested. If you are not interested in what I did ten minutes ago, you are not interested in what I did in Tubutama either!

The funny tone of the scene comes from the fact that our expectations of such an authority, namely heteropatriarchal control, are reversed or truncated, giving Heberto's attempt to hold that type of power a ridiculous tone. However, his bigger failure in this respect, and underlying cause of his obsession with the border, is explained almost at the end of the play, in a monologue that is displayed in front of the soon-to-be-killed Tony. In there, Heberto tells us how her daughter left home to marry an American man, who Heberto decides to beat up to restore his power as the main manly figure that is already compromised by race. After this, his daughter decides to leave for good and breaks contact with him, thus preventing him from knowing his grandson later on.

> HEBERTO: Que tiene un hijo, me dijo Clara, y que es igualito a mí. Me quiso enseñar la foto, pero yo no quise [...] Si uno es macho, pues se sostiene y punto. Nada de andar allí con cosas (2005, 49).[13]

The final effort to recover his lost power then consists of killing Tony, who is an Americanized Mexican who works as a migration officer and looks just like the man that married her daughter. As Herberto later tells us, this embodies his failure as a heteropatriarchal leader, as an immigrant and as a good citizen of the neighborhood watch.

Fictive Pacts and the Failure of Language

These plays follow in a reverse way the same logic that structures violence in the narrative of the stranger and hospitality. Violence, in this discourse, is understood as instrumental and exceptional in those cases where it is needed to restore power and preserve property. The plays analyzed allow for the absurdity of the situation to arise and make obvious the impossibility of coming out of this logic

---

HEBERTO: Wait, barbarian!
CLARA: and you go inside right now and eat what I prepared for dinner, I am not going to waste food!
Clara takes him inside by hitting him."

[13] "HEBERTO: She has a son, Clara told me, and he looks apparently just like me. She wanted to show me a picture, but I didn't want to [...] if you are a man, you hold on and that's it. No messing around with those things."

unharmed by reversing the roles. The hilarity of *El cazador de gringos* and the tragic atmospheres of *Alguien Silbó* and *Ternura Suite* are possible because the positions of the lawful subject and the immigrant stranger are not interchangeable. As Ahmed (2000) already showed, their bodies are already marked in a complex logic of signs and misrecognitions, making impossible the pact that Cocodrilo tried to achieve with Hombre. This same failed pact, this time established between the actors and the audience, takes place in *Ternura Suite* where, through a stage direction, Edgar Chías mentions the following: "los asistentes decidirán si lo penetra con el taladro o no. Quizá se escuchen los argumentos, quizá solo la votación general. De cualquier modo, Anfitrión va a partir su carne. Al cabo de la encuesta, no importa el resultado, lo hace" (2013, 59).[14]

Nevertheless, by reversing and reproducing the logic of instrumental violence on the border, these plays point to something else, to a primary violence that precedes those situations and that is structural and symbolic. Structural violence depends on our understanding of how identity is constructed, and therefore what constitutes a lawful subject, and a good citizen is linked to a definition of "home", as well as who has the right to dwell on that space. As has been mentioned in previous sections and is perfectly portrayed in in the case of *Ternura Suite*, the Law of Hospitality implies a primal violence: that of the division between those subjects who are allowed to dwell and those who are not. The lawful citizen is entitled then to reject the immigrant-stranger's claims to hospitality and tolerance by paradoxically alluding to a permanent state of vulnerability and tends to desire autonomy understood as dominant power.

Symbolic violence resides in the same economy that names those subjects and reduces them to stranger-others. As Ahmed shows, one of the main problems of the conceptualization of the stranger is related to its lack of referent, creating a category that is

---

[14] "The attendees will decide whether or not she penetrates him with the drill. Maybe the arguments will be heard, maybe only the general vote. In any case, Host will break his flesh. At the end of the voting, no matter the result, she does it."

ultimately empty: "the failure to name those who inhabit the signifier 'suspicious' hence produces the figure of the unspecified stranger, a figure that is required by the making or sensing of 'the common', of what 'we' are, as a form of distinction or value (property)" (2000, 26). In *Ternura Suite*, the failures of language can be observed on two levels. First, the symbolic naming of the two main characters as "Visitante" and "Anfitrión" (visitor and host) already marks them and subjects them to an economy of hospitality where unequal treatments are going to take place. Secondly, whereas Anfitrión has a name that is known by the audience and the other character, Visitante constantly changes his name, explicitly stating the insignificance, in his case, of providing a real one. The carrier of danger, the potential harassment, does not need to be linked to a specific individual; in fact, the mere narrative that supports those views rests in the emptiness (and therefore exchangeability) of that category.

The immigrant and migration officer in *Alguien silbó* significantly hold the titles of "Cocodrilo" and "Hombre" (Crocodile and Man), respectively. In here, the disparity of symbolic marking between the lawful subject and the stranger not only exposes the impossibility of individuation but also points to a process of animalization. The immigrant-stranger has been deprived of humanity to an extent that he is no longer able to remember his previous name, adopting both the label of "Cocodrilo" and the logic behind it. As he explains: "así funciona esto. Se agazapan entre los matorrales como animales al acecho y esperan la señal" (2007, 37), "todo lo que necesitamos estará entre los restos, lo suficiente para vivir. Busque entre los restos, como las alimañas"[15] (31). The animalization of the immigrant-stranger and their conceptualization as a possible threat entail a double narrative of hypervisibility and invisibility, as he is

---

[15] "This is how it works. They huddle in the bushes like stalking animals and wait for the signal", "everything that we need will be among the waste, enough to keep on living. Search within the waste, like vermin."

easily identified as the one who does not belong and yet is constantly ignored: "nosotros no estamos aquí. No existimos, aquí o en otro lugar. Los animales no existen para los hombres" (59).[16]

Spectator as Third-Party

How are we to come out of that circle then? I would like to propose an understanding of the audience as a third party in the resolution of violent and harmful conflicts. Therefore, by enacting the dramatic text on the stage and by the specific cues that are given in the plays regarding how to address the audience, it is possible to see the role of the spectator as essential in these conceptualizations of violence. As Carlos Thiebaut asserts, this figure, as the third actant in the perpetrator-victim dichotomy, can offer judgement in a third-person perspective, distant from the first-person view of the victim and the second person mode of the perpetrator. The third party is then a "concerned spectator" that has "an active role as a member of the experience of violence" (2015, 10). Complementing this view with Žižek's mention of how, even if our abstract reasoning is extremely developed, our emotional and ethical responses are still conditioned by out reactions to suffering and harm that we witness (2008, 43), we can begin to grasp the importance of the audience in a theatre setting.

The role of the audience as a third party that is in the presence[17] of that pain, being even complicit by their observation in the

---

[16] "We are not here. We don't exist, neither here nor in another place. Animals don't exist in the eyes of men"
[17] This term is being strategically used not only in its acceptation of "witnessing" but also in the theatrical meaning consolidated by Erika Fischter-Lichter (2008) of co-presence. "Presence", then, points at the distinctive quality of theatre that, according to recent debates, would reside in the confluence of space and time of audience and actors allowing for an auratic presence to appear. Advances in technology, however, have created tensions in this supposedly essential quality of theatre with scholars such as Philip Auslander (2006, 2012) or Sarah Bay-Cheng (2012) addressing the importance of mediation and documentation in the consideration of the theatrical act. In this section, however, I shall follow Pedro Manuel's (2014) approach to the concept of co-presence in which technological and theatrical advances (where a part of the actor-audience coupling might be missing) still can contribute to the feeling of such presence instead of rendering the concept obsolete.

reinforcement of the violence, is an essential feature of those plays. The spectacular condition of how that violence is perpetuated and constructed by and through certain social imaginaries is revealed in *El Cazador de gringos* by Heberto's attitude in the role play and by the space that he has constructed. As is explained by stage directions at the beginning: "Heberto ha colocado en la azotea una trinchera que copió de alguna película de Hollywood" (2005, 2).[18] The cultural constructions of this specific type of violence is going to determine in a performative way his actions and our way of approximating and evaluating them. Similarly, in *Ternura Suite* it is specified how the spectacular machinery needs to be self-evident, also encouraging through stage directions the introduction of screens that broadcast live the most violent scenes. Edgar Chías, however, goes a step further by creating characters that interrupt the action to address the audience, to engage them through sideways or direct looks in search for their approval: "la relación entre ellos se torna más estrecha e intensa, aunque no dejan de mirarnos furtivamente, esperando complicidad" (2013, 26).[19]

The role of the audience as an active witness of violence becomes evident in *Alguien silbó* right at the beginning of the play. Cocodrilo, whose voice is heard coming from the darkness, slowly shows himself sitting on the stage, directly gazing at the stalls while stating the following:

> Eh, ¡amigo! Tú no lo puedes imaginar
> Ya sé que no sabes de lo que hablo
> Hay que haber escuchado la verdadera historia de los cocodrilos
> Hay que saber la verdadera historia de la piel del cocodrilo (2007, 19).[20]

Unlike the previous plays where the visual aspect of the complicit communal construction of violence was emphasized, here the role of hearing becomes essential. The audience, comprised in that

---

[18] "Heberto has placed in the rooftop terrace a trench which he copied from a Hollywood movie."
[19] "The relationship between them turns closer and more intense but they don't stop looking at us sideways, waiting for our complicity."
[20] "Hey, friend, you can't imagine it. I know that you don't know what I'm talking about. You need to have heard the true story of the crocodiles. You have to know the true story of the crocodile's skin."

ironic vocative of "amigo", needs to actively listen to those animal stories which are usually disregarded. Such a story that we eventually and slowly get to discover through the interaction between Cocodrilo and Hombre is contradictory, fragmented, forgotten and invented at the same time. Fiction and reality fuse not only in the conscious selection of the discourses of the two characters of the images that they want to present to each other, but also in the involuntary interplay of memories and oblivion of the immigrant's past:

> No sirven los recuerdos. Se quedan agarrados al estómago. Recordar solo nos deja aire en el estómago. A partir de esta noche usted comenzará a no recordar, como sin darse cuenta. Aprenderá a mirar sólo hacia delante. ¿Sabe una cosa? A mí los recuerdos se me confunden en este lugar extraño. Sinceramente, prefiero olvidar. Simplemente ya no me llamo (2007, 31)[21]

Cocodrilo interpellates us and urges us to wake up and listen to a story that might be confusing, that might not be holistic but that nonetheless requires us to witness it. Cocodrilo reminds us of our ethical imperative of detaching ourselves from those sleeping birds that metaphorically surround the characters of the play and try to imagine, through and with him, what an animal story would be like:

> En este momento la mitad del mundo duerme
> Los pájaros ya se fueron a dormir
> ¡Estúpidos pájaros!
> Es hora de dormir
> La mitad del mundo duerme
> La mitad del mundo
> Estúpidos pájaros (2007, 21)[22]

---

[21] "Memories are worthless. They hold onto your stomach. Remembering only fills your stomach with air. From tonight on, you will start to forget, almost without realizing it. You will learn to look forward. Do you know something? Memories get mixed up in this strange place. Honestly, I'd rather forget. I simply do not name myself anymore."

[22] "At this moment, half of the world is sleeping. The birds already went to sleep. Stupid birds! It's time to sleep. Half of the world is sleeping. Half of the world. Stupid birds."

Conclusion

In the course of this analysis, two frames for understanding violence have been discussed: one that comprehends violence as instrumental and one that considers a previous level where violence intercedes at a structural and symbolic level. By following Ahmed's manner of transposing the logic of the citizen and the stranger onto the nation and the immigrant, as she herself proposes, it is possible to address the first instance of violence. The instrumental understanding of violence then relies on the narratives of the good citizen (the rightful, lawful subject) and the stranger, where a justification of violence takes place as long as the immigrant defies the obscured and unspoken rules of hospitality; this takes place whenever the rightful subject feels exposed to potential dangers, whenever they get confronted by possible perpetrators of harassment. This well-structured meta-narrative that still holds up nowadays presupposes, and is built upon, conceptions of the "home", the right to dwell, and a certain type of identity formation that fears — and tries to assimilate — alterity.

Thanks to the close reading of *El cazador de gringos*, *Alguien silbó* and *Ternura Suite*, it is possible to explore their construction of a space where the logic of such narratives is reversed, where the immigrant crosses those boundaries and positions themselves in the dominant role. The consequence of those actions, however, lead them to an impossibility of achieving the justice they wanted to restore, perpetuating instead a circle of violence that turns their initial intentions into vengeance. Nevertheless, by exposing this reversal, a new type of violence that precedes and permits the instrumental usage of it to arise is shown: a structural and symbolic violence. Through an analysis of the texts and the stage directions, the ways in which these pieces signal something greater than the mere reproduction of power structures has been addressed. These three dramatic texts call attention to the damaging myths that underlie these narratives, to the constructed status of the "home" and which subjects are entitled to it, to the way autonomy and vulnerability are articulated as opposites, to how hospitality is based on a primary exclusion and, finally, to the manner in which bodies are already marked in a symbolic economy of signs that would never permit such an interchange of roles to happen.

Finally, by positing the spectator as an active listener to the immigrants' stories, as well as a complicit co-creator of the violence that is shown on stage, these plays are able to disrupt the circle of violence and point to the ethical imperative of us taking responsibility in a situation where no one wants to be blamed. Even if the spectators are not directly addressed as the cause of those actions, the characters direct their gaze towards them in a gesture that emphasizes how their mere presence reinforces that violence. It is then by exposing the circular logic of the violent exchanges of power on the border and by underlining the spectacular condition of this situation that these plays are capable of exposing the structural violence that takes place in migratory practices and at the same time highlight its vanishing point.

Bibliography

Agamben, Giorgio. 2017. *Homo Sacer: Sovereign Power and Bare Life*. Translated by Daniel Heller-Roazen. Standford, CA: Standford UP.

Ahmed, Sara. 2000. *Strange Encounters: Embodied Others in Post-Coloniality*. New York: Routledge.

Auslander, Philip. 2012. "Digital Liveness: A Historico-Philosophical Perspective." *PAJ: A Journal of Performance and Art* 34 (3): 3-11.

— — —. 2006. "Performativity of Performance Documentation." *PAJ: A Journal of Performance and Art* 84: 1-10.

Bay-Cheng, Sarah. 2012. "Theatre is Media: Some Principles for a Digital Historiography of Performance." *Theatre* 42 (2): 27-41.

Braidotti, Rossi. 2010. "The Politics of 'Life Itself' and 'New Ways of Dying.'" In *New Materialism. Ontology, Agency, and Politics*, edited by Diana Coole and Samantha Frost, 201-218. London: Duke University Press.

Butler, Judith, Zeynep Gambetti and Leticia Sabsay, eds. 2016. *Vulnerability in Resistance*. Durham, NC: Duke UP.

Chías, Edgar. 2013. *Ternura Suite*. Colonia Juárez: Ediciones Milagro.

De Paco, Antonio. 2007. *Alguien Silbó (y Despertó a un Centenar de Pájaros Dormidos)*. Madrid: Injuve.

Derrida, Jacques. 2000. *Of Hospitality*. Standford, CA: Standford UP.

Domenech de la Lastra, Pablo. 2017. "Excepción en la Frontera: Laberintos Legitimadores de la Violencia Soberana en los Límites del Estado." *AGORA* 36 (2): 75–100.

Dzodan, Flavia. 2011. "In the Name of Safety: The Multi-National Anti Immigration Industry and Their Billionaire Profits." *The Tiger Beatdown* (blog), October 7, 2011 http://tigerbeatdown.com/2011/10/07/in-the-name-of-safety-the-multi-national-anti-immigration-industry-and-their-billionaire-profits/

Fischter-Lichter, Erika. 2008. *The Transformative Power of Performance: A New Aesthetics* Translated by Sasyka Iris Jain. Oxford: Taylor & Francis.

Manuel, Pedro. 2014. "Absent Audiences." *Performance Research: A Journal of the Performing Arts* 19 (5): 69–76.

Serrano, Daniel. 2005. *Cazador de Gringos*. México DF: Malaletra Libros.

Thiebaut, Carlos. 2010. "Tolerancia y Hospitalidad. Una Reflexión Moral ante la Inmigración." *Arbor: Ciencia, Pensamiento y Cultura* 744: 543–554.

— — —. 2015. "Harm and Violence: Does the Notion of Harm Help Us to Define Violence and Non-Violence". Research Gate. Last modified May 30, 2015. https://www.researchgate.net/publication/277345 315_Harm_and_violence_Does_the_notion_of_harm_help_us_to_de fine_violence_and_non-violence

Žižek, Slavoj. 2008. *Violence: Six Sideways Reflections*. New York: Picador.

Violence in the Lives of Immigrants

Children of *Brexit*: Violence Against Immigrants as Nativist Practice in *Night of the Party* and *We Come Apart*

Cornel Borit

An article published in *The Guardian* on the 12th of April 2018 drew attention to a controversy caused by BBC Channel 4's intention to broadcast "for 1st time EVER, Enoch Powell's Rivers of Blood speech in full on UK radio" (Sweney 2018), as BBC media editor and program host, Amol Rajan, boisterously advertised on Twitter the same day. Despite significant controversy raised in the days preceding the event, the program titled *50 Years On: Rivers of Blood* (Rajan 2018) went on air as scheduled and British people could hear the entire speech broadcast on radio for the first time in history. Actor Ian McDiarmid impersonated Powell fifty years after the former conservative MP had delivered the (in)famous speech to a meeting of the Conservative Political Centre in Birmingham on the 20th of April 1968.

Much of the criticism formulated by academics, politicians, and commentators not only questioned the contextual significance of the program itself, but also reiterated the dangers about the legacy of a speech that divided the nation at that time and has significantly influenced the way race relations have evolved in Britain ever since. In an official letter that Labor peer Andrew Adonis wrote to the Ofcom chief executive, Sharon White, he bemoaned the decision of BBC to "celebrate the 50th anniversary of 'rivers of blood' [by] broadcasting the full text of the most incendiary racist speech of modern Britain that was not even broadcast at the time" (Sweney 2018). The speech, which ended with a reference to a scene in Virgil's *Aeneid* in which a prophetess predicts civil war in Rome with the phrase "I see the river Tiber foaming with much blood" (Powell 1968), prophesized itself that, because of immigration in

Britain, "in 15 or 20 years' time the black man will have the whip hand over the white man" (Powell 1968).

The debate triggered by the broadcast of the *50 Years On: Rivers of Blood* program by BBC disclosed that in contemporary Britain, despite visible progress in terms of race relations, the legacy of Enoch Powell still haunts British politics and society, as noticed during the *Brexit* debate when many conservative politicians alongside a wide sector of population eagerly refashioned some of Powell's racist claims to unleash an unprecedentedly aggressive campaign against immigrants, particularly those from Central and Eastern Europe (CEE). Even though violent xenophobic manifestations like the murder of Stephen Lawrence in 1993 or the ethnic riots of 2001 in Oldham, Bradford, Leeds, or Burnley may be considered sporadic and insignificant in the wider picture, a scrutiny of policies and public attitudes towards immigration in contemporary Britain reveals that violence against immigrants is still present in forms that, although they are less perceivable, are nonetheless equally harmful. The general tendency is to categorize as acts of violence such obvious deeds as international conflicts, terror attacks, or ethnic riots as those mentioned above. We should, however, as Slavoj Žižek suggests, learn to increase our awareness beyond the forms of violence that are performed by visible, identifiable agents (Žižek 2008, 1) and be ready to perceive the insidious forms of violence that are not directly perceived but which create the background for and nurture such outbursts.

Given the significant societal impact that violence has had in human history, it has constantly represented an important theme in cultural representations as well as in different fields of critical social studies. Recent developments in the field of conflict studies have paid special attention to phenomena and notions related to violence in an attempt to distinguish the features of various types of violence, trace their origins, and scrutinize the connection between perceivable and invisible forms of violence. The efforts of both cultural productions and scholarship in social sciences attempt to raise awareness about the atrocious consequences that any form of violence can bring and thus contribute to increasing our propensity for tolerance and peaceful conviviality.

Despite such efforts, violent attitudes and manifestations still accompany us. Taking as a starting point the debate over immigration in Britain during the first decades of the 21st century, this chapter aims to discuss literary representations of violent behavior and attitudes displayed by a certain category of British natives and institutions against immigrants from CEE countries. Various forms of violence, from discrimination, exploitation, social exclusion, and marginalization, to bullying, expulsion, incarceration, or forced repatriation have accompanied the growing anti-migrant rhetoric permeating British society both in the period preceding and that following the *Brexit* referendum. Even though various depictions and discussions of instances of violence against CEE migrants have been present in the media, the topic has seldom been exposed to a thorough scrutiny that would go beyond observable phenomena of violence. This chapter therefore focuses especially on the problems and ambiguities raised by those unperceivable forms of violence that both sides involved tend to internalize and accept as natural manifestations of the interaction between migrants and natives in reception societies.

The forms of manifestation that violence takes may vary and sometimes the dividing lines between them are also less perceivable. Building on the theoretical model developed by Johan Galtung (Galtung 1990), which maintains that there is an intrinsic connection between a symbolic form of violence, which he calls *cultural violence,* and perceivable instances of violence, which he calls *structural* and *direct violence,* this chapter argues that elements of the British nativist discourse represent forms of cultural violence that create the premises of structural and direct violence against immigrants by disseminating detrimental migration myths, by reinforcing negative heterostereotypes about migrants, and by promoting a sense of moral panic and illegality. Since direct violence, as Galtung contends, is the most easily noticeable and identifiable form of violence, thus easier to oppose (Galtung 1969, 169), this chapter focuses on analyzing instances of *cultural* and *structural violence* to which immigrants are exposed, revealing their insidious presence, exposing the various forms of manifestation they may take, and examining the causal relation that exists between them.

Since all the above-mentioned issues have been portrayed in literature in recent years, it is particularly interesting to examine how they are negotiated by authors who engage in the debate about migration from CEE countries to Britain. As Gayatri Spivak has pointed out in *An Aesthetic Education in the Era of Globalization* (Spivak 2012), literary works play an important role in "training the imagination" (122) and it is through this lens of imaginary activism of literature that the current chapter engages with problematic questions regarding the presence of imperceptible forms of violence directed at immigrants in contemporary British society. Therefore, after discussing the main theoretical concepts framing the chapter and exploring the connection between *nativism* as an underlying ideological factor and various forms violence, this chapter turns to examining how fiction texts negotiate the relational frames established between *cultural* and *structural* forms of violence and their impact on the emotional, social, cultural, and economic aspects of immigrants' lives. Two contemporary novels, which have received rather little critical attention until now, were selected: Tracey Mathias' *Night of the Party* (2018) and Sarah Crossan and Brian Conaghan's *We Come Apart* (2017). Both texts depict the experiences of disenfranchised Romanian teenage immigrants in Britain who either are exposed to the constant threat of forced repatriation in a dystopian post-*Brexit* Britain governed according to the principles of the "British Born policy" (Mathias 2018), or undergo a routine of alienation and brutal discrimination in a system informed by pervasive anti-migrant mentalities (Crossan and Conaghan 2017). The novels are highly relevant for analysis as they depict through original writing styles and attention to detail different forms of violence to which migrants from CEE countries are exposed, thus providing a factual and pungent response to nativist attitudes and policies regarding intra-European migration in Britain in the second decade of the 21st century.

Nativism, Populism, and Violence

The anecdote opening this chapter draws attention to an important premise for this study, namely the fact that attitudes, acts, and policies directed at immigrants in Britain after World War II have constantly been informed by strong nativist traces. Powellism did not only resonate with its contemporaries, but its traces are easily noticeable to this day, as the reactions to BBC's program expressed by many public figures suggest. Serious concerns remain that in the space where British natives and CEE incomers interact today, the "structure of feeling that governs the continuing antipathy toward all would-be settlers" (Gilroy 2005, 103) as residual traces of imperial racism "combine easily with mechanistic notions of culture and a deterministic organicism to form a deadly cocktail" (144). Such resilient traces of nativism, instilled in the British collective subconscious, can act as a moral indicator justifying aggressive attitudes or acts directed at migrants on grounds of the natives' primacy principle professed by nativist discourses. In what follows, the main theoretical concepts employed in this chapter are discussed, explaining their significance for exploring the social-historical context informing this study. The discussion moves from the investigation of the concepts *nativism* and *populism* to presenting Johan Galtung's model of theorizing violence and then explores the potential of nativism to act as ideological backdrop that justifies and legitimizes structural violence against migrants.

In the aftermath of World War II, migration from colonies to Britain was instrumental for economic reconstruction, but the general assumption of locals was that migration was temporary and migrants would return to their countries of origin when economic conditions changed (Geddens and Peter 2016, 8). It was in this context that anti-migrant attitudes, primarily framed in terms of social and economic concerns, started transpiring among certain categories of British natives. Once it became clear that the "guest workers" were not returning to their countries of origin, the debate on immigration became a pivotal social and political topic. By this time, the social and economic aspects were conflated with ethno-national elements, stirring up a mix of racial resentments, which involved mistrust for foreigners, nationalistic isolationism, intolerance for multiculturalism, and a nostalgia for past glories (Mudde and Kaltwasser 2017, 7), thus giving rise to a fully-fledged nativist current in Britain. Such responses to immigration that emerged in the years following World War II remain today, as Paul Gilroy contends, the backbone of this resistance to convivial culture (Gilroy 2005, 103) that viciously permeates consistent portions of the British society.

The fundamental features of nativism, it can be said, refer to its focus on the native group that defines itself in opposition to undesirable immigrants, its preference for protecting the interests of the domestic over those of new-comers, its ethnocentric dimension, which predicates the natives' supremacy over foreigners and seeks to maintain their racial, cultural, and political privileges, and its anti-pluralistic dimension, which advocates strict control or restrictions of the flow of migrants to the destination communities (Guia 2016, 10). Drawing on these premises, Cas Mudde defines nativism as "an ideology that holds that states should be inhabited exclusively by members of the native group ('the nation') and that non-native (or 'alien') elements, whether persons or ideas, are fundamentally threatening to the homogeneous nation state" (Mudde 2016, 296).

Despite a series of fine distinctions, most scholars agree upon two common features that inform nativism today; firstly, it implies a mechanism that contributes to maintaining relations of power, domination, and exploitation (Guia 2016, 13) derived from the binary logic dividing society into "us" (the natives) and "them" (the newcomers). Secondly, nativism is conflated with populism in western societies (Mudde 2016; Riedel 2018) where immigration allegedly threatens the privileges to which the "true people" are entitled. Therefore, in the context of increased immigration to Britain after CEE countries joined the European Union, populist rhetoric has confiscated the nativist principle of the natives' pre-eminence and merged it with the "commonsensical" idea of defining the "people" exclusively in ethnic and cultural terms. In addition, populist actors have efficiently exploited the long-ingrained fears and fantasies professed by Enoch Powell a few decades before, triggering a sense of crisis built around the fear of immigrants who do not belong to the core in-group, the "true people", who are perceived as fundamentally different, and represent a threat to the group's ethnic and cultural homogeneity.

The surge of anti-migration feelings and Euroscepticism among large sectors of British population compounded with the low levels of confidence in the conventional way of running politics have allowed the rise to prominence of a new political challenger during the first decade of the twenty-first century, the United Kingdom Independence Party (UKIP), which swiftly became the "primary vehicle for public opposition to EU membership, mass immigration, ethnic change, and the socially liberal and cosmopolitan values that had come to dominate the political establishment" (Ford and Goodwin 2017, 4). UKIP's growing popularity, which materialized in a resounding victory in the 2014 elections for the European Parliament, as well as an appreciable 12,6 per cent at the general election in 2015, prompted both Labor and the Conservatives to reassess their position on the highly controversial topic of migration, a strategy that had *Brexit* as final result. Once again, as in the 1950s and onwards, the fear of immigrants materialized into an acute sense of crisis, as the alleged invasion reached, in the words of one notorious Leave campaign poster, a "breaking point" (BBC 2019), thus turning a fabricated crisis into a form of exclusionary identity politics.

It can be thus said that, in the *Brexit* campaign, Powell's specter returned to haunt British politics once more. Daniel Hannan, a Tory MP and one of the pioneers of the *Brexit* movement, hailed Powell as his political hero. Nigel Farage also glorified him, while *Leave.EU*, one of two main *Brexit* campaigning organizations, recently declared that Powell's "Rivers of Blood" speech was "the most important speech in post-war history" (Earle 2018). Even though it can be argued today that Powell's prophecies have not been fulfilled, as neither civil unrest, similar to the events in the USA in the 1960s, nor a dramatic reversal of social hierarchy has materialized in Britain, this, however, does not mean that attitudes and views similar to his have significantly changed in the institutional practices and social relations of everyday life.

It may be that mainstream political discourse has by and large become more responsible, but speeches on immigration, similar to those of Enoch Powell five decades ago, continue to play with the same powerful feelings of aggression, guilt, and fear and articulate them as a violent racist politics (Gilroy 2005, 101). Even if Powell was factually wrong in his predictions, the awful prospects of fear raised by his speech are still around and, as Paul Gilroy suggests, have "subsequently provided the justification for many a preventive strike like the one that took Stephen Lawrence's life in 1993" (101). Following thus Paul Gilroy's line of inquiry, it is the purpose of this chapter to interrogate those elements of Enoch Powell's poisonous and pessimistic rhetoric that continue to inform the political discourses, institutional practices, and social relations in Britain today.

Seen from the vantage point of today, it is clear that the immigration narrative, which was often conveyed in the language of violence and war, influenced the *Brexit* referendum result in a decisive way. Immigrants, largely those from Eastern Europe, were often represented as the enemy that dissipated the energy of the nation. Nigel Farage started the referendum campaign with the statement "We will win this war" (Earle 2018) and designated politicians who opposed *Brexit* as "quislings", a reference to collaborators of the Nazis during World War II. Such references to a major event in British history bolstered by the employment of bellicose language with reference to migration also contributed to the emergence of a metanarrative professing a legitimation of violent attitudes and acts against immigrants.

The display of aggressive anti-migrant discourse British nativism manifested during the *Brexit* campaign, which has also triggered drastic restrictions in the legal frame of migration,[1] corresponds to what Johan Galtung describes as *cultural violence* and

---

[1] The government's response to the public constraints and populist political parties' pressure has materialized in the new, stricter Immigration Bill of 2015, by which the Cameron administration tried to appease the actors exploiting immigration as a major Brexit campaign tool.

which, he argues, appears in "the symbolic sphere of our existence...that can be used to justify or legitimize direct or structural violence" (Galtung 1990, 291). Cultural violence allows for the existence of "direct and structural violence" by making them look "right—or at least not wrong" (291) and thus renders it acceptable in society. Galtung points out that this functions at a subconscious level (291–292), being a form of symbolic violence that is instilled into a culture through language and ideology, representing prevailing and prominent social norms, customs, symbols, mentalities, attitudes, and beliefs that become so embedded in a given culture that they are perceived as absolute and inevitable and are reproduced uncritically across generations. Nativist discourse has thus laid the premises of structural and direct violence against immigrants in British society during the past two decades by constructing a demonized and reductionist image of immigrants. A deep chasm has thus been constructed through emphasizing the binary opposition between *Self* and *Other* as a defining feature of the relations being established between natives and immigrants, inflating the value of *Self* and disparaging the value of *Other*.

Once the archetype of the migrant *Other* is constructed in terms of the infrahuman, structural and direct violence "can start operating" (298). Galtung places these three types of violence in a model in which a "causal flow from cultural via structural to direct violence can be identified" (295). To explain this model, he argues that the phenomenon has a similar structure to that of an iceberg, in which there is always a small, visible part and a huge, hidden part. Direct violence is the tip of the iceberg; it is more obvious and is usually visible and done by an identifiable individual or a group. It refers to the actual infliction of physical harm to a person or group of people (Galtung 1969, 169). We can see this violence in conflicts as large as wars or in individual instances of brutality. Being the most easily perceivable and impactful, it is commonly thought that direct violence is the worst of the three types, but in fact, precisely its visibility makes it easier to identify and resist. In Galtung's vision, it is the indirect forms of violence, namely cultural and structural violence that are the most wide-spread and difficult to oppose; they represent the invisible part of the iceberg, hidden deep down in social structures and in culture (Galtung 1996, 271). And if through cultural violence an overdetermined, dehumanized image of immigrants is constructed and instilled in the collective subconscious, structural violence represents the manifestation or the result of a social stratification process that cultural violence underpins, taking the form of a damage in the satisfaction of basic human needs necessary for fulfilling one's full potentials in life, such as welfare, identity, freedom, and participation in decisions that affect one's own life (Galtung 1969, 1996; Webel and Galtung 2007).

Nurtured by a constant and virulent anti-migrant discourse, promoted either in the media or through the voices of nativist-populist politicians, specific forms of structural violence directed at CEE immigrants penetrated many strata of the British society during the past decades. The normalization through discourse of such instruments of rejection or/and repression as discrimination, perpetual observation, or even abusive retention, may give the impression that *Brexit* Britain turned into a society in which, as Michel Foucault contends, the "carceral texture" is transferred from the penal institution to the entire social body (Foucault 1995 [1975], 298). It can thus be argued that the experience of many immigrants in Britain during the past two decades has significantly been informed by all-pervasive structures of control, confinement, and punishment in ways that resonate Foucault's description of the disciplinary society as "the carceral archipelago" (Foucault 1995 [1975], 297), in which various segments of the society function as a unitary mechanism of implementation of imperceptible forms of violence.

On the "Playground" of *Brexit*: Exploring the Path of Violence from Culture to Practice in *Night of the Party* and *We Come Apart*

In what follows, this chapter explores several representations in contemporary migration literature of experiences of violent treatment to which immigrants from CEE countries in Britain were exposed in the aftermath of the *Brexit* referendum. In doing so, this section scrutinizes the relationship between the culture of violence which, once ingrained in the British nativist discourse, has contributed to constructing and disseminating anti-migrant attitudes and mentalities, and manifestations of structural violence at both the societal and the individual level. By relying on the distinction between the three forms of violence theorized by Johan Galtung, this section explores the representation of images, performances and ideas in the selected texts to identify the cultural elements that underpin, legitimize, and stimulate anti-migrant attitudes and acts of structural violence.

As previously mentioned, the focus of this study is on analyzing the relationship between representations of cultural and structural forms of violence as in literary texts, since these forms of violence are more difficult to identify and address in everyday practice. Literary works, through specific techniques, such as the employment of figuration, narrative pace, representations of opposite angles and multiple perspectives, detailed depictions of characters' psychological states, and introspection, can enhance readers' knowledge and awareness about these less perceivable forms of violence by depicting the symptoms and the impact they have on characters. Therefore, examining how Galtung's theory works within the novels selected for this study may illuminate how violence functions in society, in various contexts informed by the specter of violence.

In most contemporary novels that reflect social-historical realities connected to *Brexit*, the interaction between immigrants and British natives and authorities is significantly informed by an anti-migration rhetoric directed at Eastern European immigrants and by the notoriously strict migration policies advanced by populist politicians and their supporters. The novel *Night of the Party* (Mathias 2018), by Welsh contemporary author Tracey Mathias, illustrates this clearly. It is built around the story of a teenage romance between Ash, a progressive young student majoring in mathematics and philosophy and seventeen years old Zara, an apparently ordinary girl with a strong interest in English classics and aspiring to study English literature. At the same time, as the title suggests, the narrative involves a few dark aspects revolving around the signifier "party". The word refers denotatively to a concrete event in the past, the party when Ash's sister and Zara's best friend, Sophie, died in a controversial, unspecified drug-related accident. But an equally dramatic meaning of the word implies a metaphorical reference to the populist-nativist ruling political party depicted simply as "The Party", which, in a post-*Brexit* dystopian reality, has adopted "The Immigration and Residency Act". As the major provisions of this bill represent the backbone of the "British Born policy" (Mathias 2018, 1), its implementation implies that all residents born outside Britain are forcefully expelled unless they choose to leave Britain willingly. Failing to report illegals is also a crime. The "night" that the Party ensures descends over Britain impacts the relation between Ash and Zara dramatically, as she turns out to be a Romanian-born immigrant who has lived most of her life in Britain after she and her mother moved in legally before *Brexit*.

The novel explores the roots of socio-historical trauma and its psychological impact on the characters by excavating the sources and the effects of various forms of structural violence that both authorities and compliant locals impose on immigrants who must live in constant fear of arrest and deportation. Whereas many narratives that focus on the migrant experience explore the intricacies and challenges of integration, cultural exchange, or identity (re)configuration, *Night of the Party* deals with situations that immigrants sometimes encounter in societies where pervasive nativism exposes them to extreme forms of exclusion. Mathias uses this to make a sharp comment on the dynamics of the political and social polarization around migration informing British society during the *Brexit* debate. She exposes her characters to an environment intoxicated by a Manichaean approach to reality, constructed through a virulent dissemination of nativist propaganda and myths, which both convince large masses of Britons that migration represents the paramount problem of society and professes an illusionary solution: remove all immigrants and Britain will thrive.

The reader is already introduced to the dystopian climate informing the entire narrative on the first page, as it presents a mock Wikipedia article titled the "Immigration and Residency Act" (Mathias 2018, 1). As the article explains, the provisions of this bill literally deprive all immigrants in the UK of residence and property rights, thus anchoring the story in a hyperbolic, yet recognizable context for the contemporary reader. The preface-like insertion of the bill's provisions also acts as an interface between the legal frame underpinning a near ubiquitous state of emergency and a reality in which illegalized immigrants struggle to adapt by mimicking ideal citizen conduct. Irony is employed when mentioning that the expressed purpose of the law is the "protection" of freedom, whereas in the novel's diegetic frame it appears rather as a temporary suspension of law which resonates Giorgio Agamben's "state of exception" (Agamben 2005) wherein states can remain lawful while transgressing individual rights.

Throughout the novel, the tense anti-migrant climate is constructed through the insertion of montage- or collage-like narrative structures, interrupting and supplementing the plotline with quotations from newspapers or slogans encompassing the official policy pursued by the "Party". Zara is repeatedly depicted in situations where such slogans are ubiquitous:

> "posters on the bus shelters shouting the same message she read later, on the scrolling screens on the tube, in spaces above the windows, where once, sometimes, there used to be poetry. DO YOU KNOW AN ILLEGAL? IT IS YOUR DUTY TO REPORT THEM" (Mathias 2018, 14).

Such scenes abound in the text. The effect of the nativist state propaganda not only constantly reminds Zara of her insecure condition, but it also suggests the presence of a generalized anti-migrant mind-set generated by the permeation of the collective subconscious with the idea that immigrants and natives are inexorably in a state of conflict.

The fact that Zara perceives the effects of nativist propaganda as a threat to her basic human needs, in the sense expressed by Johan Galtung (Galtung 1990, 292), such as freedom or personal development, inspires empathy in the reader. It is, however, not the slogan itself or the message it conveys that represents the real threat. The nativist ideas comprised in slogans or expressed in the re-election speech of the Prime Minister—"What rights do these people have? They are here illegally" (Mathias 2018, 133)—are manifestations of *cultural violence* in the "symbolic sphere of existence", which, as Johan Galtung contends, underpin and justify concrete forms of violence (Galtung 1990, 291). They represent the ideological backdrop that insidiously, and many times unconsciously, infiltrates the collective mind-set of a group, thus making direct or structural violence seem not just acceptable, but even necessary.

Many natives portrayed in the novel tend to internalize the ideas and values circulating in the symbolic sphere to such a degree that these become a natural component of their existence. A significant example in this sense is depicted when Ash and Zara go on Christmas day to a pub in the countryside, which has its walls covered in pro-Party symbols and election posters and displays above the bar the sign "Not born here? Not welcome here" (Mathias 2018, 58). Zara's unease is almost immediate, whereas Ash completely fails to notice all these details, which shows that what she perceives as hostile seems completely normal to him. Only at a later point, as Zara confesses her non-British Born identity, Ash starts growing in awareness of how he had been programmed into unconsciously accepting the official policies of the government about migration. Before that, he failed to realize the true dimension of the cultural violence to which immigrants fall victim, acknowledging the anti-migrant campaign as part of the banal reality.

The presence of such forms of cultural violence starts making sense to Ash only after he has to face a major moral dilemma. One of the omnipresent announcements in the newspaper stating "KNOW AN ILLEGAL? IT IS A CRIMINAL OFFENCE TO FAIL TO REPORT THEM" (Mathias 2018, 133) prompts his conscience to split between the citizen's duty to report Zara and protecting her against the law. Reflecting on what the consequences of abiding by the law may be, Ash comes to realize that the British Born policy is morally inconsistent and consequentially repressive, thus his moral duty is to resist the injustice caused by an inhumane law and engage in a crusade against the oppression instilled by the abusive authorities.

Through depicting the origins of cultural violence imposed from above by means of political discourse, Mathias draws attention to the historical consequences to which societies are exposed when a political regime resorts to arbitrariness and cynicism. Nevertheless, the interrogation of cultural violence that *Night of the Party* performs extends beyond political propaganda, as the text often shifts narrative focus between institutional and individual frames that contribute to the emergence of violent ideological structures. A plethora of myths that distort and exaggerate the effects of migration on society, recognizable to the informed reader as being from the *Brexit* campaign, also contribute to engendering a climate of cultural violence in the novel. At the level of character interaction, as well as in the novel's overall ideological gist, Mathias inserts a subtle critique of the construction of a generalized moral panic around migration caused by the dissemination of detrimental myths about migration and immigrants. One iconic example in this sense is the narrative line which juxtaposes native characters upholding contradictory views on the migration situation in the country. Ash develops throughout the novel as a character who opposes the British Born policy and all it involves. At university, political debate over migration is rife and, nonetheless, often conflicting among Ash's friends. Lewis, for instance, whose political support for the Party is apparent in many situations, professes the commonly accepted narrative claiming that immigrants represent a burden for society; therefore, he claims, their expulsion is an equitable solution to resolve Britain's overlapping crises:

> "We're a small island. We've got limited resources and limited space. […] We are getting overcrowded. Overrun. There were too many people coming in, taking benefits and jobs, putting too much demand on everything. The NHS. Housing. Schools—" (Mathias 2018, 161).

The allusion to Powellism is obvious in this scene and Mathias's text arguably aims to alert readers of the dangers that the perpetuation of this mythology in the British collective subconscious represents. Myths, as Christopher Flood maintains, offer simple explanations for complex phenomena, which people are willing to believe; the authenticity of their content is never doubted by the members of the group who believe it (Flood 2002, 8) and this is key to the powerful effect that myths have. Once converted into a myth, the mere belief that immigrants are the reason for societal, moral, and economic decline provides legitimacy for natives to disparage, reject, or act aggressively towards such foreigners who "feed uncertainty and promote ontological jeopardy" (Gilroy 2005, 142) for the local community. This is what justifies the British Born policy in the vision of natives like Lewis: "People who were born here should come first. That's all the BB policy is" (Mathias 2018, 162).

Once nativist ideas infiltrate the collective imagination, the premises for concrete manifestations of structural violence are set, as Galtung argues, since they provide justification for other, more visible forms of violence directed at the members of an out-group (Galtung 1990, 291). An example in this sense is represented by the ubiquitous presence of Neighborhood Watch, a sinister organization of volunteers signifying the willingness of people to collude with the regime in implementing the British Born policy. The integration of common people, often harmless elderly, in the violent frames of surveillance and detection of immigrants is depicted as a natural continuation of the oppressive deeds of state institutions. The protagonists in *Night of the Party* are frequently exposed to random ID checks carried out either by the police or by Neighborhood Watch patrols, an image that recalls Foucault's "carceral texture of society" (Foucault 1995 [1975], 304), in which the surveillance is "hierarchized, continuous, and functional" (176). The effects of such surveillance actions in the novel are identical to what Foucault signifies through the metaphor of the Panopticon, which he uses to describe disciplinary societies: "to induce […] a state of conscious and permanent visibility that assures the automatic functioning of power" (201). Already in the opening scene, when Zara and Ash are forced to walk home in a blackout which caused the train to stop, Ash's neighbors who are on patrol approach them: "You need to go home. Stay in till the power's back on!" (Mathias 2018, 8). The scene is banal, and the apparently kind neighbors seem to act helpfully. Yet, the scene foreshadows ominous events that would lead to Zara's exposure and subsequent arrest by the police.

In this atmosphere, the fulfilment of basic human needs, such as identity, freedom, or welfare becomes precarious. Structural violence against immigrants manifests at all levels and in all imaginable circumstances, conveying the sensation that abuse represents a state of normality. This is particularly visible in Zara's development as a character, as she struggles to avoid exposure by acting normally. Her frequent jogging tours across Hampstead Heath are a form of resistance to movement restrictions and equally represent a metaphor for the perpetual chase to which she is subjected. ID checks are less likely and surveillance is limited in the barren environment of the heath; the city, however, signifies the realm of policing and surveillance, reminding of Foucault's society *qua* prison (Foucault 1995 [1975], 298), where palpable tension in the body and the mind is omnipresent. Even if Zara and her mother succeeded in remaining in hiding during the Party's first term, re-election leads to an escalation of structural violence as the Prime Minister announces the beginning of "house to house searches in London" (Mathias 2018, 219).

From this moment on, the chase is no longer a metaphor but becomes the perpetual reality for Zara and her mother. Therefore, they agree to flee to Ireland, but before that, Zara decides to get justice for her friend, Sophie. She is the only witness who can identify the person responsible for Sophie's death, thus she goes to the police station to report him. However, the reporting scene takes an unexpected turn; the officer is not interested in the information Zara wants to provide and insists on checking her ID. This way, her true identity is revealed, and she is arrested. Throughout the entire novel, the ID card trope signifies the harsh societal control that the authorities impose on individuals, since each interaction with authorities is associated with a thorough scrutiny of identity documents. Humans are turned into statistics in the dystopian reality of the novel, in striking similarity to the norms imposed on immigrants by the UK Borders Act of 2007, which requires immigrants in the UK to apply for "biometric immigration documents" (or BIDs), the information from which will be placed on the "National Identity Register" (Bosworth 2008, 204).

"Identification first," the refrain repeated throughout the story, represents the most efficient instrument for the repressive

British Born policy to separate "true citizens" from undesirable immigrants. Those failing to identify themselves as British born are cast into the sphere of illegality: "You're illegal, Miss Ionescu. You're under arrest" (Mathias 2018, 216). The words used by the police officer are symptomatic of defining the relation between the state authority and immigrants. The syntactic construction is particularly significant, as it denotes the categorization of a person, not an action, as "illegal". But how can a human being be illegal, irrespective of the situations in which they are or the acts they commit? In reaction to the irresponsible use of the term "illegal migrant" in contemporary political and media discourse, Khalid Koser considers that the "most powerful criticism of the term 'illegal' is that defining people as 'illegal' denies their humanity" (Koser 2007, 54). The employment of such terms may have severe effects on the way immigrants are perceived, as the fact that immigrants are human and have rights, whatever their legal status may be, can be forgotten. Nativist discourse in Britain during the *Brexit* campaign persistently acted to blur the distinction between migrants as persons and their acts, by using semantic constructions that associate a technical term describing an action, such as "irregular" or "illegal", with human beings. Once adopted in the every-day language, such semantic constructs have created social categories that are difficult to combat. The term "illegal migrant", or simplified "illegal", thus became a meaningful instrument of cultural violence used by nativist propaganda in Britain during the *Brexit* campaign to justify violent attitudes and acts against immigrants.

The debate about illegal immigrants is by and large the main theme of *Night of the Party*. By following Zara's experience, the reader is invited to reflect on events and actions that seem inseparable from the reality that some immigrants must face today. Arguably, the dystopia built by an all too believable repressive state in the novel represents a bitter criticism of Britain's restrictive immigration and asylum policies. The most conclusive example in this sense is the depiction of Zara's detention in the deportation center after being arrested. In a similar way to the immigration Act 1971, amended by the Immigration and Asylum Act 1999 and the Borders Act 2007, which grant the UK authorities considerable discretion to detain and remove migrants, the fictitious "Immigration and Residency Act" represents the key instrument of structural violence that authorities commit against immigrants in *Night of the Party*. The mere fact of being non-British born places Zara in a state of illegality, which makes her subject to deportation, a practice that Melanie Griffiths compares to the ancient-world practice of banishment, with its spectacle of punishment and façade of maintaining social order (Griffiths 2017, 540).

According to the legislation enforced in Britain today, immigration detention represents the practice of holding people who are subject to immigration control in custody, while they wait for permission to enter or before they are deported or removed from the country (Association of Visitors to Immigration Detainees, n.d.). Oake Leigh, the deportation center for women in *Night of the Party*, corresponds to this description. In the booklet "Your stay at Oake Leigh" the center is described as Zara's "new temporary home" where the "trained staff will do all they can to help" (Mathias 2018, 226). The reality is, however, dystopian; Oake Leigh is a place where people are stuck in limbo at the whim of the state, where forms of structural violence to which immigrants are exposed are extreme. Privations, abuses, and mistreatment are common practice. Zara is often woken up in the middle of the night for interrogation or is denied basic hygiene rights, such as access to tampons or going to the toilet. Her hope is to be on the deportation list and be sent "out of England, in a place where she doesn't belong" (Mathias 2018, 225), but instead she is detained without explanation for a much longer period than legally allowed.

The deportation center works very well, both symbolically and practically, as a tool of social control, rather than a transit residence. It is, as Zara reflects, a "community of the illegal—the unknowable" (245) where the detained are dispossessed of their identity and of their humanity, an image that invokes Giorgio Agamben's figure of the *homo sacer* — bare life — the human being stripped of political and legal attributes (Agamben 1998). In a space surrounded by a "six-metre razor-wire-topped fence, with the first two metres of dense green mesh that stops you from seeing out" (Mathias 2018, 246), freedom is a chimera that detained immigrants can chase only in their imagination. Discontinuity becomes an ontic state of permanence, and this is highlighted through a juxtaposition of tropes signifying movement and stasis, freedom and confinement. The only decisions Zara can now make concern the micromanagement of time and space, as she struggles to keep track of the calendar and to maintain her routine of running: "Sunday, Monday, Tuesday, Wednesday pass" and she continues her "obsessive looping runs around the yard under the free circling birds in the sky" (Mathias 2018, 251). The metaphor of birds occurs repeatedly to emphasize the contradiction between the freedom that lures Zara beyond the fences and the cage-like place where she is confined. However, Zara knows that outside the detention center there is another larger bird cage, as the entire country has turned, under the rule of the Party, into a dystopian space of intricate structures of confinement and control, a "carceral archipelago" as that described by Michel Foucault (Foucault 1995 [1975], 297).

The novel has an optimistic ending, as the protagonist escapes the detention center during a riot and, with Ash's assistance, she manages to escape to Scotland. Yet even though the readers may be rewarded with a cathartic experience, *Night of the Party* is a novel that challenges in many ways the arbitrariness of policies, as well as their casual popular support regarding immigration in Britain as we know them today. Nicolette Jones contends in her review in The Sunday Times that the novel's greatest strength is its "thought-provoking political scenario, decrying inhuman detention centres and the dangers of apathy" (Jones 2018). Her concerns about just how credible and immediately recognizable the frightening dystopia depicted in the *Night of the Party* seems are also shared by other critics who have reviewed the novel (Hennessy 2018; Williams 2018). By highlighting the dangers of an overall development of structures of violence targeting immigrants, Mathias provides social commentary about the urgency of a need for tolerance and for promoting a cosmopolitan outlook among Britons; perhaps the book's young adult audience proves to be more perceptive than previous generations.

The relations between Eastern European immigrants and British natives during the second decade of the twenty-first century were often informed by tensions that frequently took the shape of violent acts. In what follows, this chapter directs attention to the novel *We Come Apart* (2017) co-authored by Sarah Crossan and Brian Conaghan, which, in a similar way to Mathias' novel, depicts a story that approaches as major theme a teenage romance between a Romanian immigrant and a British native set against the hostile backdrop of *Brexit*.

We Come Apart is a lyrical novel that tells the story of Romanian Roma teenager Nicu, who migrates to Britain with his family and struggles, despite his best efforts, to pass for a "normal" citizen, but implacably becomes a victim of a system imbued with prejudices and violent attitudes against immigrants from Eastern Europe. The experiences of interacting with authorities as well as with his peers at school reveal a disagreeable side of the British society, which shatters Nicu's initial utopian projections about life as an immigrant in the United Kingdom. His exposure to discrimination, exclusion, and downright humiliation for the simple fact of being a Romanian immigrant engender a dystopian migrant experience that only seems to be alleviated when Nicu's schoolmate, Jess, starts to look at him from beyond the veil of prejudice and ignorance. Nevertheless, the adventure of discovering each other's humanity, which develops into an affectionate relationship, eventually proves to have fatal consequences.

The authors create an all too recognizable world in which the interaction between immigrants and natives is informed by social injustice, where various manifestations of cultural and structural violence intertwine. It becomes clear quite early in the narrative that prejudices and heterostereotypes represent significant "underlying cultural codes" (Gilroy 2005, 142) endorsing hostile attitudes and acts to which the protagonist and his family are exposed. The prejudices against immigrants in Britain are expressed in *We Come Apart* through the integration of the powerful vocabulary and imagery recognizable from the tabloid press of the period, which has constantly described Eastern European immigrants in derogatory, infrahumanising terms. An emblematic example of this is a dialogue during a family breakfast between Jess and her stepfather, Terry. After she casually mentions her new Romanian school mate,

Nicu, a raging Terry, newspaper in hands, releases a tirade that describes immigrants as "scroungers who'd pimp out their own kids for a pound" living on "taxpayers' money [...] in council's houses down Lordship Lane" (Crossan and Conaghan 2017, 136). Terry, like many British natives of his generation, uncritically adopts such preconceived images about immigrants, based on distorted depictions in the tabloid media. Terry's attitude in this scene signifies how easily features of symbolic violence may become embedded in and govern people's everyday lives.

The exploitation of immigration as a major topic by nativist media to propagate cultural violence is especially emphatic in *We Come Apart*. What is more, a particularly interesting comment on the dissemination of cultural violence refers to the generational transmission of nativist values and attitudes both in families and in the institutional context of schools. Terry's way of referring to migrants as "dirty immigrant, rat scum" (Crossan and Conaghan 2017, 92) is mirrored by Jess who, prejudiced by her domestic education, perceives Nicu as a "gypsy wolf boy" (80) when she first meets him. Some of her school mates prove to be equally prejudiced about immigrants; without making any effort to know him, they designate Nicu as a "stinking gyppo," "rat boy gypsy scum" (133) or "filthy fucking thief" (193). The source of such prejudices is revealed by one of the boys: "my old man's right about them lot" (193). Generational transmission of nativist values, the novel suggests, prompts children to mimic the bigoted remarks and attitudes of their parents. In this way, they unconsciously become part of a historical continuum which, as Fred D'Aguiar argues, underpins "the underlying conditions for the existence of racist views safeguarded in institutional practices and expressed in views and behaviour" (D'Aguiar 2016, 759).

As mentioned before, the major dangers of cultural violence are related to its power to promote and justify other forms of violence that directly affect those who are targeted. The highly influential nativist narrative promoted by *Brexit* supporters claiming that Eastern European immigrants represent a socially and morally inferior 'Other', who, in addition, is responsible for the ills of the society, has often served as an ideological backdrop for acts of marginalization, discrimination, and social exclusion. In their novel, Crossan and Conaghan address events and situations in which the protagonist is exposed to this kind of treatment by his teachers who put him "in no-hope group" (Crossan and Conaghan 2017, 67) assuming that he lacks knowledge without even assessing him: "I know things, but teachers never ask" Nicu bitterly reflects (67). He is thus denied any possibility of integration into the education system, something to which he had looked forward, and this is connected to the teacher's preconceived opinion about Nicu: "I doubt you'll be able to catch up. Just keep your head down and behave" (57).

The lack of integration support and the outright discrimination displayed by the school officials stimulate Nicu's equally prejudiced school mates to display intolerant attitudes and perform exclusionary gestures. From this point on, for Nicu, the experience of school becomes merely a series of discriminatory acts combined with instances of bullying and psychological abuse. The sense of feeling unwelcome develops gradually, from racist hints and remarks, including the hanging of pictures of *Big Fat Gypsy Wedding* all around the school area (122), to writing hateful messages on his books such as: "*Isis slag [...], Stinking Gyppo, [...], Voted out of Britin. Fuck off*" (133). Although such gestures may look like isolated mishaps in the wider context of the story, the reader realizes that they have a symbolic value that extends beyond students' individual preferences or traits of personality. And even if the novel refrains from commenting directly on historical events that make up the backdrop in which the story unfolds, the depiction of discrimination, bullying, and marginalization of immigrants as banal events in the every-day life of a school provides a bitter social comment on those very historical realities.

The spread of nativism, the emergence to power of populist politicians, or Britain's exit from the European Union are, of course, historical events with major impacts at societal and state institutional levels. But they are not, the novel suggests, merely discursive, abstract phenomena informing the political sphere. They have concrete effects that may be less conspicuous compared to grand political events, but which impact countless anonymous individuals in ways that make their lives wretched and meaningless. Nicu acknowledges the impossibility of achieving the utopia he had envisioned before moving to Britain the day "someone put a note on no-hope table: *Brexit*" (149). This incident, although banal, anchors all events, attitudes, and emotions depicted in the novel in a recognizable historical reality informed by hostility to immigrants and permeated by instances of structural violence. The signifier *Brexit*, with all its implications, can be interpreted as a metaphor for obstruction, a symbol of what Paul Gilroy describes as "a way to keep the migrants cast outside of both culture and historicality" (Gilroy 2005, 32). The novel's ambiguous ending does not clarify what Nicu's destiny is. The extreme pressure put on him by the hostile environment, which Jess shares after they become emotionally involved, literally pulls the two protagonists in different directions, as the title of the novel suggests. Being chased by the police after he retaliates to his schoolmates' assault, Nicu chooses not to get on the train which takes Jess to safety, away from him and the stigma which he, as an immigrant, seems to carry inexorably.

Final Considerations and Conclusion

We Come Apart is a lively book that stimulates the reader's empathy and aspirations for living in a world where difference can represent a strength and not a burden. As Annabel Pitcher writes in a review of the novel, the "problems that the protagonists face are unsurmountable, but the narrative never feels overburdened, soaring above the issues it explores to offer a beautiful tale of love, hope and survival" (Pitcher 2017). *Night of the Party* is a dystopia that disturbs the reader with its depiction of duress and a suffocating, gloomy atmosphere, but it equally suggests the possibility of surpassing tribulations through love, solidarity, and loyalty. Imogen Russell Williams describes the novel as "a hundred-decibel alarm call, skewering both the inhuman bureaucracy of the detention centre and the casual acceptance of horrors" (Williams 2018) in contemporary Britain.

It can thus be said that both novels provide incisive comments concerning the long-lasting consequences of marginalisation, discrimination, and abuse, that immigrants often experience in societies that tend to prioritise an inward-looking, exclusionary ethos. However, the parallelism of these novels stretches beyond thematic similarities and the intention to scrutinise abusive practices in connection to migration in Britain. The authors employ similar narrative strategies to structure the novels by juxtaposing the perspective of a native and a migrant protagonist on the same events in successive chapters, thus creating the sensation of a dialogue not just between the characters themselves, but metonymically, one which implies the entire groups they represent. If the communication between protagonists is hesitant in the initial stage, the relationship they develop throughout the story provides a strong message: intercultural dialogue and cosmopolitan conviviality can become a factual reality. Ash and Jess enter the narratives as standard British natives, preoccupied with trivial aspects of existence in a social environment in which the fault line between the native 'Us' and the migrant 'Others' goes unquestioned. In both cases, it is precisely the omnipresence of the oppressive culture underpinning such divisions that triggers their transformation into agents of cosmopolitanism. Their characterisation represents a strong argument through which the novels dispel the narrative of division, the myth of the intractable conflict between different cultures and individuals proclaimed by the prophets of nativism in the campaign for *Brexit*.

The transformation that Ash and Jess undergo is significant in at least two aspects: it demonstrates the futility of cultural violence when direct contact and open intercultural dialogue prevail, and it invites readers to reflect on aspects of the migrant experience that they easily tend to overlook if not exposed to contact with migrants in real life situations. We encounter in the novels a category of characters who internalise aspects of cultural violence that make them act as oblivious nativist agents, such as Jess' schoolmates who find pleasure in bullying Nicu, or Ash's colleague, Lewis, who considers it to be his unconditional duty to report a pub worker whom he suspects to be non-British Born. In such a climate, where the banality of evil, of which Hannah Arendt warned sixty years ago (Arendt

2006 [1963]), may emerge as an everyday feature, novels like *Night of the Party* and *We Come Apart* represent, one may say, unfortunately, necessary but also efficient literary responses to a reality in which tolerance, acceptance, and cosmopolitan conviviality are a desirable abstraction rather than a fact. The novels can be read as an exploration of the positive power of overcoming violent attitudes and acts directed at immigrants by promoting constructive dialogue as a key element for achieving the "cosmopolitan vision" to which Ulrich Beck (2006) refers, in the sense of acknowledging the otherness of, and practicing non-violent co-existence with, those who are culturally different (57).

By telling the affecting stories of young immigrants who resiliently navigate a menacing environment, the novels make accessible to readers the daily experience of migration in a way that most of those who never had to move can hardly imagine. Perhaps the greatest strength that is common to both novels is the capacity to raise awareness about the insidiousness of violence that is inflicted upon immigrants through unconscious, sometimes involuntary gestures and attitudes which anyone could produce at a certain time. For, as Johan Galtung suggests, on a historical scale, it is often common to pay attention mostly to the noticeable acts of direct violence; but once these cease to be manifest, and "only two labels show up, pale enough for college textbooks: 'discrimination' for massive structural violence and 'prejudice' for massive cultural violence" (Galtung 1990, 2), the risk to ignore these forms of symbolic violence always lurks. Therefore, reflections on such elusive aspects of violence that, among others, the novels in question provide, raise awareness about the existence of ethical issues around us that otherwise may pass unnoticed.

Although descriptions of nativist ideas or accounts about the marginalisation and discrimination of migrants can be found in various media, both academic and journalistic, representations of these events and their outcomes through memorable, sensitive, and relatable narratives can have more powerful effects on the recipient. When discussing the immigrant experience in particular, its portrayal in literature offers the opportunity to present individual stories in a wider context, referring both to past and future, explaining both rational and personal motivations. Nevertheless, even though *Night of the Party* and *We Come Apart* may be regarded as predominantly dark and pessimistic novels, a note of optimism transpires as, through the interaction and dialogue established between the protagonists, the narratives also celebrate the possibility of dismantling societal and state structures that support violence against immigrants.

These novels may therefore be added to the category of British cultural productions that seek to address the contradictions and contentions that immigration continues to raise in contemporary Britain fifty years after Powell delivered his speech. The unsettling shadow of Powell in the age of *Brexit* is as present as it was at the time when the speech was first uttered. Powell's prophesies of doom have never materialised, but, as Samuel Earle sustained in an article in *The Atlantic,* "he proved prescient in a different sense: as a figure who embodied fears that continue to animate Britain's present and will help define its future" (Earle 2018). Despite this, and perhaps because of it, literature will continue to contribute significantly to constituting critical approaches to the intricate realities of multicultural societies, which continue to be informed by contradictions and contention.

Bibliography

Agamben, Giorgio. 1998. *Homo Sacer. Sovereign Power and Bare Life.* Stanford, CA: Stanford UP.

Agamben, Giorgio. 2005. *State of Exception.* Chicago: The U of Chicago P.

Arendt, Hannah. 2006. *Eichmann in Jerusalem: A Report on the Banality of Evil.* New York: Penguin.

Association of Visitors to Immigration Detainees (AVID). n.d. "What Is Immigration Detention?" Accessed April 12, 2022. http://www.avid-detention.org.uk/immigration-detention/what-immigration-detention.

BBC. 2019. "Nigel Farage: Breaking Point Poster 'Transformed Politics.'" Last modified May 12, 2019. https://www.bbc.com/news/av/uk-politics-48244663.

Beck, Ulrich. 2006. *The Cosmopolitan Vision.* Translated by Ciaran Cronin. Cambridge: Polity Press.

Bosworth, Mary. 2008. "Border Control and the Limits of the Sovereign State." *Social & Legal Studies* 17 (2): 199–215.

Crossan, Sarah, and Brian Conaghan. 2018. *We Come Apart.* London: Bloomsbury.

D'Aguiar, Fred. 2016. "Letter to Beryl Gilroy." *Callaloo* 39 (4): 757–761. https://doi.org/https://doi.org/10.1353/cal.2017.0006.

Earle, Samuel. 2018. "'Rivers of Blood': The Legacy of a Speech That Divided Britain." *The Atlantic* (blog). Last modified April 20, 2018. https://www.theatlantic.com/international/archive/2018/04/enoch-powell-rivers-of-blood/558344/.

Flood, Christopher. 2002. *Political Myth. A Theoretical Introduction.* London and New York: Routledge.

Ford, Robrt, and Matthew Goodwin. 2017. "Britain After Brexit: A Nation Divided." *Journal of Democracy* 28, 17–30.

Foucault, Michel. 1995. *Discipline and Punish. The Birth of the Prison.* New York: Vintage Books.

Galtung, Johan. 1969. "Violence, Peace, and Peace Research." *Journal of Peace Research* 6 (3): 167–191.

– – –. 1990. "Cultural Violence." *Journal of Peace Research* 27 (3): 291–305.

– – –. 1996. *Peace by Peaceful Means. Peace and Conflict, Development and Civilization.* London: Sage.

Geddes, Andrew, and Peter Scholten. 2016. *The Politics of Migration & Immigration in Europe.* 2nd ed. London: SAGE Publications. https://doi.org/10.4135/9781473982703.

Gilroy, Paul. 2005. *Postcolonial Melancholia*. New York: Columbia UP.

Griffiths, Melanie. 2017. "Foreign, Criminal: A Doubly Damned Modern British Folk-Devil." *Citizenship Studies* 21 (5): 527–46. https://doi.org/10.1080/13621025.2017.1328486.

Guia, Aitana. 2016. "The Concept of Nativism and Anti-immigrant Sentiments in Europe." Max Weber Programme Working Paper No 2016-20, European University Institute, Fiesole. https://doi.org/10.13140/RG.2.2.25755.67360.

Hennessy, Claire. 2018. "British YA Gets Political: Teen Reads for July." *The Irish Times*. Last modified July 17, 2018. https://www.irishtimes.com/culture/books/british-ya-gets-political-teen-reads-for-july-1.3550218,

Jones, Nicolette. 2018. "The Best Summer Reading for Children and Young Adults." *The Sunday Times*, June 24, 2018. https://www.thetimes.co.uk/article/the-best-summer-reading-for-children-2z6bs68l9.

Koser, Khalid. 2007. *International Migration: A Very Short Introduction*. Oxford : Oxford UP.

Mathias, Tracey. 2018. *Night of the Party*. London: Scholastic.

Mudde, Cas. 2016. "Populist Radical Right Parties in Europe Today." In *Transformations of Populism in Europe and the Americas: History and Recent Tendencies*, edited by John Abromeit, Gary Marotta and York Norman, 295–307. London: Bloomsbury.

Mudde, Cas, and Cristóbal Rovira Kaltwasser. 2017. *Populism: A Very Short Introduction*. New York: Oxford University Press. https://doi.org/10.1093/actrade/9780190234874.001.0001.

Pitcher, Annabel. 2017. "We Come Apart Review—a Bittersweet Teenage Romance in Verse." *The Guardian*, February 18, 2017. https://www.theguardian.com/books/2017/feb/18/we-come-apart-review-sarah-crossan-brian-conaghan.

Powell, Enoch. 1968, April 20. *Speech to a Meeting of the Conservative Association*.

Rajan, Emol. 2018. "Archive on 4—50 Years on: Rivers of Blood—BBC Sounds." Last modified April 14, 2018. https://www.bbc.co.uk/sounds/play/b09z08w3.

Riedel, Rafał. 2018. "Nativism versus Nationalism and Populism—Bridging the Gap." *Central European Papers* 6 (2): 18–28. https://doi.org/10.25142/cep.2018.011

Spivak, Gayatri Chakravorty. 2012. *An Aesthetic Education in the Era of Globalization*. Cambridge, MA: Harvard UP.

Sweney, Mark. 2018. "BBC under Fire over Enoch Powell 'Rivers of Blood' Broadcast." *The Guardian*, April 12, 2018. https://www.theguardian.com/media/2018/apr/12/bbc-to-air-reading-of-enoch-powells-rivers-of-blood-speech.

Webel, Charles, and Johan Galtung. 2007. *Handbook of Peace and Conflict Studies*. London: Routledge.

Williams, Imogen Russell. 2018. "Children's and Teens Roundup: The Best New Picture Books and Novels." *The Guardian*, May 26, 2018. https://www.theguardian.com/books/2018/may/26/childrens-teens-roundup-best-new-picturebooks-novels.

Žižek, Slavoj. 2008. *Violence: Six Sideways Reflections*. New York: Picador.

Indefinite Detention in Britain: A Literary and Philosophical Understanding of Detainee Lives in the Twenty-First Century

Rebecca Deluce

Introduction: The Media Image of Migration vs the Emerging Genre of Refugee Literature

Recently, certain elements of political and media discourse on migrants and refugees have encouraged a detached view of those seeking asylum in Britain, owing to which violence against them is seldom questioned or even noticed. With increasingly nationalist, xenophobic and racist discussions of migration, the distance between citizen and migrant lives has arguably increased. This change is both a result of explicit political policies and of attempts to manipulate the perception of the UK's immigration policies as well as those caught within them. With riots (in 2023), protests, and hunger strikes (in 2018) at Yarl's Wood Detention Centre and the unjust threat of removal as a result, public debates even more intensively revolve around the position and figure of the migrant, and the ill-defined restrictions and regulations of detention in Britain. The idea that migrants are essentially unhinged in space and time during indefinite detention leaves them in a position of simultaneous inclusion and exclusion; a "zone of indistinction" where they are cast as the Other to the public and country yet ruled by the same figures that exclude them from society (Agamben 1998, 19).

In this chapter, Michel Foucault and Giorgio Agamben's theories on biopolitics and sovereignty are utilized in concert with Judith Butler's concept of grievability to comment on the precarity of migrant lives in host countries. The authority of state power is considered through ideas on sovereignty in twenty-first century Britain to identify the extent to which contemporary sovereign powers influence the acceptance of violence and injustice of detainees. This is to help in analyzing instances of exploitation and abuse in select literary renderings of both non-fictional migrant accounts and British authors' works that challenge the negative perception of migrants and the unethical practices and exploitation within the immigration and detention process.

The emerging genre of refugee literature (used here to mean literature authored or co-authored by those with direct experience of refugees' lives) is investigated in its discussion of detention and the physical and psychological abuse frequently overlooked by legal authorities. Literature's attempt to produce an alternative, nonofficial perspective on immigration and detention is studied through the organization Refugee Tales' collection of Chaucerian narratives of that title (*Refugee Tales* 2016), alongside a similar anthology, *A Country of Refuge* (2016), to evaluate the dialogues these texts create in response to violence within the immigration system and detention experiences. In Popescu's compendium, *A Country of Refuge,* the violence often faced by refugees during migration, detention and removal to and from countries is explored directly through Ruth Padel's poetry, whilst Joan Smith's essay "To Avoid Worse" explores the comparisons of identity and ignorance towards refugees through the figures of Anne Frank and Aylan Kurdi. The collaborative efforts of authors and migrants in *Refugee Tales* depict experiences of living indefinitely in Britain, each exposing a different manner of discrimination suffered. "The Appellant's Tale as told to David Herd" investigates the immigration control standards and the arbitrary gathering of asylum seekers and refugees for detention and deportation. "The Interpreter's Tale as told to Carol Watts" studies the power and restriction of words within the immigration system. The narrative further explores the importance of an accurate interpretation and administration of life forced upon individuals in detention and the immigration process.

In 2013, attempted suicides in detention centers "hit a record high of 325" with "one attempt on average every 27 hours" (No Deportations 2015), while a Freedom of Information publication from March 2014 considering the preceding five years, documented 230 cases of staff who were "dismissed for misconduct," including racism, bullying, harassment and discrimination, immigration abuse or corruption, negligence, and verbal or abusive behavior (Gov.uk

2014). In reference to the purpose of immigration detention, these centers were renamed "immigration removal centres [IRCs]," in 2001 "to signify more clearly their purpose, […] were to provide short-term secure housing prior to administrative removal or deportation" (Bosworth 2012, 127). With the continuation of indefinite detention in Britain, the temporary and vulnerable positions of detainees are further distorted by a dismissal of citizen rights within these confines.

Additionally, the lack of documentation often found during the identification of detainees and within detention procedures produces an ambiguity between individual and state, and portrays them to be "unknowable", "ungovernable" and thereby "dangerous" to the country (Malloch and Stanley 2005, 54).

The related concept of the "illegal" immigrant, and economic migrant, in twenty-first century Britain, has become wrongly imbedded in the definitions of refugee and asylum seeker. Through the indistinction of politicians and the media, along with the reiterated idea that they are only here to "secure an improved standard of life" (Malloch and Stanley 2005, 55), the distorted perception and criminalization of individuals fleeing hostile environments continues. Branded as terrorists and hindrances to national health and welfare services, they are said to "pose a very real risk to liberal democratic states" (54). Furthermore, the general regard that the vast majority of asylum seekers and refugees are "economic migrants" has led to the British asylum policy seeming "inadequate, overly-liberal and ineffective in keeping 'them' out" (58). With the start of the Syrian civil war in March 2011, contributing to the largest displacement of people since the second world war, the anxieties regarding the number of refugees migrating raised suspicions and enforced stricter border controls within the U.K. The demonization of immigrants, particularly of Syrian refugees, implies that they are "implicitly associated with the dangerousness of the regimes they flee" (55). This misrepresentation overpowers the reality of war-inflicted crises and creates a "rhetoric of crime and prevention" that views migrant populations as "clandestine or 'illegal'" (Angel-Ajani 2003, 435).

Following this, in July 2013, the British Home Office initiated Operation Vaken as a part of the Hostile Environment policy. An advertising campaign "encouraging irregular migrants to leave the UK 'voluntarily'" using vans stamped with the phrase "go home or face arrest" (Burnett 2017, 90). Not only was this said to mimic the language used by the far-right group, The National Front, in the 1970s, but the failure of the operation, along with its disapproving rejection by the public and media, caused the termination of this campaign by October 2013. This alarmist perception and isolation of immigrants enforces the belief that they are "'not one of us', and are, therefore, a threat to 'our way of life'" (Kundnani 2001, 52). The hostile space created by the campaign and the media's presentation of the refugee crisis and immigration control further disassociates citizens from immigrants, leaving each unaware of the other's reality and constructing a reliance on media and political sources to inform.

Sovereignty, Power, and the Precarity of the Other in a State of Exception

This ties rather seamlessly into the concept of sovereignty. While sovereignty is traditionally understood as a single authority figure's possession of absolute reign and governance, emblematized by the doctrine of the divine right of kings, this idea of the sovereign power is no longer employed today. Legal and governmental actions are no longer considered to be taken in the name of God, and no single being is responsible for the laws, legislations, governance or rights of individuals.

Sovereignty, however, still exists today, constituting—in addition to disciplinary mechanics and biopower—"the general mechanisms of power in our society" (Foucault 2003, 39). Contemporary sovereignty is exercised as a collective power gained by those in government and parliament through the active maintenance of the state of exception. Foucault contends that sovereignty is seen not in the sources of power but in the "various operators of domination" that support, "converge and reinforce one another in some cases, and negate or strive to annul one another in other cases" (2003, 45). With the removal of a divine power governing all, the operators who control and legitimize one another's claims contribute to a sovereign power's goal. This creates a unified power that collectively claims absolute authority. Though all the operators of domination may not always synchronize, the necessity is simply for a majority to legitimize, and to cast others in opposition as incorrect.

The unity of power that has been founded here is defined by Foucault as one of the three required elements of sovereignty. The other two elements are identified as "a subject who has to be subjectified" and "the legitimacy that has to be respected" (2003, 44). It can be argued that the subject is the detainee and refugee through the criminalization and oppression of these individuals in society. The final element can be seen as the most precarious of the three, in that the respect towards the "unity of power" and the manner of legitimacy can alter at any time. The ambiguity towards the validation of legitimacy can be seen through these two interpretations: the validity of the actions of the unity of power through sovereign and legal respect, or the respect that originates from the "sovereigns" or peoples to validate the legitimacy of their actions. While the legitimacy from the perspective of the "operators" within the unity of power is ordinarily secure, the respect from the public for the actions and treatment of those subjected can be volatile. The respected legitimacy is often seen through the acts of law which are validated by the value of law in contemporary democracy. However, as mentioned earlier, the legitimacy simply needs to be validated by both the sovereign and the unity of power that enforces the subjection of the subject: "a power can be constituted, not exactly in accordance with the law, but in accordance with a certain basic legitimacy that is more basic than any law and that allows laws to function as such" (2003, 44). Arguably, Foucault highlights here the insignificance of law in justifying the actions put upon subjects when the actions are considered more vital than any jurisdiction of law.

A similar logic is used to validate the treatment of detainees and refugees in contemporary society through the state of exception. The indefinite state of detainees and refugees causes both an isolation and rejection of life, casting them as the other within a society. Fiske describes this, quite aptly, as the "distancing of the refugee from the citizenry" (2016, 3). This is where literature broaches a connection between the two spheres to enable an alternative discourse and account of events, whilst further reconnecting the segregated lives.

The sovereign power, or the unity of power that dominates today, manipulates the position of the detainee and refugee through various justifications of their influence upon the condition of the country. The otherness that pertains to these individuals, reinforced by those within the unity of power, implicitly defines them as "capable of threat" with "unknown intentions, proclivities, associations and histories" (Hall 2010, 890). This indistinction is therefore a cause for speculation rather than a recognition of individuals and their lives. The "rhetoric of crime and prevention" (Angel-Ajani 2003, 435) and the "crimmigration"[1] that has become prominent in the discussion and treatment of detainees emphasize the fear of immigrants from select regions of the world. The attention given to terrorist groups in the media and in political speeches, and the national connection they have to a number of refugee and asylum seekers, is used by the operators of domination to reiterate the association between immigrants and criminality that is the source of so much distrust within the community. Butler illustrates this through the recognition that terrorism is no longer "historically or geographically limited," giving way to a limitless state of emergency (2006, 65). She theorizes this to be the potential for a "lawless future […] given over to the discretionary decisions of a set of designated sovereigns" (65). This reality may come to fruition through

---

[1] Crimmigration is a term coined by Juliet Stumpf in 2006 in her paper "The Crimmigration Crisis: Immigrants, Crime, and Sovereign Power." It identifies the reasons behind "the confluence of criminal and immigration law and maps […] how and why these two areas of law have converged, and why that convergence may be troubling," suggesting especially that a central role in this process is played by "membership theory, which limits individual rights and privileges to the members of a social contract between the government and the people," with the crucial consequence that the application of this theory "has the potential to include individuals in the social contract or exclude them from it" (Stumpf 2006, 377).

the escalation of the exercise of sovereignty over immigration control in current times.

A sense of management and power over the issue of immigration has also been asserted through the control over the opinion of immigrants in the twenty-first century. Even detainee protests on the violence and abuse taking place in detention are, when they are detected by the public sphere, misrepresented as manipulative, political acts. This emphasizes "the government narrative" on their actions of disobedience "as evidence of 'their' moral bankruptcy, deviousness and difference from 'us'" (Fiske 2016, 122). Through these acts, detainees and refugees are "othered" by the suggestion that they are "non-integrationist" and "opposed to assimilation" within Western democracy (Malloch and Stanley 2005, 56). Through the manipulation of their vulnerable position as a refugee or asylum seeker, the unity of power can distort the intention of these individuals and exile them politically from society whilst physically remaining within its borders. It is through this that the sovereign power's "decision on which lives count as political, and which are to be 'excepted'" is identified (Hall 2010, 84). The state of exception identified in Agamben's work explores the idea of exemption and exclusion from society whilst physically, and as a figure, remaining within its perimeters.

Agamben identifies this as a "topological zone of indistinction" (1998, 37) where individuals are subjected to indefinite distinctions of their rights, their place in the country and as a political body. The concept of the state of exception allows the sovereign to work beyond the rule of law in suggesting that it will be for the benefit of the country's citizens. In Mills' understanding of Agamben's theory, this allows there to be a simultaneous appropriation and abandonment of life for those employed within the state of exception (2014, 67). In terms of detention, Agamben demonstrates this concept through the concentration camps in Germany in the 1930s to the 1940s. A parallel can be drawn from the camp and contemporary detention centers in that it presents a place "where people are 'taken outside' yet governed more tightly, where sovereign power intervenes directly on bodies and individual lives which do not have the normal protection of law" (Hall 2012, 13).

Literature of/in Detention Camps

The parallels between private sector-operated detention centers and concentration camps have recently been explored by contemporary writers, as in Robert Schenkkan's 2018 play *Building the Wall*. The presence of the juridico-political structure in the twenty-first century evinces that this hidden form of violence towards migrants and refugees is not "an anomaly belonging to the past [...] but the hidden matrix and *nomos* of the political space in which we are still living" (Agamben 1998, 166). The adaptation of sovereignty in the twenty-first century then functions within the system through its ability to remain concealed in the workings of the law. Foucault asserts that "the right of sovereignty was the right to take life or let live;" in contemporary times, the manipulation of this doctrine has altered to become "the right to make live and let die" (Foucault 2003, 241). This calls to mind Judith Butler's idea in *Frames of War* (2016) of the grievability of individual lives and what determines a life to be protected based on its political significance, as it is explored below in the context of Agamben's "bare life" theory.

It is crucial to recall that, as discussed above, the injustices and violence committed towards detained refugees and asylum seekers have also been documented in literary form. One recent, globally significant incident was the distribution of poetry produced by the prisoners residing at the Guantanamo Bay Detention Camp. The collection titled *Poems from Guantánamo: The Detainees Speak* (Falkoff 2007) contains a variety of poems by seventeen inmates who expressed their experiences in this format. The response from the public, media and the government during the circulation of these poems has given an opportunity for detainees and the silenced individuals of the world to work together, collectively with authors and other recognized citizens, in a fight to reclaim their voice in society.

Narratives based exclusively on British detention center experiences and refugee and asylum life in Britain have been documented, amongst others, in Lucy Popescu's edited anthology, *A Country of Refuge* (2016). The compilation was produced by a diverse range of authors, who themselves have either experienced the injustices and violence of the immigration system firsthand, met with mistreated individuals within detention and during immigration, or aimed to challenge the negative connotations associated with these individuals in contemporary culture. This text allows for a discourse on the topic of immigration in Britain today to evidence and fight against the treatment and perception of refugees and asylum seekers in the twenty-first century.

The experience of detained life in Britain is explored through several of Ruth Padel's poems in this collection. The effects of sovereign power and manipulation of government and law can be seen more clearly through her poem, "The Prayer Labyrinth." The hellish and limbo-like portrayal of the state of detention seen in the poem mirrors frequent descriptions by detainees themselves. Padel references this analogy throughout the first stanza of her poem (2016, 166):

> She went looking for her daughter. How many
> visit Hades and live? Your only hope
> is the long labyrinth of Visa Application
> interviews with a volunteer from a charity
> you're not allowed to meet.
> You've been caught: by a knock on the door
> at dawn, hiding in a truck of toilet tissue
> or just getting stuck in a turn-stile. (1–8)

The figure of Hades, commonly known as the ruler of the underworld in Greek mythology, represents the sovereign figure or indeed the detention centers in this passage. The threat to life and power over death that this image portrays questions the ability to survive in such a situation and implies the doubt an individual has in deciding to travel there. The menacing tone of this question also implies fear over this figure, "Hades", who appears destructive and governing over life. The intimidation this figure creates in the protagonist correlates to the unity of power, the sovereign power, that rules over contemporary society today. The destination of this fear is then affirmed following the arrest during the first stanza: "You're on Dead Island: The Detention Centre" (166). The direct declaration beginning the second stanza not only serves to remind the reader of residing in an infernal state, but that the living beings do not belong here.

In other words, Padel arguably highlights a parallel between the zombie figure and the treatment of refugee and asylum seekers in representing them as the "living-dead." And, if this is the case, Padel may even be alluding to the identically named survival video game "Dead Island," which is set during a zombie infestation, including a "maximum security facility for international terrorists" that is "surrounded by a minefield" off the coast (Dead Island Wiki 2018).[2] With the state of exception acknowledging biological life whilst excluding their political and lawful presence within the state, the zombie-figure could be the ideal representation for the treatment of the twenty-first century detainee.

The violence and abuse of detainees is also emphasized through the "evidence of cigarette/ burns" (166), "a broken finger, a punctured lung" (167) and the suicidal imagery of detainees "[tying] themselves together/ before they jumped" (166). Through communicating and exhibiting their evidence of abuse, Patel not only calls attention to the dismissive "Lack of Credibility" stamp that asylum seekers and applicants for refugee status often receive, but also highlights the corruption of officials, their abuse of detainees, as well as the extent to which this may drive them to self-harm and suicide. The effect that violence and abuse have upon those in detention can be seen through the suppression of their quality of life and state of health. The final stanza illustrates the various instances of neglect and cruelty, from being "dragged/ from your room, denied medication" (166), "locked/ in a corridor for three days without water" (166) to being "handcuffed through [a] biopsy" (167). The abuse stated here portrays a lack of respect and dignity for the individual, highlighting the unjust treatment of commonly innocent detainees. The subordination and secondary state put upon detainees causes forms of domination and violence to occur since they are not protected by national citizen laws, while prisoners, individuals who have committed crimes against the state,

---

[2] For more on the analogy between refugees as zombies, see e.g. Mouflard (2016), Toivanen (2019) and Zaborowski and Georgiou (2019).

have access to them. In the state of exception, physical restriction and restraints are then interpreted as public safety procedures and identification of their violent behavior. The destruction of self is reiterated through the recurrent statements, emphasizing detainees' lack of political power and recognition of life within and outside the confines of the detention center: "You've no choice" (167) "or a voice" (166), "[t]hey say you don't belong" (167). These phrases not only express the internal insecure beliefs of the detainee but the reality of effect and influence, or lack thereof, that they have on their place in the state. This clearly shows the importance of the literary representation of abuse and life within detention as it provides a platform from which stifled narratives can be told and will be recognized.

An acknowledgement of these stories via the written word has also taken the form of the collaborative work of authors and detainees, such as those identified in the various projects of Refugee Tales. This organization, with its slogan requesting "a call to end indefinite immigration detention," aims to inform the public on the definition of indefinite detention; through its solidarity walks to share "other people's tales, the project gathered and [communicated] experiences of migration" (Refugee Tales 2018), as well as through the publication of selected detainee and refugee tales, such as those in the volumes *Refugee Tales* (2016), *Refugee Tales II* (2017) and *Refugee Tales III* (2019). Similarly to Popescu's *A Country of Refuge*, these narratives explore the injustices experienced by refugees and asylum seekers in their confrontation with the British immigration system. In David Herd's "The Appellant's Tale" in *Refugee Tales,* the arbitrary detention and unjust, physical restraint of detainees is apparent in the treatment of the appellant in his experience with the detention system. It follows an individual who worked and resided in Britain for almost thirty years, and who is suddenly detained for reasons unknown to them. "[T]hey call the Home office and the Home Office confirms you and says you have no criminal record. / Anyway they arrest you" (2016, 71). While no legal infringement has occurred by actions of the individual, the "sovereign", in this case, the security services who govern the detention centers, are making use of the state of exception, through identifying the appellant as potentially illegal. The evidence that the appellant has "no criminal record" seems irrelevant to the imprisonment, therefore the authorities exercise their sovereign power over the individual, veiled as intentions for national security and public protection.

The suppression of evidence is also recurrent, from the inability of the "appellant" to collect evidence from their home to the manipulation of court procedures and administration. "The Appellant's Tale" emphasizes the necessity of evidence in depicting it as "the song of your occupations" (72). The musical connection made here gives a sense of voice from the detainee. The absence of this "song", the physical testimony of his consent to be in the state, highlights the disenfranchisement of the detention process regarding human and detainee rights. The acknowledgment of music in society, both through the lyrics and how they are formed, illustrates the impact and effect they have upon the world and its communities. The importance of communication is recognized in the tale as an imperative factor of proof in detention. Herd further stresses this during the appellant's bail tribunal by his absence in the courtroom; "It matters you are not in the courtroom. The judge accepts what the UKBA says" (78). Without physical communication and firsthand accounts, the understanding of, and empathy for, the appellant is lost amongst the administration of life in the deportation and detention system. The subjection put upon detainees and migrants through immigration control and sovereign powers is underscored by the sovereignty of the UKBA in this extract within the legal framework, here identified through the judge's actions. With the Windrush Scandal in mind, and the wrongful detention of immigrants, this tale calls to attention the changes needed to be made throughout the immigration system, whilst emphasizing the corruption of the government and legal constitutions in the confines of immigration policy.

The exploitation of life in the immigration system can be assessed through Butler's theory of the grievability of life alongside Agamben's "bare life" concept in *Homo Sacer*. As Foucault suggested, the power of sovereignty in modern societies is taken over by disciplinary systems and biopolitics, in which "the old power of death that symbolized sovereign power [is] now carefully supplanted by the administration of bodies and the calculated management of life" (2012, 298). The biopolitical focus on bodies that continues today highlights the use of beings contained within "bare life" conditions as a use for political exploitation. Similarly to the state of exception, bare life places a being in a "zone of indistinction between outside and inside" the political sphere (Agamben 1998, 19), whilst being "stripped of its political status and becom[ing] abject" (Hall 2012, 12). Agamben claims that the inclusion of bare life in the political realm remains the "nucleus of sovereign power [...] placing biological life at the center of its calculations" (1998, 6). In relation to the refugee and asylum seeker in detention, the fundamental right of the "sacredness of life [...] expresses precisely both life's subjection to a power over death and life's irreparable exposure in the relation of abandonment" (83). Agamben believes that refugees bring to light the condition of bare life within the political domain through embodying "the man of rights" figure who holds "rights outside the fiction of the citizen," arguing that this is "what makes the figure of the citizen so hard to define politically" (131). This argument leaves refugees not in a state of powerlessness, but in a state of precarity in being indefinable as a citizen or alien. Mills claims that Agamben is mistaken in the belief that bare life is "fundamentally passive [...] to sovereign violence, singularly exposed without recourse or response" (2014, 75). As we can see through the detainee protests, calls for change from the public, and literary, photographic and artistic communication with those caught in the state of exception, passivity towards the indistinction and injustices of their lives is rarely apparent.

While this dialogue is on-going, the political and general view of refugees and asylum seekers is through a biological definition of being, rather than showing a comprehensive understanding of the circumstances from which they have requested refuge. Hall's earlier suggestion that they are removed from political status within the state of exception seems contradictory to her later work. She subsequently argues that while the "modern habit" is to view the "political realm in terms of citizen's rights," the very existence of bare life from the point of view of sovereignty is the only "authentically political" being (2012, 106). Though it is apparent that detainees have minimal rights in detention, ultimately subjecting them to a lack of political force, their embodiment of the sacred man—"homo sacer"—defines them as political through their indistinction and ungovernable state within the borders of the country where they have been detained.

The figure of homo sacer is defined as he "who may be killed and yet not sacrificed" (Agamben 1998, 8), highlighting the possibility of death without it being classified as murder. Agamben identifies the paradox or fiction of sovereignty through homo sacer and bare life as being the "originary activity of sovereignty" leaving the life caught in the "sovereign ban" as "the life that is originarily sacred" (83). The fundamental right to life in opposition to sovereign power resists the power to be murdered through the rights of law. Agamben situates this "in the age of biopolitics" to suggest that the sovereign's power over those within the state of exception to be "killed without the commission of homicide" has been "transformed into the power to decide the point at which life ceases to be politically relevant" (1998, 142). With this power, the sovereign can demand death upon any selection of individuals whom it decides to be politically irrelevant and outside legal jurisdiction. These instances have occurred in history, through the atrocities of concentration camps, and more recently seen through the prisoners of Guantanamo Bay and the Rohingya persecution in Myanmar. As Agamben recalls, it was only after the Jews had been denationalized, stripped of their residual citizenship, that they were able to be detained within the extermination camps (1998, 132). These examples of violence illustrate how the presence of bare life lies at the very center of society just as much today as during the totalitarian régimes of the twentieth century (181–182). The presence of bare life leaves vulnerable the right to life and the grievability of these individuals.

Often disguised under the pretense of security, national identity and the public good, the politicization of lives removes the recognition of another living being as, to reference Judith Butler's text, a *Precarious Life* (2006). The condition of bare life that detainees are subjected to deems them to be unqualified lives, since they are "not conceivable as lives within certain epistemological frames" (Butler 2016, 1). This perspective suggests that these lives are "never lived nor lost in the full sense" (1). The argument made here by Butler is that the inability to perceive a life as potentially grievable and precarious renders said life irrelevant and apathetical within societal sentiment. The influence of sovereign power is illustrated through the detachment of these individuals within society. This is shown through the ignorance towards the shared condition of precarity in policy and the public (28). The effect of "this differential distribution of precarity" evinces the "justified" treatment of those deemed ungrievable, and how they are made to "bear the burden of starvation, underemployment, legal disenfranchisement, and differential exposure to violence and death" (25). Butler argues that it would be almost impossible to understand the suffering of oppression without first recognizing how "this primary condition" of precarity is "exploited and exploitable, thwarted and denied" (2006, 31). Only through an awareness of shared precarity are we able to recognize the injustices put upon these lives, often found during the conditions of war. The "forms of domination" that occur during this time "leads not to reciprocal recognition, but to a specific exploitation of targeted populations" (Butler 2016, 31). As conflict recognizes a threat to regular life, these national sources, and the citizens who inhabit the space, ultimately become "threats to human life" rather than "living populations in need of protection from illegitimate state violence, famine, or pandemics" (31). The only way in which to terminate the injustices and anonymity of these lives is through the recognition of precarity and empathy for another life both including and beyond the biological element of living.

     A.L. Kennedy's short story, "Inappropriate Staring" in *A Country of Refuge* (2016) portrays the British public's perception of refugees through depicting the reactions of a mother and son when visiting the zoo. The two characters are viewing what is suggested to be a collection of primates, or a species like their own, behind electric fences. In fear of one of the male animals, a discussion between mother and son on their safety is expressed:

> "You're all right — he can't get to you. He can't get near you."
> "Sometimes they get out."
> "There's electric fences and all sorts of stuff. We're safe here." (Kennedy 2016, 68)

The recognition of detainee life here illustrates the obvious comparison between the isolation of refugees in detention and the perception of animals in enclosure. The threat to life and anxiety produced by these creatures parallels the general regard for refugees and asylum seekers in Britain today. The enclosure highlighted though the presence of "electric fences" both portrays the secondary status of those within the enclosure, and the authoritarian status of those in control of the space who keep safe the spectators in the story. The segregated space between the two groups of bodies demonstrates the bare life conditions of those in confinement (those without political status and with little influence on their own quality of life), against the citizens who are only involved with their existence through their discussions of those imprisoned. The minute elements of empathy and emphasis on difference exhibits the misunderstanding and distancing of those in detention.

Other than the recognition of a familial and protective bond between the animals in the enclosure, the mother and son's discussion is based on a comparison of life. While they acknowledge that "sharing's an instinct" (70), they also make apparent the distinctions of distribution — "we take care of our own — they take care of their own" (70). The identification of the principle that all living beings need certain necessities in life exposes a connection between the two, whilst the division and the domination of one group by the other leaves the authoritarian group in control of the management and of the aid the other one receives in acquiring these necessities. Their lack of empathy and the stress on authority and order is a form of the administration of lives that takes precedence over lives themselves in the twenty-first century, particularly in the case of those migrating and seeking refuge.

In contrast to the segregation shown in Kennedy's narrative, "The Dependant's Tale as told to Marina Lewycka" in *Refugee Tales* (2016) illustrates the unjust detention and immigration process of a family living in Bradford who are eventually saved through the community's and organizations' support and assistance. The beginning of the account depicts the family's arrest at their home and the protagonist's, an eight-year-old boy's, response to this. The unnecessary security portrayed by the participation of four men in detaining two children is emphasized by the boy as he mocks them: "We were so dangerous!" (86). He further begins to question the management of policy and process during this period: "who draws up the guidelines for how they should treat people they are deporting or keeps a check on how they behave" (86). The obvious lack of supervision in the immigration sector by the Home Office in Britain has been more publicly recognized after the Windrush scandal in 2018. This scandal revealed that the UK Home Office lost the records of several immigrants who had been granted permission to stay, who were thus unable to prove they were in the country legally and were prevented from accessing healthcare, work or housing and occasionally even became threatened with deportation.

Lewycka's text indicates that, within detention, the lax attitude to abiding by the immigration policy and human rights standards is often overlooked by those in authority and those supervising this process. Medical malpractice and negligence within detention is brought to attention by the protagonist through the behavior of his father and the infirmity of his mother. The "shouting and crying" from his father evinces not only the frustration of living indefinitely, but the anxiety and stress put upon a parent and a life in this situation. Besides recognizing the deterioration of mental health in the detention, how "some people went a bit crazy" (87), the account of his mother's health is largely physical. Instances of "high blood pressure and panic attacks" along with "asthma" and weight loss (87) are indicated as reasons why "she didn't seem like [his] mother at all" (87). The debilitating quality of life in detention is recognized even by a young child through the loss of what he knew his parents used to be like. The abrasion of life is clearly illustrated through the deterioration of mental and physical health, evincing the effects that living in "bare life" conditions can have.

The isolated atmosphere and indeterminate duration of indefinite detention is a prominent factor both through its influence on detainee health, and the detachment of public knowledge and acknowledgement of life in detention centers. Kennedy's short story, however, demonstrates an occasion when the British community and organizations supported this family in their application to remain in Britain. The protagonist, through notifying a friend of his family's repeated arrest for detention, initiated protests, pleading and campaigns in support of letting the family remain at home (90). Yarl's Wood Befrienders began protests in England and Wales against the detention of women and children and put the family "in touch with a solicitor, who had more experience of immigration law" (90). The evident support and influence of the national public and organizations demonstrates the impact that public and detainee communication can have upon the result of detainee lives.

Without the attempt to proliferate dialogue and public knowledge, the undefined identity of refugees and asylum seekers is left ambiguous for the manipulation of power and ideas relating to those who are left voiceless. The state of exception and bare life that has been considered in this study as significant to detainee lives has further influenced the identity of these individuals and their position in Britain. Bosworth argues that their anonymous identity "renders them unable to make claims they would assert," demonstrating "just how important identity is in a world of global mobility" (2012, 126). Their position of inferiority in detention and their non-citizen status reinforces their otherness against the national identity of the country in which they are detained. Fiske asserts in her study based on "in-depth interviews with refugees who protested against their incarceration" (2016, 3) that "the less contact that 'ordinary citizens' have with detained refugees, the less likely they are to have access to refugees' own explanations of their actions" (3). This refers to the protests and strikes within detention centers and how these cases are often purposely misconstrued by the authorities as a method of reiterating their allegedly uncontrollable, violent nature. What is perceived as disobedient nature is then the justification for detention as it "both enables, and is itself enabled by, the distance between asylum seekers and citizens" (3). Fiske recognized, however, that direct communication with "the Australian community was a high priority for asylum seekers" as a "strategy towards regaining rights" (41). This also "created a political space in which their words and deeds were meaningful" to the society they wished to insert themselves into (41). By enforcing a discourse, detainees themselves can regain a voice and identity through communication with society against the unity of power's attempts to distance them from it.

Joan Smith's essay in *A Country of Refuge* acknowledges the refugee identity through comparing the lives of Aylan Kurdi, a three-year-old Syrian refugee found on a Turkish beach after drowning in the Mediterranean Sea, with the fifteen-year-old Anne Frank and the recorded story of her and her family's life in hiding. The ignorance in the countries of safety of those seeking refuge is no more highlighted in these two individuals than in the case of any other refugee. Smith acknowledges this in her consideration of how we, in the countries determined as safe, consider refugees and continue to distance ourselves from the realities of the crises:

> But the portrayal of Anne in popular culture speaks volumes about how we think — how we allow ourselves to think — about refugees. The diaries are a story without an end, broken off when Anne's hiding place was discovered, and that fact is crucial to their enduring appeal. They allow us to think about loss and wasted lives but without dwelling on either the day-to-day horrors of the Holocaust or the missed opportunities that would have brought about her physical — as well as literary — survival. (Smith 2016, 94)

Not only has culture accepted Frank's diary in documenting life during the Nazi rule, it has "been transformed into a wistful tale about a plucky teenage girl" (94) without acknowledging the barriers and division which caused a young girl to document for years the atrocities and inhuman conditions of her life.

The global reception of the image of Aylan Kurdi in 2015 froze the world's opinion on refugees and asylum seekers through the recognition of life in a young boy's death. The horror of the Syrian refugee crisis was brought ashore and forced the world to face the brutalities that occurred and continue to occur during the time of writing in Syria. However, this image has begun to wane, not through a desensitization of the image, but by a distancing of this figure reiterated again through the operators of domination. As Smith states, "Aylan Kurdi did not need to die, any more than Anne

Frank. Seventy years apart, their stories are characterized by the same depressingly bureaucratic response to refugees fleeing fascist regimes" (98). The unchanging, unfeeling response to the global refugee crisis presents today is shown through the regurgitated mistrust and manipulated perception of refugees, along with the suppression of their voices. It is only through the flickers of a photograph or an escaped record, or, more recently, the self-documentation of mobile videos of global incidents, that our attention is drawn back to the reality and inhumanity of these lives.

Conclusion: Literature as Phonopolitics

The theories explored above comment on the discourse, and on the figure of the twenty-first century refugee and detainee, documenting the state's ongoing ability to exploit and abuse these individuals. Conditions of bare life under sovereign rule have made detainees politically irrelevant by situating them outside the legal sphere of citizenry and through the general criminalization of those seeking refuge. The biopolitical body of the detainee in the present has permitted a disregard for the quality of life within detention but illustrates how the fundamental right to (biological) life is the only defense against murder under sovereign power. The distorted identity and suppressed voice of detainees within the public sphere has caused a prejudiced perspective of the current economic and global affairs on migration, as well as a with the marginalization of this group, allowing for instances of abuse and neglect whilst in detention. Judith Butler's concept of grievability highlights the vulnerability of detainees and refugees by calling attention to the public's inability to empathize with and recognize a life that has been or is being lost. Through this distancing of citizens from exiled groups, the failure to visualize a life, as well as the failure to communicate experience and abuse, sentences detainees and refugees to a life of isolation, oppression and abandonment. This deprivation of voice also allows sovereign powers to manipulate a country's public concerns to suggest their issues were instigated by immigration and the individuals involved.

The significance of direct communication between citizens and detainees has been highlighted through an analysis of the literary depictions of refugee experiences in *A Country of Refuge* and *Refugee Tales*. The discussion produced by allowing a platform for hushed voices through literature grants the ability to discover faults within the immigration and detention system through evincing experiences and implementing change through public discussion.

Further, as I have explained above, the state of exception in which detainees and refugees are placed, the situation of being both outside and inside, also applies to the position of this specific type of literature. Being both fiction and non-fiction, while it is placed outside of legal and governmental spheres, it nevertheless has the ability to confront issues emerging in these arenas. In the age of the internet, the distribution of these narratives is also ever easier and more accessible. While it is possible to ban literary texts, as we have previously seen predominantly in totalitarian régimes, or as a form of censorship over public discourse through governmental control, the inability to erase or limit this form, whether written or orally delivered, admits this practice of expression to evade control. Agamben suggests that we cannot return "from the state of exception to a state of law. Because the state of law foresaw the exception as the ultimate core," this emphasizes the "dual machine" which he depicts between "law and management" (Loggos 2013). He further suggests that a third element needs to be added to disintegrate the binary poles where one "dominates over the other" while the other is there simply to ratify (2013).

The proposal I thus put forward to destabilize these poles, highlighted through the significance and inviolability of literary representation, is the introduction, or indeed value of *phóné*. Through the expression of voice, or a "phonopolitical" philosophy on political, legal and governmental matters, a broader discourse could include the experience of violence, injustice and neglect of minority sectors, for example, within the detention of refugees and asylum seekers. The impossibility of detaining a voice of any expression—literature art, music, photography, oral dialogue, or memory to name a few—demonstrates this component's ability to redistribute the sovereign's power over the state of exception.

Bibliography

Agamben, Giorgio. 1998. *Homo Sacer: Sovereign Power and Bare Life.* Translated by David Heller-Roazen. Stanford, CA: Stanford UP.

Angel-Ajani, Asale. 2003. "A Question of Dangerous Races?" *Punishment & Society* 5 (4): 433–448.

Bosworth, Mary. 2012. "Subjectivity and Identity in Detention: Punishment and Society in a Global Age." *Theoretical Criminology* 16 (2): 123–140.

Burnett, Jon. 2017. "Racial Violence and the Brexit State." *Race & Class* 58 (4): 85–97.

Butler, Judith. 2006. *Precarious Life: The Powers of Mourning and Violence.* London: Verso.

— — —. 2016. *Frames of War: When is Life Grievable?* London: Verso.

Dead Island Wiki. 2018. "Prison." Last modified January 1, 2018. http://deadisland.wikia.com/wiki/Prison.

Falkoff, Marc. 2007. *Poems from Guantánamo: The Detainees Speak.* Iowa City, IA: U of Iowa P.

Fiske, Lucy. 2016. *Human Rights, Refugee Protest and Immigration Detention.* London: Palgrave Macmillan.

Foucault, Michel. 2003. *"Society Must be Defended": Lectures at the College de France. 1975–76.* Translated by David Macey. New York: Picador.

— — —. 2012. "The History of Sexuality (from the History of Sexuality, Vol. I: An Introduction)." In *Contemporary Sociological Theory*. 3rd ed, edited by Craig Calhoun, Joseph Gerteis, James Moody, Steven Pfaff and Indermohan Virk, 295–304. Malden, MA: Wiley-Blackwell.

Gov.uk. 2014. "FOI Release: Former UKBA Staff That Have Been Dismissed for Misconduct from 2008 to 2013." Last modified March 16, 2014. https://www.gov.uk/government/publications/ukba-staff-dismissed-for-misconduct2008-to-2013/former-ukba-staff-that-have-been-dismissed-for-misconduct-from-2008-to-2013.

Hall, Alexandra. 2010. "'These People Could Be Anyone': Fear, Contempt (and Empathy) in a British Immigration Removal Centre." *Journal of Ethnic and Migration Studies* 36 (6): 881–898.

— — —. 2012. *Border Watch: Cultures of Immigration, Detention and Control.* London: Pluto Press.

Herd, David. 2016. "The Appellant's Tale as told to David Herd." In *Refugee Tales,* edited by David Herd and Anna Pincus. Manchester: Comma Press.

Herd, David, and Anna Pincus, eds. 2016. *Refugee Tales*, Vol. I. Manchester: Comma Press.

— — —, eds. 2017. *Refugee Tales*, Vol. II. Manchester: Comma Press.

— — —, eds. 2019. *Refugee Tales*, Vol. III. Manchester: Comma Press.

Kennedy, Alison, L. 2016. "Inappropriate Staring." In *A Country of Refuge*, edited by Lucy Popescu, 65–72. London: Unbound.

Kundnani, Arun. 2001. "In a Foreign Land: The New Popular Racism." *Race & Class* 43 (2): 41–60.

Lewycka, Marina. 2016. "The Dependant's Tale as told to Marina Lewycka." In *Refugee Tales*, edited by David Herd and Anna Pincus. Manchester: Comma Press.

Loggos, Michalis. 2013. "Giorgio Agamben on Biopolitics (Eng Subs)." July 1, 2013. Video, 1:11:30. https://www.youtube.com/watch?v=skJueZ52948.

Malloch, Margaret. S., and Elizabeth Stanley. 2005. "The Detention of Asylum Seekers in the UK: Representing Risk, Managing the Dangerous." *Punishment and Society* 7 (1): 53–71.

Mills, Catharine. 2014. *The Philosophy of Agamben*. Oxford: Routledge.

Mouflard, Claire. 2016. "Zombies and Refugees: Variations on the 'Posthuman' and the 'Non-Human' in Robin Campillo's *Les Revenants* (2004) and Fabrice Gobert's *Les Revenants* (2012–2015)." *Humanities* 5 (3): 48–58.

No Deportations. 2015. "Self-Harm in Immigration Detention January through December 2013." Last modified January 2, 2015. http://www.no-deportations.org.uk/Media-1-2012/Self-Harm2013.html.

Padel, Ruth. 2016. "The Prayer Labyrinth." In *A Country of Refuge*, edited by Lucy Popescu. London: Unbound.

Popescu, Lucy, ed. 2016. *A Country of Refuge*. London: Unbound.

Refugee Tales. 2018. "About Refugee Tales." http://refugeetales.org/about-refugee-tales/.

Schenkkan, Robert. 2018. *Building the Wall*. New York: Arcade Publishing.

Smith, J. 2016. "To Avoid Worse." In *A Country of Refuge*, edited by Lucy Popescu, 91–98. London: Unbound.

Stumpf, Juliet. 2006. "The Crimmigration Crisis: Immigrants, Crime, and Sovereign Power." *American University Law Review* 56 (2): 367–419.

Toivanen, Anna-Leena. 2019. "Zombified Mobilities: Clandestine Afroeuropean Journeys in J. R. Essomba's *Le paradis du nord* and Caryl Phillips's *A Distant Shore*." *Journal of African Cultural Studies* 31 (1): 120–134.

Zaborowski, Rafal, and Myria Georgiou. 2019. "Gamers versus Zombies? Visual Mediation of the Citizen/Non-citizen Encounter in Europe's 'Refugee Crisis.'" *Popular Communication* 17 (2): 92–10

The Representation of the Immigrant Population in Leïla Slimani's *Chanson Douce*: A Sociological Perspective

Vedran Ćatović

Introduction

Leïla Slimani's Goncourt prize winning novel, *Chanson douce* ("The Sweet Song", translated as "The Perfect Nanny" in the US), is a complex portrayal of France's capital city that examines the core values of contemporary French society. The novel casts a stark and detached look at the current state of Paris and France, and at the way fast-paced modern life affects human capacity for empathy. At the heart of *Chanson douce* is a relationship between the main character, an enigmatic and somewhat unusual (in the sense that she is white) nanny named Louise, and a middle-aged couple of aspiring Parisian "hipsters," Myriam, a young lawyer of Arabic origin, and Paul, a white Parisian musical producer. The couple hires Louise to look after their two children, and she does so for several years with great care and success. However, the prospect of a breakup of ties as the children grow old makes the nanny feel as if she is losing her family, the only community she has and where she feels welcome. In an act of wild despair, the nanny kills both kids and wounds herself badly. *Chanson douce* thus ends up as a psychological and social study of alienation in the modern bourgeois society, under a deceptive surface of a sensationalist newspaper article.

In this study, I will emphasize one very important aspect of the novel, that of the status of the migrant population in Paris as represented by the author. The characters are migrating to, but also within the Paris of the novel. Louise herself is migrating on a daily basis from the suburbs (in French often designated by the increasingly pejorative term "banlieue") to reach her workplace in the central Parisian flat. It is a long, strenuous, even costly ride that is necessary for her to work and that is simply assumed by her employers. It is not a "commute," but a genuine migration across the class boundaries, from the impoverished world of the *banlieue* to the busy, well-off milieu of the bourgeoisie.

But Louise is not the only character in this kind of situation. In fact, a closer look at the novel, a look beneath the attention-grabbing central plot line, reveals an abundance of interesting characters, a world of "migrating bodies" in search for well-being. I will focus on episodes and moments that seem to be the most significant regarding the subject of migration. My analysis will show that the restrained style and sparse syntax of *Chanson douce* make for a particularly effective strategy of representation and render the reader alert to the complex and often unjust social dynamic at play.

Representation of Migrants in the Novel

"No illegal immigrants, agreed? For a cleaning lady or a decorator, it doesn't bother me. Those people have to work, after all. But to look after the little ones, it's too dangerous" (Slimani 2018, 5).[1] These are the words of Emma, a friend of Myriam, a presumably assertive, self-confident, feminist urban professional as she advises her friend on the choice of a nanny. The narrator remarks that if somebody were to speak of *them* in such a way, these women would scream at discrimination, but here, since it is their own interest in question, Emma is entitled to proceed: "Apart from that . . . not too old, no veils and no smokers. The important thing is that she's energetic and available. That she works so we can work" (5).[2]

However, Myriam is not so insensitive in this regard. She finds such a line of reasoning repelling and makes a trip to the employment agency by herself. There she is crossly greeted by a female manager or clerk who bluntly informs her that to sign up she needs

---

[1] I will quote from Sam Taylor's 2018 translation of the novel, titled *The Perfect Nanny* in the US edition. I will use Gallimard's 2016 French edition only when the English translation is not precise enough, or when French idiom may be lost.
[2] The original uses a stronger verb, "bosser", in the sense of working really hard at something (Slimani 2016, 16).

to provide a complete dossier, a CV, and signed references from previous employers. She does so because, as we soon discover, Myriam is of Arabic descent, and her skin color made the manager assume that she was looking for employment, not an employee. However, upon discovering that Myriam is looking for a nanny, the clerk switches to cajolery and politeness, as Myriam is now a "client" ('une cliente') for her. She presents her a catalog of available workers, as "dozens of photographs of women, most of them African or Filipino, flashed past Myriam's eyes" (15). The portraits are "blurred", or "poorly framed" and not a single woman is wearing a smile. It is a gallery of ephemeral pictures and faces whose untold stories bear a particular weight.

Later, Myriam has chosen (partly out of moral displeasure) not to hire a nanny through an agency, but to look at the Internet ads. In the ensuing episode, she and her husband interview six candidates, each getting a thirty-minute slot. All these women lead a life of predicament and struggle. The first one is twenty minutes late, a Filipino woman who expresses herself poorly in French. Paul, Myriam's "pragmatic and egoistic" husband, switches to English, and soon shows this candidate a way out with a "Thank you." Then comes Grace, an Ivorian without papers, or in French, *sans papier*, which is a (sometimes pejorative) term for illegal immigrants. She is smiling. We cannot know if it is a smile of despair, of desire and the need to please and "sell" herself; or perhaps it is a smile of pride and dignity in spite of her difficult condition. She is merely mentioned in one single sentence. She appears to be utterly insignificant to her potential employers. She is quickly followed by Carloine. The narrator describes her as an "an obese blonde with dirty hair, who spends the interview complaining about her backache and her circulation problems" (Slimani 2018, 18). Then, before Louise will show up and win over everyone in the family, enters a Moroccan woman, Malika. Myriam, who was upset by the condescending treatment she received from the female manager of the agency and found that woman's attitude to be hypocritical and disgusting, shows a surprising side to herself. Even though she is the only person of color in the novel who is well-off, excelling professionally, moving up the social ladder, and has integrated—as opposed to merely immigrated—into French society, she insists that she does not want a Maghrebian woman to look after her children. When her pragmatic and egoistic, but otherwise agreeable, liberal, open-minded husband disagrees and points out that a Maghrebian nanny would talk to the children in Arabic, and that it would be a good thing, since Myriam herself does not want to, Myriam refuses it "steadfastly" (18). She is afraid that a tacit complicity, a familiarity may arise between the two of them. She is afraid the other woman might start addressing her in Arabic, that she might start asking for small favors in the name of their common language and religion. The narrator sums up her attitude in this way: "She (Myriam) has always been wary of what she calls immigrant solidarity" (18) ('Elle s'est toujours méfiée de ce qu'elle appelle la solidarité d'immigrés') (Slimani 2016, 28).

This is not the whole picture, however. For all the cruelty and selfishness of the environment, the exploited underclass populace has their meeting places, their moments of mutual sympathy and responsibility. One of the more beautiful and poetic parts of the novel is Slimani's depiction of the small social scene of mostly immigrated nannies gathering around the small urban squares in Paris, a union ('syndicat'), or a hiring office ('bureau de recrutement') under an open sky, as the narrator puts it. It is a world where the insouciance of children is mixed with troubles and worries of the nannies. Around the slides and sandboxes resonate the words in Baoulé, Dioula, Arabic, Hindi, Tagalog or Russian. These are all women who have moved in and are trying to stay. They form a "swarm" ('nuée') around the infants. Some of them are "veiled" ('voilée') and, therefore, "have to be even gentler, cleaner, and more punctual than the others" (Slimani 2018, 221). Others change their wigs every week. Some are very old and meet on the streets the adolescents they have once reared; others are new to the trade, and work only for a few months after which they "vanish without saying good-bye, leaving trails of rumors and suspicions behind them" (221).

Louise, the protagonist, is among them. She appears to be inaccessible, a little haughty. She does not say much, she has things to hide, and other nannies understand that silence. They discover a sort of complicity, solidarity even, in silence that bonds them. They all have shameful secrets that cannot be confessed ('des secrets inavouables') (Slimani 2016, 174). They are wary of each other. They do not talk much about themselves, or only through allusions. They mostly talk about their masters instead. They also talk about their own children a little (not the children they are nursing), but they hardly get to see them, as they must take care of other people's children. They help each other a little, they circulate gossips and job offers, and are led by their self-proclaimed leader Lydie, an Ivorian woman of fifty wearing fake fur coats and drawing her eyebrows in thin red lines. Here, as in the rest of the novel, the detached, dry tone of the narrator enables an effect of surprising beauty and empathy. The reader eventually feels attached and drawn to that realm of hard-working women who are accustomed to their predicament to the point of being stronger than it.

Probably the most moving character in this circle is Wafa, a young Moroccan woman of no more than twenty-five years of age, the only near-friend Louise has, and a person of great simplicity and earnestness. She eats honey cookies and candy all the time, has a slightly vulgar smile, round, sensual, slightly chubby shapes, long black hair, but dirty and uncombed. The narrator remarks that "she could be pretty. Or attractive, anyway" (Slimani 2018, 126). She makes one think of a large cat without much subtlety but disposing of a great resourcefulness. She ends up becoming a sort of "success" by society's own standards—she will, it appears, become a French citizen—but the price she had to pay is rather cruel. Her relationships with men have paved her way to Paris, as well as to citizenship.

She came to France thanks to an old man to whom she would provide massages in a seedy hotel in Casablanca. Starting with her hands, the man got attached to Wafa's whole body. Her mother advised her to allow that man to possess her, and she was eventually led by him to Paris. There they lived off welfare in a shabby apartment before the man's children ousted Wafa out of fear their father might impregnate her. Then she subscribed to a website for young

Muslim women without "papers". Then a man named Youssef invited her to a *rendez-vous* in a McDonald's in the *banlieue*. He liked her, courted her and then tried to rape her. She, however, managed to calm him down. They then got onto business. Youssef agreed to marry Wafa for twenty thousand euros. He explained: "That's cheap for getting your French papers" (127) ('C'est pas cher payé pour des papiers français') (Slimani 2016, 99). After the price is set, they do eventually get married. The episode makes for a sort of escapade, a travesty of French bureaucracy. The whole ritual is duly executed: a couple of near strangers meet in the municipal building of a suburban commune, with Louise as their witness. Signatures are made, rounds of applause and shouts of enthusiasm seem sincere, and the whole thing has an air of truth. Youssef even organizes a celebration in a restaurant, with music, dance and laughter. Even Louise herself cannot believe it as she smiles at Wafa, having forgotten that the whole thing is "but a masquerade, a fool's game, a hoax" (Slimani 2018, 163). But it is also a success, as Wafa's stolen youth and degradation will be compensated by that for which twenty thousand euros is not too much to pay.

Chanson douce in a Contemporary Context

As we can see from the examples presented above, migrants of Slimani's book are not integrated, nor assimilated in the genuine sense of those words, into French society. They experience an ongoing struggle. They are constantly moving and migrating, from other countries and continents, but also—even in the case of some French citizens "proper"—within the city, from the suburbs to the city center and back, every day. Their existence is precarious. They are exploited and oppressed. Slimani does not conceal or embellish their condition. What is more, she emphasizes it, with sharpness rather than hyperbole, rendering it evident without exaggeration. Slimani's approach is not "dramatic", but simply accurate, realistic. As the author of the book's blurb suggests, through the artist's precise descriptions, "it is our epoch that is revealed, with its conception of love and education, relationships of domination and money, prejudices of class and culture" (Slimani 2016; my translation).

In turn, French society, as measured by its own greatest accomplishment—that of proclaimed equal rights and enlightened solidarity and empathy between people—turns out to be unjust, unfair, unequal, even brutal. Consequently, the oppressed are shown as capable of intense passive suffering, but they have little room for socially transformative action. Even so, I argue that Slimani's stark, at times even deprecatory depiction of the subaltern subjects in France makes for a particularly powerful strategy of representation. The harshness of the narrator's descriptions exposes the cruelty of the French immigration policy and mobilizes empathy and critical awareness of social injustice in the readership.

Slimani's narrator is a witness, a chronicler of this world. The narrator refrains from explicit moralism or outright value judgment, and even refrains from showing pity for the troubled characters. Nonetheless, a morally severe critique emerges in the process. The narrator's dry, detached, but also remarkably sustained and slightly resentful tone paradoxically enables empathy and recognition of pervasive oppression, but also a realization of the widespread confusion, and a lack of conscience or sense of possible agency among the oppressed.

In the context of contemporary post-colonial literature written in French, Slimani could be said to continue the legacy of French-speaking writers of African and Maghrebian origin who have adopted French, and moved to France, without sacrificing the depth and substance of their writing, or the thematic scope of their works. Not unlike older writers of repute, such as French-Algerian Leïla Sebbar or Moroccan Mahi Binebine, Slimani exhibits a keen sense of her layered identity and shows unwavering critical attitude. She does not limit her criticism just to a critique of the colonial power of France but often takes aim at the issues of her native Moroccan society, especially in her journalistic work. Thematically, her literary creations delve deep into the world of violence and existential terror, which recalls the intense writings of Alain Mabanckou, a Congo-born novelist of high stature residing in Paris.

At the same time, Slimani readily adopts influences of classical Western literature and authors. Her strong and well-honed prose exhibits the fluency of the realist masters, as well as the concision of the twentieth-century masters of parataxis, such as Nathalie Sarraute or Albert Camus. *Chanson douce* cites two epigraphs, one from Rudyard Kipling and another from Fyodor Mikhailovich Dostoevsky. This diversity of influences and versatile education makes Slimani a transnational writer, who can be meaningfully situated in different cultural contexts, even if her works are exclusively written in French. Without reaching for strained metaphors, one could say that a sense of layered and migratory identity is a force that quietly shapes the creative output of this writer. Still, one might put all these parallels and influences aside. What makes Slimani's writing interesting and compelling is her storytelling ability and the capacity of her narratives to stand on their own, as self-enclosed and well-rounded creations.

This is why I chose to use *Chanson douce* as an occasion for a broader reflection on the subject of migration as well. The author's layered identity, critical attitude and well-crafted novel that focuses on the problematics of migrant labor invite detailed commentary as well as a broader theoretical reflection. This is especially true after a well-received English translation of the novel, which came out as *Lullaby* in the United Kingdom, and *The Perfect Nanny* in the United States.

Migration and Different Models of Integration

In this section, I will venture to pose a few questions of more general and theoretical nature. On the one hand, I will try to shed light on the issues of immigration tackled by Slimani's creative discourse, and I will do so by addressing some of the important points raised in recent research on migration in social and humanistic sciences, with special focus on the case of France. On the other hand, I will try to engage questions of the creative, that is literary discourse itself and discuss how literature can meaningfully contribute to conversations about migration without losing its critical edge or compromising its primary purpose—to be a powerful and creative verbal expression.

The main point I wish to make in relation to this case study of *Chanson douce* and with regard to the first issue, namely that of immigration, is that the mere and continuing presence of migrant population in the host country is not "integration", and certainly not equality yet. Finney, Catney and Phillips (2016) describe this as *spatial assimilation*, a condition that condemns migrants to a mere contiguity, not a substantial participation in the host country's wealth and resources. In a similar vein, Catney and Simpson (2010) established that upward mobility as well as movement from immigrant settlement areas are primarily socio-economically conditioned. In other words, integration comes through entitlement and wealth, whereas "likelihood of migrating away from settlement areas decreases as economic well-being decreases" (cited in Finney et al. 2016, 39). The concept of segmented assimilation is also helpful to describe the unsatisfactory state to which Slimani bears witness. Karen O'Reilly suggests that such assimilation can "sometimes only be into certain sectors of society, into low-paid jobs, and into continued experience of racism" (2012, 57), and that what is actually happening is an assimilation into an "alternative, third culture and structure" that, while helping preserve the immigrants' sense of self-worth, deprives them of genuine participation in the consumption of society's wealth.

Hence, this lack of immediate and warranted access to privilege-granting resources seems to be the key hindrance that migrants experience in the host countries of the developed world. If other issues exist, such as those of institutionalized racism or sexism, they would still appear to be of a corollary nature, and would be easily mitigated if policy makers would genuinely implement politics of access to material means and possessions. To put it simply, if people are poor and deprived of labor and citizenship rights, they are going to suffer gravely, regardless of their racial, gender or religious identity. Conversely, if they are well educated and make a lot of money, they are likely to thrive, regardless of their racial, gender or religious identity.

This realization has been at the heart of recent revisionist criticism in literature on migration. As Yolande Jansen (2013, 89) explains, the work of "liberal assimilationists" such as Joppke and

Morawska, is concerned with such policy proposals that would streamline and simplify occasionally abstract theoretical debates and infuse them with a sense of worldly pragmatism regarding crucial issues. Joppke and Morawska thus make an interesting, and at first glance surprising, proposal that the often attacked and seemingly obsolete notion of "assimilation" as the agenda-setting policy should be kept in favor of the deceptive notion of integration. Instead of discarding the notion of assimilation as entailing an "old style enforced cultural homogenisation", a revival of the concept would preserve the awareness of the "legitimate, structural side of assimilation" (Jansen 2013, 89) that would, in the words of Joppke and Morawska, concern itself with "socio-economic equalisation of the life-chances between immigrants and native population (in employment, income, education, etc.)" (2002, 6).

This proposition aims to introduce a measurable standard against which all social policies as well as scholarly theorizations can be leveled. Good education, fulfilling jobs and high income have a way of mollifying identity differences, differences that are otherwise easily inflated for manipulative purposes of the ruling classes. In this context, the debate between assimilationists and integrationalists appears to be needlessly choosy and sophisticated. Whether a host state should aim to integrate its migrant population into a presumable but hardly existing social whole while somehow respectfully observing and maintaining identity differences, or its goal should be to assimilate all its subjects regardless of their identities into a normative and all-encompassing paradigm (in case of France, that would clearly be the paradigm of *laïcisme*), efficiency of politics should be measured by simple and verifiable criteria of social mobility and access to privilege-giving resources. Clearly, at this point, research concerned primarily with these parameters is bound to give consistent and revealingly predictable results. The host countries of the developed world, it turns out, take more than they give, and they do not make systematic and budget-taxing efforts toward facilitating their migrant population's way toward high income and accumulated property. These people are meant to be poor and duped into debates about less tangible and less lucrative affairs.

The Case of France: The French Model of Assimilation

I will now illustrate this argument using the specific case of France, and the specific section of immigrant labor—namely, the prevalently female labor of nannies, nurses and caregivers, on which Slimani's novel also focuses.

Gabriella Lazaridis has recently undertaken excellent research that sheds light on what she describes as feminization of migration. Bringing into focus an increased awareness of the significance of the agency of women in migratory processes, she has investigated the status of female migrants that were likely to be overlooked in the traditionally "androcentric" research on migration. Focusing on maids, nannies and nurses, her research paints a compelling social picture that dovetails with the narrative threads picked up in the case study of the first part of this chapter.

Lazaridis shows that "women who have no legal means of entry or who lack work permits are confined largely to privatized spheres of work (domestic and other forms of care work, the sex industry and so on," and that "many are working on short-term contracts or are undocumented, subjected to the vagaries of their employers" (2015, 63). These include employers keeping the passports of these women for alleged "security", a lack of contracts while working longer and unpaid hours, and a lack of social security and other benefits (66). Additionally, domestic work entails "stigmatisation and low social status combined with social isolation" as well as downward social mobility and brain waste, since a lot of the workers are highly educated" (67). In this regard, the damage is twofold: there is a brain drain from the standpoint of the home country, and a brain waste from the standpoint of the host country. Lastly, due to what Lazaridis describes as a "trampoline effect", many women can end up "moving from unemployment to maid, from maid to quasi-nurse, back to unemployment, up to maid or quasi-nurse and sometimes back to prostitution or unemployment again" (68).

We can observe a similarity between Lazaridis's account and the episodes of Slimani's novel analyzed above, which speaks to the harsh realism of the artist's depictions. That the conditions of the nannies in *Chanson douce* are similar to Lazaridis's scholarly findings is of considerable importance here. Both testimonies underscore what Lazaridis calls "abjectification" of migrant women, a refusal to grant dignity and rights otherwise venerated and promised to all by the host state — by the French Republic in this case.

But these women have come of their own free will, one might say. They were not invited, nor promised anything. In addition, they live illegally in a foreign society, taking on ("stealing") the jobs of the citizens proper. Such rhetoric, of course, is frequently emitted from the far right, but the factual falsehood behind it makes it not only morally reprehensible, but also illogical. Lazaridis describes the phenomenon of nanny and nurse labor as one of the "emerging forms of migrant care labour in today's Europe, where social and health care systems would collapse without migrant care workers" (70). It turns out that, far from having the irregular workforce off the radar or out of control, the government needs migrant workers and counts on them, uses them and exploits them with peculiar ruthlessness, extracting cheap, underpaid labor to sustain the flimsy health care system. As is often the case with the gray economy, it is integral to the system, and it is planned and managed to a considerable degree.

Moreover, the ailments that plague illegal migrant workers are largely shared by the legal residents originating from the former colonies. The same issues apply to the second and third generation residents. In an effort to interrogate the long-standing myth of the French Republic that is "welcoming to foreigners and caring to promote their ascent to citizenship and equality" Gérard Noiriel and Stéphane Beaud highlight the continued discrimination endured to this day even by the youth originating from the former colonies, especially on the job market (Noiriel 2002; Beaud and Noiriel 2005; my translation). Noiriel notes that people from the former colonies are confined to the least valued sectors of the labor market ("les secteurs les plus dévalorisés du marché"), making France surprisingly unattractive to the immigrants, quite contrary to the established perception. As it happens, a rather small fraction of the foreigners who have moved to France stayed there, choosing eventually, in the words of Noiriel, to "vote with their feet" and go somewhere else (Noiriel 2002).

These authors also contest the supposed efficiency of France's model of integration, the one that, inasmuch as it does have a definitive shape, rests on the classical definition of assimilation, that is, on the homogenizing subsumption of various groups within the framework of *laïcisme*. When assimilation does not go smoothly, the rhetoric of differentialism is activated to exert pressure on the minorities and subsume them under the official culture and values of the Republic, as well as to inculpate them for their inability to assimilate. Consequently, such an approach leads to "exclusion rather than recognition", making the French model of multicultural integration opposite to that of Canada, where all members of society are "supposed to consider their membership as multicultural in some way", rather than only minorities being expected to adapt to the established set of cultural values (Jansen 88; see also Joppke and Morawska 2002).

This results in the merely spatial, or segmented, assimilation discussed above and aggravates the already glaring issue of poor access to education, good employment and wealth. Bauman's interpretation of the concept of the "hyperghetto" seems to encapsulate this situation and summarize its shortcomings accurately. Depicting hyperghettos as "truncated, artificial and blatantly incomplete groups of people," as "aggregates but not communities," as "topographical condensations unable to survive on their own" and as being "suspended on strings that originate beyond its boundaries and most certainly beyond its control" (Bauman 2005), this author gives a concise summary of a segmented (if not segregated) society, a summary that is easily applied to the French society as well. In fact, it does not require much imagination to realize the proximity of Slimani's descriptions of the nannies' "union under an open sky" to Bauman's description of the truncated, artificial and incomplete aggregate of people unable to survive on their own and suspended from strings beyond their control.

It should be noted however, that the metaphorical strings are primarily of material nature. Possession of substantial material resources would easily reverse the cultural dynamic. James Hampshire rightly notes that the bulk of the integration debate not focusing on education and unemployment issues but rather on "rhetorical denouncements of multiculturalism" is a mistake. While it is more difficult to propose specific labor market and educational reforms, these impose themselves in light of "substantial, if variegated, evidence of poor educational outcomes and high relative unemployment among immigrant groups, especially in mainland Europe" (Hampshire 2014, 158). Without better outcomes in these spheres, it is hard to expect positive changes in the culture at large. There will be a persistent and usually justified sense of identity-based discrimination, and the culture will suffer all the more. In the absence of a thriving cultural life, the disenfranchised groups are likely to latch on to simplified and radicalized notions of identity and culture (especially religious notions), while remaining unable to insert themselves into the dominant cultural paradigm and assert their cultural identities.

Therefore, it would be fair to say that the French model of integration is a case of multiculturalism conceived as an exclusive form of assimilation. It is a paradigm that is unable and possibly unwilling to accommodate differently envisioned identity politics. However, it would be all too easy to indulge in excessive scrutiny and find fault with any proposed model or agenda, be it assimilation, integration, multiculturalism, and so forth. What is more difficult and important is to insist on simple, material things that reach into the public budget and demonstrate genuine political will for change. What is needed is economic participation, inclusion, and access that eventually lead to more money for the poor and enable the upward mobility and permeability of class barriers. However flawed a paradigm may appear when put to rigorous theoretical observation, these small and tangible aspects can be insisted on and measured to a considerable extent within each given paradigm. Furthermore, it is easy to see when they do not work. Excessive (and conspicuously ineffective) insistence on identity politics is a strong indicator of such a condition.³ Joppke and Morawska are therefore right when they seek to envisage a new notion of assimilation based on "stronger politics of citizenship" and aimed towards segregation and socio-economic marginalization (quoted in Jansen 2013, 87–90).

We have seen in the episode of Wafa's wedding how significant, yet how formal and bureaucratic, citizenship is. It has its procedure, its decorum, its price. It has nothing to do with some ethnic essence. You do not have to *be* French to *become* French. Twenty thousand euros, a small administrative charade, and a person not wanted and not recognized by the society (although her labor is counted upon) becomes entitled to the privileges and rights of a citizen. The problem is that giving everybody these rights would be a difficult thing to do for the government. The nationals already in possession of citizenship expect protection and demand exclusive rights bestowed upon them by the state. They will punish the government that betrays their demands through different electoral choices. However, yielding entirely to these demands is not possible for the government either, as the government would have to bear the brunt of moral reproach and would fail to live up to the proclaimed constitutional principles of liberty and equality.

As James Hampshire explains "liberal norms of equality cannot long tolerate persons being excluded from access to rights, hence there is an inherently inclusionary logic at work in liberal states" (2014, 158). However, "when citizenship is put on the political agenda, and especially when it is framed as an issue of national identity, it has proven quite possible to oppose and roll back liberalization" (158). This results in a paradox that "it is exceedingly difficult, perhaps even impossible, to design migration policies that will command majority support and fully respect the rights of migrants; nor is it easy to imagine popular consent for labour migration policies that maximize economic growth" (159). This would

---

[3] In fact, in yet another study, Noiriel makes a thought-provoking point that "the broad diversity of cultural practices among immigrant laborers from North African countries is associated with an abstract political geopolitical entity (the Maghreb), one that is no more (and is often less) familiar to them than is French culture" (Noiriel 1996, 278).

imply that the government of France, for example, may not restrict access to citizenship to people deserving of it out of cynicism or express malice and that, even assuming the noblest of intentions, the government is torn between conflicting and irresoluble imperatives. Liberal institutions and norms entail perpetual conflict between these contradictory demands, so much so that citizenship, according to Hampshire, embodies "a liberal paradox insofar as it is at once an inclusionary and an exclusionary status" (157). Hampshire concludes with a disquieting remark on the "intractable nature of immigration policymaking" as "an inherent feature of liberal statehood" (160) forcing the governments of liberal states to "muddle through" as they strive to reconcile conflicting urges and demands (161).

Hampshire is probably right to predict a long, strenuous and only partly efficient process as the only way through this political impasse, but such a prediction should by no means occlude the grave injustice perceptible on both a small and large scale. The "liberal paradox" is far costlier for the disenfranchised, underpaid and poorly educated people, and its existence surely serves some political interests better than others. It should also be stressed that a large number of undocumented workers providing cheap labor in the gray economy sector is not altogether contrary to the "labour migration policies that maximize economic growth" (159). For all the issues it entails, the gray economy labor can still be beneficial to the state, which for its part is not obliged to reciprocate and reward such labor through its legalization and adequate remuneration. Like cheap labor obtained through outsourcing, domestic labor in the gray economy can be quite beneficial in the short run for the governments. We have already seen that this labor is not off the state's radar and that the state, in fact, counts and depends on it.

At the "big picture" level, the liberal paradox—especially if understood as the paradox of the liberalization of the labor market *within* the European Union—engenders the corollary border paradox. For those with EU citizenship, all of the Union is open, borderless, and they can move as they wish. They can also sell their labor as they see fit, with all the associated rights and benefits guaranteed. However, for those who are trying to enter without citizenship, Europe has become a "gated continent", or a "fortress", as Matthew Carr puts it (2012).[4]

As Carr describes it, "today responsibility for monitoring Europe's borders is shared between national governments, police forces and immigration officials and some 400,000 border guards in different countries" (23). This indicates yet another paradox relating to the fact that "through each of the EU's successive enlargements, the incorporation of new member states into the new borderless European space has been dependent on a persistent hardening of Europe's 'external' frontiers" (25). This is all happening "in an age of international migration and mobility, with more people living outside their country of birth or citizenship than at any time since territorially bounded states came into existence" (Hampshire 2014, 156).

In such a context, it is quite clear that no innocent, playful dynamic between inclusion and exclusion can take place. It is a rough, political and interest-driven game, and, once more, the only way to lead an equitable and conscientious struggle is to perpetually plead for an acknowledgment of rights and fair acquisition of material gain for those deprived of such luxuries. This is all the more evident as deprivation is taking place equally in the "small" world of the French *banlieue* as it does across the expanses of the "gated continent".

Conclusion

I will conclude this study with some remarks on how literature as art can plead for the "wretched of the earth", to borrow the phrase from Frantz Fanon's classic (1963). Good intentions do not suffice and will often not help in literature. Moreover, sometimes good intentions will even work against the quality of writing, making it naive and benign. In a world as politically harsh as the one I have been discussing above, a detached and somber attitude will prove

---

[4] Carr's metaphor of a "gated continent" disregards the fact that not all European countries are in the European Union, and are, therefore, outside the gates, but for all practical intents and purposes, the metaphor is appropriate and accurate.

to be more beneficial, as it will bring about more truthfulness, lifelike vigor and artistic candor from a writer. A writer may indeed profit from his or her peculiar position in the political arena, a position that is often not understood by scholars and not easily acknowledged by writers themselves. It is the position of disenfranchisement, of insurmountable exclusion from the world of political power.

Hakim Abderrezak is right to say that "just as the poet was excluded from Plato's *Republic*, writers are traditionally excluded from international policy decision making" and all the more so in the realm of media coverage "susceptible to hijacking by discourses saturated with demagoguery" (Abderrezak 2016, 87–8). Therefore, writers occupy a curious and ambivalent position. Excluded from political power, and at risk of compromising their talent when trying to approach it—as Slimani arguably did, having subsequently assumed the role of a personal representative for the French language and culture to increasingly unpopular president Emmanuel Macron—writers can nonetheless convey the most urgent political truths of their time. They can provide unsparing testimonies of the social reality to a reader hungry for uncontaminated truth.

Chanson douce is one such testimony to the fates of the "intimate others" (Helma Lutz, cited in Lazaridis 2015, 79), that is, the nannies who were, according to Slimani herself, "both women we loved as mothers, and strangers" (cited in Morene 2016). The novel places a mirror in front of the French public and shows a not so flattering image of its values. Slimani's poetics of detached observation make the reader aware that there are deep-seated problems at the heart of society and inspire a sense of a genuine and ongoing crisis. Slimani's immigrants suffer at the hands of a society that has promised much more to them than it delivered. It is precisely this condition of partial, unfulfilled "integration", with an accompanying lack of education, money, and privilege that the novel *Chanson douce* is describing. It offers a particularly clear-eyed and sharp testimony of the ongoing struggle and oppression even in the wealthiest of the world's societies and cities, eerily recalling the alluring but brutal Paris of Balzac, Zola or Edmond and Jules Goncourt, in whose memory the award to Slimani has been given.

Bibliography

Abderrezak, Hakim. 2016. *Ex-Centric Migrations Europe and the Maghreb in Mediterranean Cinema, Literature, and Music*. Bloomington, IN: Indiana UP.

Bauman, Zygmunt. 2005. "Archipelago of Exceptions." *Public Space*. Last modified June 3, 2009. http://www.publicspace.org/en/text-library/eng/b015-archipelago-of-exceptions.

Beaud, Stéphane, and Gérard Noiriel. 2005. "Les nouveaux parias de la République." *Le Monde*, November 3, 2005. www.lemonde.fr/societe/article/2005/11/03/les-nouveaux-parias-de-la-republique-par-stephane-beaud-et-gerard-noiriel_706278_3224.html.

Carr, Matthew. 2012. *Fortress Europe: Dispatches from a Gated Continent*. New York: New Press.

Catney, Gemma, and Ludi Simpson. 2010. "Settlement Area Migration in England and Wales: Assessing Evidence for a Social Gradient." *Transactions of the Institute of British Geographers* 35 (4): 571–584.

Fanon, Frantz. 1963. *The Wretched of the Earth*. New York: Grove Press.

Finney, Nissa, Gemma Catney, and Deborah Phillips. 2016. "Ethnicity and Internal Migration." In *Internal Migration: Geographical Perspectives and Processes*, edited by Darren P. Smith, Nissa Finney and Nigel Walford, 31–47. London: Routledge.

Hampshire, James. 2014. *The Politics of Immigration: Contradictions of the Liberal State*. Oxford: Wiley.

Jansen, Yolande. 2013. *Secularism, Assimilation and the Crisis of Multiculturalism: French Modernist Legacies*. Amsterdam: Amsterdam UP.

Joppke, Christian, and Ewa Morawska. 2002. "Integrating Immigrants in Liberal Nation States: Policies and Practices." In *Toward Assimilation and Citizenship: Immigrants in the Liberal Nation-State*, edited by Christian Joppke and Ewa Morawska, 1–36. Basingstoke: Palgrave Macmillan.

Lazaridis Gabriella. 2015. *International Migration into Europe: From Subjects to Abjects*. Basingstoke: Palgrave Macmillan.

Noiriel, Gérard. 1996. *The French Melting Pot: Immigration, Citizenship, and National Identity*. Translated by Geoffroy de Laforcade. Minneapolis, MN: U of Minnesota P.

Noiriel, Gérard. 2002. "Petite histoire de l'intégration à la française." *Le Monde Diplomatique*, January 2002. https://www.monde-diplomatique.fr/2002/01/NOIRIEL/8320.

Morene, Benoît. 2016. "Leïla Slimani Wins Prix Goncourt, France's Top Literary Award." *New York Times*, November 4, 2016. https://www.nytimes.com/2016/11/04/books/prix-goncourt-Leïla-slimani.html?_r=0.

O'Reilly, Karen. 2012. *International Migration and Social Theory*. Basingstoke: Palgrave Macmillan.

Slimani, Leïla. 2016. *Chanson douce*. Paris: Gallimard.

— — —. 2018. *The Perfect Nanny*. Translated by Sam Taylor. New York: Penguin Books.

Turkish for Advanced: Domestic and Ethnically Motivated Violence in Turkish-German Cinema

Sándor Klapcsik and Zénó Vernyik

Introduction

This paper analyzes domestic and ethnically motivated violence in migrant cinema and films inspired by this filmic tradition, which we will name as migrant-themed cinema. We investigate to what extent the recent ramifications of commercialization dominate popular Turkish-German films. This process can be understood as a somewhat controversial case of transcultural diffusion or cultural exchange (Jackson 2021, 81–83, 87) and, for some viewers, perhaps even becomes similar to the cinematic "commodification of Otherness." This is a popular and common phenomenon "because it is offered as a new delight, more intense, more satisfying than normal ways of doing and feeling. Within commodity culture, ethnicity becomes spice, seasoning that can liven up the dull dish that is mainstream white culture" (Hooks 2006, 366). Yet, by focusing on the portrayal of aggression, we conclude that acculturation (Berry 2006, 27–29; Sam 2006, 17), especially when this term is located in the theoretical framework of postcolonialism (Bhatia and Ram 2001, 2–3), is the notion that characterizes these films better.

The term "migrant cinema" designates films whose creators (writers, directors, and cast) include immigrants, focus on the lives of immigrants, and are often, to a certain extent, biographical. This definition of migrant cinema draws on Hamid Naficy's (2001) "accented cinema," Daniela Berghahn's (2014) "diasporic family films" and Berghahn and Claudia Sternberg's (2010) "migrant and diasporic cinema." In his paradigm shifting volume, *Accented Cinema*, Naficy discusses films whose creators have some connections with "exilic, diasporic or ethnic" communities. In this book, he mostly focuses on artists who "operate independently, outside the studio system or the mainstream film industries, using interstitial and collective modes of production that critique those entities. As a result, they are presumed to be more prone to the tensions of marginality and difference" (Naficy 2001, 10, 11). Berghahn and Sternberg's (2010) "migrant and diasporic cinema" is not defined according to the producers and contributors, but rather according to themes, such as "a preponderance of journeys and a heightened sense of mobility," as well as "identities in flux" and "a predilection for claustrophobic interiors and the use of locations on the peripheries" (2010, 41). Berghahn discusses "diasporic cinema," which "challenges and frequently disavows borders of all kinds. Its protagonists transcend the borders of the nation-state on account of their dual heritage" (2014, 8). She classifies these films according to genre, primarily discussing three distinct categories: films may invoke "the generic conventions of the road movie," those of "the family melodrama" and, finally, those of "the romantic comedy" (5). As this paper will point out, it is important to add to these genres the gangster or crime film, for example the Norwegian-Pakistani *Izzat* (2005; dir. Ulrik Imtiaz Rolfsen), Turkish-German *Kurz und schmerzlos / Short Sharp Shock* (1998; dir. Fatih Akin) and *Chiko* (2008; dir. Özgür Yildirim), as well as Jacques Audiard's *Un prophète /A Prophet* (2009) and *Dheepan* (2015).[1]

Migrant films until the 1990s lacked access to big budgets, as well as the attention of mainstream cinema and the distributive resources of major studios. This phase of migrant cinema is distinguished by critics as the "cinema of duty" (Malik 1996; Malik 2010, 135), "cinema of the affected" (Burns 2007, 4–7) or "social problem film" (Berghahn 2014, 38). Such films are saturated with the documentary-realist representations of racial and ethnic issues, while they often reinforce the position of the immigrant as a victim of family and social violence (Göktürk 2002, 248).

---

[1] In rare occasions, science fiction or fantasy productions also foreground immigrant families and the obstacles of immigration, such as the Latino-US *Sleep Dealer* (2008; Alex Rivera), South-African *District 9* (2009; dir. Neill Blomkamp), transnational *Children of Men* (2006; dir. Alfonso Cuarón) and the British *Code 46* (2003; dir. Michael Winterbottom).

This trend is changing or, at least, is losing momentum, as accented cinema slowly turns into mainstream multiplex cinema (Naficy 2009). By the late 1990s and early 2000s, a new generation of directors became well-known and received the opportunity to work with higher budgets. The interest of worldwide audiences towards their films was aroused following the success of Mira Nair's, Emir Kusturica's, Gurinder Chadha's and Fatih Akin's artistic and entertaining productions. In 2016, *Lion* (dir. Garth Davis), an Australian-Indian biographical film based on the memoir *A Long Way Home* (2013) by Saroo Brierley, received six Oscar nominations and gained a huge commercial success. Consequently, migrant filmmakers are now capable of targeting a more involved, open-minded and diverse audience (Bayraktar 2016). Furthermore, directors and producers of non-minority origin are inspired by migrant filmmakers and create similar films without relying on a biographical background — hence we use the term "migrant-themed cinema" for these productions. Notable examples here can be Ken Loach's realist representations of migrants in *Ae Fond Kiss…* (2004) and *It's a Free World…* (2007), as well as the American drama *A Better Life* (2011; dir. Chris Weitz) and Stefan Holtz's romantic comedy *Meine verrückte türkische Hochzeit / Kiss me Kismet* (2006).

Migrant cinema and migrant-themed films after the late 1990s often bring together the conventions of high art and popular entertainment (Göktürk 2002; Hake and Mennel 2012; Berghahn 2012), in the process of producing "a new mainstream cinema," especially in the US and Europe (Naficy 2009, 3). This phenomenon also means that the social-issue-based migrant cinema often loses its documentary-realist aesthetics and opens up to lightweight tones. The "cinema of duty" is gradually diversified by the migrant-themed cinema of the last 20–25 years. The films from this newer era often feature lighter narrative elements and focus on characters who may be outsiders to some extent, but they are strong-willed, and they feel at ease in the cultural and linguistic environment of the host country.

An example that illuminates this process lucidly is provided by Ayub Khan-Din's British comedy-drama films *East is East* (1999;

dir. Damien O'Donnell) and *West is West* (2010; dir. Andy De Emmony). As reviewers and critics observe, *East is East*, albeit bearing the characteristics of the comedy genre, is characterized by social criticism and artistic realism, insofar as its style is like that of the British "kitchen-sink" dramas of the 1960s and 1970s (Rings 2011, 122; Zapata 2010, 178). The film mainly focuses on generational conflicts and occasionally shows brutal family violence, because George Khan (Om Puri) intends "to impose upon his English wife and mixed-race children the religious and cultural traditions of his native Pakistan," especially when it comes to his children's marriage plans (Berghahn 2014, 135). *West is West* evokes a lighter tone, insofar as, although it starts with generational conflicts, it rather describes how such issues are being resolved. Mr. Khan eventually accepts that his children have a different ethnic identity, and his youngest child Sajid (Aqib Khan) becomes more welcoming to his Pakistani origin. The sequel shows tensions but eschews the depiction of domestic violence; George Khan's authoritarian brutality becomes less oppressive.[2] The second film follows the genre characteristics of melodramas and romantic comedies and finishes with a happy ending, a wedding which is based on a relationship that is a combination of a love marriage and arranged marriage.[3]

This article discusses Turkish-German films from a period of 20 years, between 1998 and 2017. This is a stage in German film history which coincides with the commercialization of migrant-themed cinema. During this era the migrant-themed film industry opened up towards wider audiences, which can be seen, among others, in the box office figures: whilst Fatih Akin's *Im July / In July* (2000) and *Gegen die Wand / Head-On* (2004) were rather successful

---

[2] The film history of migrant cinema, even in the last 20-30 years, went through various complex changes that would be too extensive to discuss in detail here. It is important to note, however, that *West is West* was made after the 2004 Madrid train bombings and the 7 July 2005 London bombings, which significantly altered Muslim and South Asian acculturation in Britain and Europe, leading to a more hostile attitude towards these groups (Mirza 2009, 273-275).

[3] Melodrama is understood here, in a way similar to Berghahn (2015, 86), not as a genre *per se* but more as a "modality" that can be detected in several genres: a dramatic narrative where music underscores the heightened emotions in the narrative.

commercially and critically, but attracted only between 5–700 000 spectators in Germany, *Almanya – Willkommen in Deutschland / Almanya: Welcome to Germany* (2011; dir. Yasemin Samdereli) and *Türkisch für Anfänger / Turkish for Beginners* (2012; dir. Bora Dagtekin) gained 1.4 and 2.4 million viewers, respectively (FFA 2022; see also Berghahn 2015, 30).

The influence of documentary-realist depictions of domestic violence can still be detected in certain cases, but this is often combined with the modality of melodrama, romantic comedies and, in certain cases, with the narrative elements of the gangster film. Although the agency of certain female protagonists is still somewhat controlled by their patriarchal fathers and brothers, the films use eroticized scenes, humor, international soundtracks, and urban violence, to show the protagonists as strong multicultural characters.

Ethnically motivated violence is similarly echoed in these films. The portrayal of clashes between racist gangs and racial minorities has a long cinematic convention. Such conflicts are explicitly highlighted, for example, in the Turkish-German *Lola und Bilidikid / Lola and Billy the Kid* (1999; dir. Kutluğ Ataman), Fatih Akin's *Aus dem Nichts / In the Fade* (2017), the British-Asian drama *Anita and Me* (2002; dir. Metin Hüseyin) and *Yasmin* (2004; dir. Kenneth Glenaan), as well as the German drama *Kriegerin / Combat Girls* (2011; David Wnendt) and cult films like the Australian *Romper Stomper* (1992; dir. by Geoffrey Wright) and British *This Is England* (2006; dir. Shane Meadows). Similar social tensions and brawls are briefly displayed in the analyzed films; yet, just as in the case of domestic violence, their significance and brutality are downplayed. Neo-Nazi attacks and street riots occasionally still lurk in the background as a distant threat, but they usually do not play a key role in the storylines.

The Conventions of Art Cinema

As Göktürk observes, domestic violence has been significantly tangible in Turkish-German cinema since the beginning. As she says, "the cinema of migration as a social-realist genre, which established itself in Germany following the mass immigration of labourers from Southern-European countries from the 1960s... has set out to represent these migrants as victims on the margins of society" (Göktürk 2002, 248). Turkish women especially are often portrayed, in the West-German films of the 1970s and 1980s, as isolated, imprisoned, terrorized and abused characters. They are "double victims," targeted both by the racist elements of German society and the brutal patriarchs in their family, especially by their husbands and fathers. A film classic that illustrates this lucidly is *40 Quadratmeter Deutschland / 40 Square Meters of Germany* (1986; dir. Tevfik Başer), which tells the depressing story of the Turkish migrant worker Dursun (Yaman Okay) and his wife Turna (Özay Fecht). Dursun tries to live according to the traditions of his fathers and thus to preserve a piece of his lost home. Sensing his new German environment as immoral and hostile, he keeps his wife locked in a 40 square meter apartment and abuses her physically.

This thematic tradition, which becomes an instrument of "cultural resistance" in "the cinema of the affected" (Burns 2007, 3–4), still appears in certain films of the 1990s and the early 21st century. The films which follow this convention the most closely are probably Fatih Akin's *In the Fade* and Feo Aladag's *Die Fremde / When We Leave* (2010). In both cases, the story is based on actual tragic events: in the former, the 2004 Cologne bombing; in the latter, the honor killing of Hatun Surucu on 7 February 2005 in Berlin. *In the Fade*, however, inverts the traditional gender representations insofar as the victim of ethnically motivated violence is Nuri Şekerci (Numan Acar), a husband of Kurdish-Turkish origin, and his son Rocco (Rafael Santana). Nuri is a former drug dealer who spent time in prison, but then started his own legal business to help ethnic minorities in Germany. He and his son die in a right-wing terrorist bomb attack, and although the police find the culprits, they are acquitted after the false testimony of a Greek hotel owner, Nikolaos Makris (Yannis Ekonomides). The story focuses less on the multiethnic male victims than on the dramatic description of the revenge of the German wife, Katja Şekerci (Diane Kruger). Katja first falls into depression after her loss, but then she travels to Greece, takes justice into her own hands and kills the perpetrators in a suicide bomb attack.

In *When We Leave,* Umay (Sibel Kekilli), after a secret abortion and physical abuse by her husband, escapes from an Istanbul suburb to her parents in Berlin with her young son Cem (Nizam Schiller). Her parents, Kader (Settar Tanriogen) and Halyme (Settar Tanriogen), welcome her for a while, but her father and older brother turn into patriarchs when they find out that she is not on a casual home visit but intends to move back to Germany without her husband. Umay escapes from home and finds refuge in a woman's shelter after she realizes that her family intends to kidnap and return Cem to her husband. She starts a new a job and has a short romantic relationship with a young German, but her family track her down, try to execute an honor killing on her and fatally wound the young Cem in the attempt.

Critics had a hard time explaining that, as late as 2010, a successful, well-made and award-winning film is centered on the documentary-realist description of family violence and the young Turkish woman as a victim. David Gramling interprets the film as myth in Roland Barthes's sense, which is "independent of and indifferent to truth-value." In his interpretation, the film represents a more semiotic than ideological stance, insofar as it is based on an iconographic surplus which derives from references to the iconic elements of the Turkish-German film tradition (2012, 33). Berghahn praises the nuanced family portrait in the film and focuses to some extent on Kader's character, identifying him "as an emotionally torn victim-perpetrator." Yet, she confirms that the film "reprises a theme that has dominated Turkish German cinema since the beginning — that of the victimised young Turkish woman" (2012, 131).

Unlike many other productions of Turkish-German cinema, both films feature minimalist soundtracks. *In the Fade* utilizes a few pop songs for diegetic music, describing the happy moments of the Şekerci family before the terrorist attack. This forms a sharp contrast with the lack of non-diegetic music, which characterizes most parts of the film, apart from a few dramatic moments. *When We Leave* operates with total silence in crucial scenes such as Umay's abortion and Kader's travel to Turkey, where Umay is sentenced to the honor killing. The representation of domestic violence receives full attention here and it is not mitigated by humorous scenes. Ethnically motivated violence does not appear in *When We Leave*, as the German society outside Umay's family appears completely safe and empathetic towards the main character.

A significantly more notable divergence from the pattern of portraying immigrants as victims of violence is realized in Fatih Akin's award-winning *Head-On*. A palpable method with which the film distances itself from social problem films is the conscious usage of a multicultural soundtrack. The film includes musical interludes of an orchestra on the shore of the Golden Horn, which makes the film somewhat similar to the melodramas of Bollywood cinema (Göktürk 2010, 221). Furthermore, the diegetic music ranges from Turkish popular music to international hits like Depeche Mode's "I Feel You," a song which underlines the strong emotional connection between the two main characters in a somewhat melodramatic mode (Siewert 2008, 204).

In addition to the soundtrack, the fresh voice and popularity of the film derive from the extreme resilience of the main characters. Several of Akin's predecessors and fellow migrant directors portray female characters of immigrant origin who transgress social norms with a fate that culminates in serious punishment. They commit suicide or become the victims of social exclusion, domestic violence or honor killing (Göktürk 2002; Berghahn 2015, 47–49). On the other hand, Akin's films, primarily *Head-On*, show the possibilities of relatively successful rebellions while they tell stories of strong-willed characters with powerful and occasionally eroticized bodies. In a way similar to how Akin appears in the media (Machtans 2012, 158–160), they refuse to represent the Turkish minority as an underprivileged social group. Akin's characters may be outsiders, but they are not portrayed as members of a marginalized ethnicity; instead, they are shown as punk and rebellious characters. Thus, domestic violence is underrepresented, while self-inflicted and urban violence come to the foreground.

Sibel (Sibel Kekkili), the heroine of *Head-On*, marries Cahit (Birol Ünel), a frequent visitor of the music pubs and night clubs in Hamburg, to avoid the strict patriarchal rules of her family. The alibi-marriage serves only one purpose: to make it possible for Sibel to freely live a promiscuous life outside her conservative family with a Turkish background. Cahit accepts these terms for a while and so the newly-weds become roommates with separate love lives, while both consume alcohol, take drugs and enjoy the Hamburg night life excessively. Soon, however, Cahit falls in love with Sibel. Forming a tragic turning point typical of a melodramatic love story, Cahit kills Nico (Stefan Gebelhoff), one of Sibel's lovers, which leads to his imprisonment but also to a change in Sibel's feelings as the love between them now becomes reciprocal. They both go through a period of penance, Cahit in prison and Sibel in Istanbul, after which they start to adhere to conformist dress codes and lifestyles. They meet in Istanbul, have a short relationship again and plan to elope together, but Sibel eventually chooses to stay with her daughter and remains in her newly formed middle-class family.

The film contains several violent scenes: the main characters deliberately cut their palms with glass shards, become the victims of urban violence and try to commit suicide. Sibel is threatened by his brother and at one point she gets stabbed on the street. Yet, the intense and dangerous episodes of the protagonists are mainly portrayed as the results of self-destruction and urban violence, not as a consequence of their mixed ethnic background or social marginalization. As Göktürk observes, the characters "show little concern with problems of acculturation" (2010, 216).

In Cahit's case the Turkish roots are distinctively downplayed, and his life shows a balance between Turkish and German elements. When he resides in Hamburg, Cahit hardly speaks Turkish and he is distanced from his Turkish roots, but this never causes significant disruptions in his life. When questioned by his future brother-in-law about his meagre Turkish language skills, he proudly answers that he left his Turkish language behind. Yet, despite his language difficulties, he feels relatively comfortable and confident in Turkey after his release from prison and eventually returns to his birth town. His homecoming is well-expressed by the final frames of the film, which show him looking ahead but moving backwards, away from the camera, as his bus to Mersin is reversing from the station's parking lot. It remains unclear whether after his return he will become akin to those characters of migrant cinema who go through the journey of reverse culture shock and trauma (Naficy 2001, 98) or his trip culminates in a "deeply psychological and philosophical" pilgrimage (6).

Sibel has somewhat greater difficulties in handling her family background of Turkish origin and German lifestyle. In a way similar to the main character Umay in *When We Leave*, she has a patriarchal father and brother who want to control her life, so much so that at one point she is ready to commit suicide if she cannot escape from her Muslim family. Yet, Sibel proves to be an equally strong character as Cahit. Although she is disowned by her family after her promiscuity is exposed and she is beaten up and raped during her penance in Istanbul, she remains in control of her major decisions throughout the film. The violent events in her life after Cahit's imprisonments are depicted as self-punishment, a process of purification which she deliberately goes through. She repeatedly teases her male attackers on the street and is ready to fight with them, assaulting them physically and verbally. She is portrayed as an active and independent woman at the end of the film, as well, when she decides to abandon her hedonistic way of living; the final turning point reads not as a defeat but as the fulfilment of motherhood and the willing acceptance of opening new chapters in her life (Berghahn 2015, 49).

The film avoids showing the main characters as victims with the frequent eroticization of strong bodies. Sexually charged scenes and erotic bodies have been recurring elements of migrant-themed art cinema for a long time. Critics often refer to Rainer Werner Fassbinder's *Angst essen Seele auf / Ali: Fear Eats the Soul* (1974) as one of the archetypical examples of German cinema where the exotic male body is highly eroticized and victimized. As Gueneli points out, after this film, German cinema gradually shifted towards the increased eroticization of the immigrant's body, while the victimization is downplayed, insofar as the characters become "a subject with agency" (2012, 137; see also Cormican 2013).

Cahit's masculine body is often shown in a leather jacket, and he is looked at amorously not only by Sibel, but also Sibel's cousin Selma (Meltem Cumbul). The spectator sees him naked several times, once while having sexual intercourse with his German lover on sheets with leopard patterns. Consequently, the actor who plays this role, Birol Ünel, received relative fame as a sexually attractive star actor after the film's success. This, complemented by his eccentricity, excessive drinking and occasionally uncontrollable behavior, leads to him being recognized as the new Turkish-German embodiment of Klaus Kinski (Gueneli 2012, 144; Berghahn 2015, 24).[4]

Sibel's revealing clothes and naked body also form a recurring element in the film. Just as in the case of Cahit, the actor's persona contributes to this eroticism, insofar as Kikkeli, before shooting *Head-On*, participated in several hardcore porn films (Berghahn 2015, 27). Sibel shows interest in a strong body during the scenes of her penitence in Istanbul. She crops her hair short and wears the puritan uniform of a chambermaid at work or clothes similar to those of Cahit when she visits the night life in Istanbul. She further transgresses the taboos of gender distinctions when she sits at the table of two young men in a kebab restaurant. Although the film shows her at this point as a relatively fragile character who mourns for Cahit and feels somewhat alienated from her body, the camera shows her watching Sibel Şimşek on television, a female European champion of Turkish origin with the same first name as hers, successfully lifting weight in a competition.[5]

---

[4] Another scene that sheds light on Cahit's highly masculinized body and machismo is when his masculinity is implicitly questioned by Sibel. The film shows Sibel buying a bottle of raki and preparing a meal, using several close-ups on the food and drinks. Sibel at one point licks the knife that she uses, making an erotic gesture towards Cahit. He enjoys the food and compliments Sibel for it, up until she makes a remark that to avoid her family's inquiries about pregnancy, she will tell her mother that Cahit is infertile, which will also form a good reason to initiate a divorce. Cahit stands up from the table and rushes out of the room; soon after this, we see him in a pub alone, playing with his wedding ring and thinking about Sibel, which may be the moment when his indifferent attitude toward his alibi-wife starts to change.

[5] Thus, in this short scene three Sibels are displayed. The identicalness of the actor's and character's name is explained with anecdotic details by Berghahn: Kekkili had meagre acting experience before *Head-On* and first had difficulties playing the character's role, and so "Akin spontaneously decided to change her name from Leila to Sibel in the hope that this would allow her to fully identify with her role and thereby enhance the authenticity of her performance" (2015, 27).

Romantic Comedies

The Turkish-German cinema of the 1970s and 1980s frequently shows the destructive elements of multicultural weddings, for example, in *Shirins Hochzeit / Shirin's Wedding* (1975; dir. Helma Sanders-Brahms), *Düğün – Die Heirat / Düğün: The Wedding* (1991; dir. Ismet Elçi) and *Aprilkinder / April Children* (1998; dir. Yüksel Yavuz). These films display a sharp contrast between the Turkish tradition of arranged marriages and the Western idea of romantic love. The films after the 1990s, however, rather "celebrate inter-ethnic romance and culminate in weddings and unite families across ethnic divides," resulting in feel-good romantic comedies which re-imagine Bollywood, British-Indian and American migrant-themed films (Berghahn 2012, 19).

Accordingly, domestic and ethnically motivated violence can be traced in the migrant-themed films of the early 21st century, but this theme appears with modifications which are similar to what has been shown in *Head-On*. The young female Turkish-German characters are usually strong-willed, they act independently, and they are often shown via eroticized shots. Thus, the patriarchal fathers and brothers who use physical aggression usually lack genuine threats against the multi-ethnic couples. The pointed usage of a multicultural and melodramatic soundtrack, enhanced by the addition of international hits, is often conspicuously present in these productions. A case in point which illustrates this is *My Crazy Turkish Wedding*, where the catchy multi-ethnic and international pop music—by artists such as British-Indian Panjabi MC, the Turkish singer Tarkan Tevetoğlu, Fatboy Slim and U2—occasionally becomes diegetic, since its main character Götz Schinkel (Florian David Fitz) runs a record store and works as a part time DJ. As Benjamin Nickl observes, "*Kiss me Kismet*'s protagonists bond over a permeating creative force, which is music" (2020, 77).

Kiss me Kismet is saturated with references to earlier migrant-themed comedies. The film is similar to *Berlin in Berlin* (1993; dir. Sinan Çetin), one of the early examples of Turkish-German cinema which "marks a significant step in this shift away from the 'cinema of the affected,'" insofar as both films are set in, and conspicuously display, Kreuzberg, a district in Berlin which is "popularly known as 'little Istanbul' on account of the density of its Turkish population" (Burns 2007, 7, 9). The German title of *Kiss me Kismet*, literally translated as *My Crazy Turkish Wedding*, indicates a clear reference to one of the most iconic pieces of this tradition, Nia Vardalos's Greek-American themed comedy *My Big Fat Greek Wedding* (2002). The initial scene of the film evokes Fatih Akin's *In July*, insofar as in both cases intelligent but reserved young German boys fall in love with Turkish-German girls under seemingly supernatural circumstances. In *My Crazy Turkish Wedding*, a divine intervention is indicated when Götz's nationalist and misogynist friend Horst (Charly Huebner) plays a romantic song and claims that if love does not turn up while the music is on, it does not exist. At this point a kid accidentally breaks their shop window and Götz gets beaten up in a street brawl. After he is rescued by Aylin (played by Mandala Tayde, a German-Indian actor), the camera uses a POV shot of Götz, who is half-unconscious and sees Aylin in a dreamlike haze. They start to date and, despite the efforts of their family members who occasionally display extreme views on migration and Muslim religious traditions, eventually they get married.

Never letting out of sight the genre traditions of a feel-good romantic comedy or melodramatic marriage film, *Kiss me Kismet* contains some violent scenes and keeps it in the audience's mind that ethnically motivated street fights, destructive arranged marriages, honor killings, and domestic violence are still displayed in the Turkish-German cultural tradition.[6] Just before their first date, Tarkan (Gandi Mukli) harasses Aylin in a discotheque; when Götz helps Aylin to escape, their date ends when Aylin's brother, who is a policeman, asks for Götz's identity card. Later, Aylin's father Süleyman (Hilmi Sözer) and uncle use force to cajole Götz into joining the family business. During one of their secret dates, Aylin reveals that her father will kill her if he finds out about their relationship. Götz is surprised and seems a bit terrified. The film suspends

---

[6] Accordingly, Nickl describes this film as a "culture clash" comedy, where "the hostility between characters with different cultural identities living in the same country is the main focus" (2020, 65).

the tension momentarily when Aylin admits that it was only a joke, but then she quickly adds that the father will rather kill Götz instead of her. This time, however, she does not clarify whether she is serious, and the film leaves it to the audience to decide, creating a melodramatic suspense.

Kiss me Kismet was made thirteen years after the neo-Nazi Solingen arson attack in 1993 and the following Turkish-German riots and is to some extent influenced by the reverberations of 9/11 and the European terrorist attacks in the early 2000s. The film displays ethnically motivated violence when it shows a street brawl between Götz's racist friend Horst and the Turkish-Germans living on their street. Horst is proud to be one of the last fully German residents who live in Kreuzberg, and he repeatedly calls his neighbors Islamist terrorists. Furthermore, Götz gets into a fistfight with Aylin's fundamentalist brother and a few times also needs to fight Tarkan, with whom Aylin's marriage was arranged before. At one point Tarkan wrecks Götz's car and the film ends with a street scuffle.

All in all, however, the ethnic tensions and violent scenes in the film are outnumbered by the feel-good comic sequences. As in a typical romantic comedy, the film ends with the marriage of Götz and Aylin. Nevertheless, aggression returns for a brief moment when Götz uses some force in their wedding to convince Aylin to say "yes" the third time to the imam's question. This scene highlights that even though the representation of domestic violence is downplayed in these films, patriarchy and hyper-masculinity are still an important topic. In a way similar to other Turkish-German romantic comedies, such as *Evet, ich will! / Evet, I Do!* (2008; dir. Sinan Akkuş) and *Einmal Hans mit scharfer Soße / A Spicy Kraut* (2013; dir. Buket Alakuş), *Kiss me Kismet* indicates that the way to a successful cross-cultural experience necessitates that Aylin's male family members tone down their stereotypical machoism, while Götz must somewhat "man up" to get integrated into the Turkish-German community.

In the 2010s, Turkish-German film productions became even more heterogenic and viewer-friendly. A clear trend highlights that although the patriarchal father still plays a key role in the Turkish-German families, they frequently turn into comedy clichés in these films. They become melodramatic or comic figures who occasionally intimidate their daughters and other family members, but their threats do not go beyond a mocking theatricality. A case on point that illustrates such a character is the role of Vedat Erincin—who is also a theatre actor—as the father of a Turkish-German family in *Almanya: Welcome to Germany* and *300 Worte Deutsch / 300 Words German* (2013; dir. Züli Aladağ).

Turkish-German Yasemin Şamdereli's *Almanya: Welcome to Germany* has been interpreted as a "feel-good integration comedy" (Berghahn 2014, 41) with distinguishable traits of Hollywood-style mollification. It was a surprise hit at the 61st Berlin Film Festival "with the German President and the Turkish Ambassador in attendance" (Hake and Mennel 2012, 1). It has gone through "multiplexing" (Naficy 2009), the process of commercialization whereby, due to market forces, feature films intend to appeal to a wider audience by accepting mainstream genre conventions (Hake and Mennel 2012, 7).

Three generations of a Turkish-German family are shown in two separate, well-constructed and beautifully photographed, types of sequences. In the first storyline, we see the everyday lives of the Yilmazes in contemporary Germany. In the second storyline, Canan (Aylin Tezel) tells her cousin Cenk (Rafael Koussouris) a story in which the film shows in flashbacks, often using slapstick comedy and newsreel images, how the grandfather Hüseyin (Vedat Erincin) first arrived in Germany in the 1960s and then his wife and children followed him a few years later.

In the beginning, the film highlights the emotional turmoil of Hüseyin and Cenk. The grandfather is anxious because he and his wife will soon become German citizens and need to collect their German passports. Cenk, in the meanwhile, has conflicts in kindergarten as he is not accepted in a football match between Germans and Turks on either side. He gets frustrated because he thinks he needs to decide on his ethnicity and because he cannot speak Turkish. Both male characters react to their inner conflicts with aggression: Cenk gets into a scuffle with the other kids and becomes black-eyed, while Hüseyin uses force to convince his family to join him on a Turkish holiday to visit his newly bought house in Turkey.

Hüseyin, however, only briefly appears as the stereotypical Muslim patriarch as he constantly provides moral support for his children, granddaughter and grandson, and Cenk also calms down by the end of the film.

Züli Aladağ's *300 Words German* extensively shows, and puts an ironic twist on, both types of cross-cultural violence: firstly, the stereotypical representation of aggression in the migrant family resulting from the cultural difference between the first generation's preference for Eastern arranged marriages and the Western love marriages sought by the second-generation immigrants is shown; secondly, the clash between immigrants and chauvinistic members of the host culture is shown.

Lale (played by Pegah Ferydoni, an actor of Iranian origin) is a strong female Turkish-German character who rides a motorcycle, attends martial arts classes, and pursues other Western habits, but she still wears a headscarf in the company of her father Demirkan (Vedat Erincin). The disagreement with her father escalates when he intends to arrange a marriage for her with an uninteresting businessman of Turkish-German origin. She solves the issue by attacking the proposed fiancé in the street and threatening him with further physical violence if he does not cancel the marriage. Demirkan, who works as a hodja (teacher) in the mosque, finds the clothes and western habits of his daughter problematic, and an even bigger conflict arises between them when Demirkan finds a new potential Turkish-German fiancé, Murat (Züli Aladağ). Murat could be a better match for Lale as he is well-mannered, intelligent, and knows martial arts, but Lale already started to date a young German immigration officer, Marc Rehmann (Christoph Letkowski). Thus, similar conflicts arise here as in *When We Leave*, but they serve only as sources of comedy and the female protagonist remains in control. The stereotypical Muslim patriarch turns into the stock character of the seemingly strict, but actually very empathetic, father who eventually provides moral support for his daughter.

300 Words German echoes the representations of ethnically motivated clashes, but constantly parodies German nationalist images and stereotypes and turns cross-cultural violent clashes into slapstick comedy. This becomes highlighted already by the soundtrack during the opening credits, which turns the first lines of the German national anthem into a Bollywood style pop song. The stereotypically racist character is personified by the head of the immigration office in Cologne, Ludwig Sarheimer (Christoph Maria Herbst). He repeatedly uses the racist slur "Kanak" to refer to Middle Eastern immigrants and has clashes with the Turkish-German community. This could easily escalate into further violence, for example, when he enters the mosque in shoes and behaves disrespectfully, and so his nephew Marc needs to remind him that his behavior can possibly lead to dangerous protests in the local community.

Ludwig makes great efforts to deport a group of young brides from Turkey who arrive in Cologne with minimal language skills after their language tests were forged in the Goethe Institute in Ankara. Yet, with the help of Lale, who speaks perfect German, and Marc, who knows a few sentences in Turkish, the girls learn the necessary 300 words to pass their language tests. In the meantime, Lale also teaches them judo and the basic cultural knowledge that is needed for their successful acculturation in Germany. Ludwig must come to terms with the surprise that her lover is of Turkish origin, and he must also accept that his nephew Marc will marry Lale and they will have a multi-ethnic son. The ethnically motivated conflict between Ludwig and Demirkan, which at one point turned into a brief fistfight, turns into a rivalry to get the attention of Marc and Lale's baby.

Gangster Films

By the mid-1990s, the film market in Europe and the US started to open up towards migrant-themed cinema. In France, notable relevant changes of filmic trends were brought about by the artistic movements of the beur and banlieue cinema. While the former frequently refers to films of Franco-Maghrebi directors and writers after the mid-1980s, the term "banlieue cinema" began to be employed by critics after the mid-1990s. Although they frequently portray multiethnic "black-blanc-beur" characters, banlieu cinema was embraced by white French filmmakers, most notably in Mathieu Kassovitz's *La Haine* (1995), which had a significant commercial success (Higbee 2013, 13-16). Banlieue films negotiate the social realist description of the ethnic youth living in the disadvantaged urban periphery with the narrative elements of the crime and gangster films, displaying juvenile delinquency, guns, drugs, violence and dysfunctional families. They also frequently include references to film classics of American popular cinema, especially crime and gangster films such as Brian de Palma's *Scarface* (1983), *The Godfather* series or Martin Scorsese's 1976 film *Taxi Driver* (Berghahn 2014, 122).

Gangster films, in a way similar to migrant cinema, often show the aspirations of multi-ethnic characters to integrate and help their friends and family members gain success in the host society. As Berghahn puts it, they want to "to be upwardly mobile and to become somehow similar to the normative model of the white hegemonic family" (Berghahn 2012, 4).

Certain gangster films, such as *Scarface* and *The Godfather Part II* (1974; dir. Francis Ford Coppola) explicitly foreground migration (Sternberg 2010, 263). Ethnically motivated violence is often foregrounded in this cinematic tradition, because the mobster is often shown to protect the families of minorities from the harassment of white and other ethnic gangs and that of the policemen (Márquez 2012, 628).

Furthermore, the detailed description of domestic violence and patriarchal family values in gangster films also shows strong connections with migrant-themed cinema. Although the typical masculine hero intends to have a stable relationship with his wife and family, his intentions often become corrupted in the process whereby he achieves a higher role in the organization of the mafia. Archetypical examples of such characters in the American gangster films can be Michael Corleone (Al Pacino) in *The Godfather* series and Charlie (Harvey Keitel) in *Mean Streets* (1973; dir. Martin Scorsese). In the meantime, female characters are pushed into the background, often literally in scenes of domestic violence, as their main role is to give moral support to the male hero (Haenni 2010, 70; Johnson 2007, 269-271).

Nevertheless, to serve the interests of popular entertainment, the genre traditions of the gangster film foreground male intimacy and chivalry to draw the attention away from domestic and ethnic violence (Fields 2004). As Márquez observes, it is especially white gangs which are traditionally described with romanticized images, according to well-established American cultural and Hollywood conventions (2012, 628–629). Turkish-German cinema follows these steps in, for example, *Short Sharp Shock* and *Chiko*. Both films, to some extent, display domestic and ethnically motivated violence, but they focus on the idealized descriptions of male intimacy and chivalry.

Short Sharp Shock revolves around the multiethnic friendship between the Turk Gabriel (Mehmet Kurtulus), the Serb Bobby (Aleksandar Jovanovic) and the Greek Costa (Adam Bousdoukos). Frequenting the shady bars and streets of Hamburg, they get into brawls several times. Gabriel behaves like a patriarchal brother at one point when he fights with the new boyfriend of his sister after she breaks up with the heartbroken Costa, but he soon reconciles with his sister. Later, Bobby hits his girlfriend Alice (Regula Grauwiller) in an argument. The most violent scenes, however, take place between the three friends and the Albanian mobster Muhamer (Ralph Herforth). After a failed arms deal, Muhamer kills Bobby, Costa stabs Muhamer and Gabriel eventually kills Muhamer with a shot in the head. Thus, the stereotype of the chivalrous ethnic mobster is embodied in Gabriel, who intends to protect his peers from white and other ethnic gangs.

The film navigates the borderline of a melodramatic gangster film and a self-reflexive parody of the genre (Isenberg 2011, 53; Sternberg 2010, 262–263). The story is peppered with references to Al Capone, *Scarface* and *Mean Streets*, and revels in national stereotypes, as the bond between the three friends is based on their habit of constantly teasing each other about their ethnic backgrounds.

In *Chiko*, the family relations of the main character Isa Çikar "Chiko" (Denis Moschitto) are emphatically displayed. He severed ties with his mother and father but shows strong attachment to his friend Tibet (Volkan Özcan), who is like a brother to him, and Tibet's mother (Lilay Huser), who is dying of kidney disease. The two Turkish-German youngsters ambitiously enter the drug scene of Hamburg when they start to work for Brownie (Moritz Bleibtreu).

For a while their cooperation is successful, but eventually Brownie's thugs beat Tibet's mother to death, Chiko kills Brownie in revenge, and Tibet kills Chiko.

The film indicates that, apart from ambition, the main goals of starting the drug business for Tibet and Chiko is to help Tibet's mother. Chiko, whose first name is the Turkish equivalent of Jesus, eventually sacrifices himself for his friend, and he intends to be generous and chivalrous with other female characters as well. He gives money to his ex-lover and their daughter, and although at one point they have an argument which ends with domestic violence, he also tries to improve the life of his girlfriend, the Turkish-German sex worker Meryem (Reyhan Sahin). His friendship with the somewhat simple-minded Tibet resembles the story of *Mean Streets* and the friendship between George Milton and Lennie Small in John Steinbeck's *Of Mice and Men* (1937). Reversing the events in Steinbeck's classic story, however, in this case the intelligent Chiko is killed in the end by the childlike Tibet.

Thus, both in *Short Sharp Shock* and *Chiko*, the glamorized sacrifice of the ethnic mobster, who intends to protect his family and friends from non-Turkish gang members, counterbalances the relatively brief scenes of domestic violence.

Conclusion

The paper described domestic and ethnically motivated violence in Turkish-German cinema. The occasional brutal scenes in these productions resemble, and are to some extent inspired by, the dramas of "the cinema of duty." Accordingly, ethnically motivated and domestic violence is not entirely absent in these productions. Racists and neo-Nazis threaten and harass the multi-ethnic characters, and patriarchal fathers and brothers use physical aggression to, as they believe, protect the honor of their family. Such devastating behaviors still dominate in certain dramas of art cinema, as in *In the Fade* and *When We Leave*, but in other cases they become complemented by the eroticized descriptions of strong bodies and self-destruction, as in *Head-On*. Domestic and ethnically motivated urban violence appears also in romantic comedies, but such scenes lack genuine threats against the multi-ethnic couples and turn into theatrical comedy clichés, for example, in *Kiss me Kismet* and *300 Words German*. The usage of a multicultural and melodramatic soundtrack, enhanced by the addition of popularized international hits, also tones down the effect of violent scenes. In gangster films or their parodies, the glamorized sacrifice of the ethnic mobster, who intends to protect his family and friends from the members of other gangs, counterbalances the brief scenes of domestic violence.

Our analysis of violence in Turkish-German migrant cinema sheds lights on the process whereby migrant cinema, formerly dominated by "the cinema of duty," turns into a more light-hearted migrant-themed cinema. As these works are commercially successful, also amongst non-minority audiences, and are occasionally produced by non-minority filmmakers who cast non-Turkish-German actors in the leading roles, this phenomenon is to some extent reminiscent of, and perhaps correlates with, often discussed controversial processes such as cultural appropriation (Jackson 2021, 84–86), "consumer cannibalism" or "the commodification of Otherness," (Hooks 2006) and "cultural violence" (Galtung 1990). Yet, our analysis maintains that reminiscence and correlation do not necessarily mean a full overlap. First, "appropriations are typically a source of pain and feelings of loss or violation for source communities" (Jackson 2021, 88), which is not typically the case here. As Nickl indicates, "culture clash" comedies like *Kiss me Kismet* appeal "to a large audience, both majority and minority communities, by appropriating elements of foreignness and Otherness and… find[ing] pleasure in the avoidance of being contained within a stereotype attached to a certain place in society" (62).[7]

Second, Hooks's cultural appropriation or "getting a bit of the Other" entails superficial sexual encounters that mainly serve as "rites of passage" for white males (2006, 368). In many of the analyzed films, however, the (female) Turkish-German characters are still in the center and the romantic relationship usually results in

---

[7] The film was awarded the prestigious Grimme Award, whose jury praised the film for not trying to avoid cultural clichés and stereotypes, but making fun of them (see Nickl 2020, 74).

consensual marriage. Hence, the term "acculturation," as used in cross-cultural psychology (Berry 2006, 27-29) and reinterpreted in a postcolonial sense (Bhatia and Ram 2001), describes these films better (see also Klapcsik 2016; Pal and Rahman 2020). This indicates that in the multicultural contact between different ethnic groups, there is a relatively balanced "mutual or reciprocal influence" (Sam 2006, 17, 20) between the participants and cultural productions.

Bibliography

Berry, John W. 2006. "Contexts of Acculturation." In *The Cambridge Handbook of Acculturation Psychology*, edited by David L. Sam and John W. Berry, 28-42, Cambridge: Cambridge UP.

Bhatia, Sunil, and Anjali Ram. 2001. "Rethinking 'Acculturation' in Relation to Diasporic Cultures and Postcolonial Identities." *Human Development* 44 (1): 1-18.

Bayraktar, Nilgun. 2016. *Mobility and Migration in Film and Moving Image Art: Cinema beyond Europe*. New York: Routledge.

Berghahn, Daniela. 2012. "My Big Fat Turkish Wedding: From Culture Clash to Romcom." In *Turkish German Cinema in the New Millennium. Site, Sounds and Screens*, edited by Sabine Hake and Barbara Mennel, 1-18. New York: Berghahn Books.

– – –. 2014. *Far-flung Families in Film: The Diasporic Family in Contemporary European Cinema*. Edinburgh: Edinburgh UP.

– – –. 2015. *Head-On (Gegen die Wand)*. London: British Film Institute.

Berghahn, Daniela and Claudia Sternberg. 2010. "Locating Migrant and Diasporic Cinema in Contemporary Europe." In *European Cinema in Motion. Migrant and Diasporic Film in Contemporary Europe*, edited by Daniela Berghahn and Claudia Sternberg, 12-49. Houndmills: Palgrave Macmillan.

Burns, Rob. 2007. "Towards a Cinema of Cultural Hybridity: Turkish-German Filmmakers and the Representation of Alterity." *Debatte: Journal of Contemporary Central and Eastern Europe* 15: 3-24.

Cormican, Muriel. 2013. "Masculinity and Transnational Paradigms: The Cinema of Fatih Akin." *Colloquia Germanica* 46 (1): 21-46. http://www.jstor.org/stable/43653048.

Fields, Ingrid Walker. 2004. "Family Values and Feudal Codes: The Social Politics of America's Twenty-First Century Gangster." *Journal of Popular Culture* 37 (4): 611-33.

FFA. 2022. "Filmhitlisten." *Filmförderungsanstalt. German Federal Film Board.* February 10, 2022. https://www.ffa.de/filmhitlisten.html.

Galtung, Johan. 1990. "Cultural Violence." *Journal of Peace Research* 27 (3): 291-305.

Göktürk, Deniz. 2002. "Beyond Paternalism: Turkish German Traffic in Cinema." *The German Cinema Book*, edited by Tim Bergfelder, Erica Carter and Deniz Göktürk, 248-56. London: British Film Institute.

— — —. 2010. "Sound Bridges: Transnational Mobility as Ironic Melodrama." In *European Cinema in Motion: Migrant and Diasporic Film in Contemporary Europe*, edited by Daniela Berghahn and Claudia Sternberg, 215-34. London: Palgrave Macmillan.

Gramling, David. 2012. "The Oblivion of Influence: Mythical Realism in Feo Aladag's *When We Leave*." In *Turkish German Cinema in the New Millennium: Sites, Sounds, and Screens*, edited by Sabine Hake and Barbara Mennel, 32-43. New York: Berghahn Books.

Gueneli, Berna. 2012. "Mehmet Kurtuluş and Birol Ünel: Sexualized Masculinities, Normalized Ethnicities." In *Turkish German Cinema in the New Millennium: Sites, Sounds, and Screens*, edited by Sabine Hake and Barbara Mennel, 136-48. New York: Berghahn Books.

Haenni, Sabine. 2010. "Geographies of Desire: Postsocial Urban Space and Historical Revision in the Films of Martin Scorsese." *Journal of Film and Video* 62 (1): 67-85.

Hake, Sabine and Barbara Mennel. 2012. "Introduction." In *Turkish German Cinema in the New Millennium. Site, Sounds and Screens*, edited by Sabine Hake and Barbara Mennel, 1-18. New York: Berghahn Books.

Higbee, Will. 2013. *Post-beur Cinema: Maghrebi-French and North African Emigre Filmmaking in France since 2000.* Edinburgh: Edinburgh UP.

Hooks, Bell. 2006. "Eating the Other: Desire and Resistance." In *Media and Cultural Studies*, edited by Durham Meenakshi Gigi and Douglas Kellner, 366-80. Malden, MA: Blackwell.

Isenberg, Noah. 2011. "Fatih Akin's Cinema of Intersections." *Film Quarterly* 64 (4): 53-61.

Jackson, Jason Baird. 2021. "On Cultural Appropriation." *Journal of Folklore Research* 58 (1): 77-122.

Johnson, Merri Lisa. 2007. "Gangster Feminism: The Feminist Cultural Work of HBO's 'The Sopranos'." *Feminist Studies* 33 (2): 269-96.

Klapcsik, Sándor. 2016. "Acculturation Strategies and Exile in Marjane Satrapi's *Persepolis*." *Journal of Multicultural Discourses* 11 (1): 69-83. doi: 10.1080/17447143.2015.1110159.

Machtans, Karolin. 2012. "The Perception and Marketing of Fatih Akin in the German Press." In *Turkish German Cinema in the New Millennium. Site, Sounds and Screens*, edited by Sabine Hake and Barbara Mennel, 149-60. New York: Berghahn Books.

Malik, Sarita. 1996. "Beyond 'the Cinema of Duty'? The Pleasures of Hybridity: Black British Film of the 1980s and 1990s." In *Dissolving Views: Key Writings on British Cinema*, edited by Andrew Higson, 202-215. London: Bloomsbury.

– – –. 2010. "The Dark Side of Hybridity: Contemporary Black and Asian British Cinema." In *European Cinema in Motion: Migrant and Diasporic Film in Contemporary Europe*, edited by Daniela Berghahn and Claudia Sternberg, 132-51. Basingstoke: Palgrave Macmillan.

Márquez, John D. 2012. "The Black Mohicans: Representations of Everyday Violence in Postracial Urban America". *American Quarterly* 64 (3): 625-51, 681.

Mirza, Munira. 2009. "Multiculturalism, Religion and Identity." In *Pakistani Diasporas: Culture, Conflict, and Change*, edited by Virinder S. Kalra, 273-84. Karachi: Oxford University Press.

Naficy, Hamid. 2001. *An Accented Cinema: Exilic and Diasporic Filmmaking*. Princeton, NJ: Princeton UP.

– – –. 2009. "From Accented Cinema to Multiplex Cinema." In *Convergence Media History*, edited by Janet Staiger and Sabine Hake, 3-13. New York: Routledge.

Nickl, Benjamin. 2020. *Turkish German Muslims and Comedy Entertainment*. Leuven: Leuven UP.

Pal, Bidisha, and Mojibur Rahman. 2020. "Acculturation, Cultural Resistance, or Cultural Rigging: A Study of Folk Performances in Popular Films." *South Asian Popular Culture* 18 (3): 261-69.

Rings, Guido. 2011. "Questions of Identity: Cultural Encounters in Gurinder Chadha's *Bend It Like Beckham*." *Journal of Popular Film and Television* 39 (3): 114-23.

Sam, David Lackland. 2006. "Acculturation: Conceptual Background and Core Components." In *The Cambridge Handbook of Acculturation Psychology*, edited by David Lackland Sam and John Widdup Berry, 11-26. Cambridge: Cambridge UP.

Siewert, Senta. 2008. "Soundtracks of Double Occupancy: Sampling Sounds and Cultures in Fatih Akin's Head On." In *Mind the Screen: Media Concepts According to Thomas Elsaesser*, edited by Jaap Kooijman, Patricia Pisters and Wanda Strauven, 198-208. Amsterdam: Amsterdam UP.

Sternberg, Claudia. 2010. "Migration, Diaspora and Metacinematic Reflection." In *European Cinema in Motion. Migrant and Diasporic Film in Contemporary Europe*, edited by Daniela Berghahn and Claudia Sternberg, 256–74. Houndmills: Palgrave Macmillan.

Zapata, Sarah. 2010. "Contesting Identities: Representing British South Asians in Damien O'Donnell's *East is East.*" *Journal of English Studies* 8: 175–86.

Active Submission as a Form of Defense against Gender-Based Violence: Threats for Women Migrants in Amy Bloom's *Away*

Michaela Weiss

Introducing the Concept of Active Submission

The present chapter introduces the, originally zoological, concept of active submission into literary studies, exploring its potential to serve as a defense mechanism against various forms of violence. For the purposes of literary analysis, its meaning and functions shall be reinterpreted and extended, proposing a broader understanding of active submission, not only as a term denoting social behavior in animals, but encompassing a conscious response to violence, and, more specifically for the purpose of this study, gender-based violence against women migrants as presented in Amy Bloom's historical novel *Away* (2007). Set in the 1920s, Bloom's novel narrates a journey of a Jewish immigrant woman travelling from Eastern Europe to America and then back to Siberia, depicting the struggles of a minority woman on the move and her survival strategies. Due to the invisibility and social inferiority of migrant women, the concept of active submission is adopted as a precise tool for denoting the mental attitudes of the protagonist to oppression, violence, and other forms of maltreatment, manifesting the applicability and contribution of the concept in literary and cultural studies.

Despite the fact that the term originates from zoology, it is primarily concerned with pack behavior, or, in other words, social behavior. As such, it can be applied to any relationship between and among living organisms or communities. Its use is not exclusive to minorities, be it ethnic or racial groups, women, or nationalities. By denoting power dynamics in groups and communities, active submission (in opposition to passive submission) provides a universal point of reference and a tool for interpretation of identity-formation narratives as well as communal narratives. Such reassessment of the term might open a discussion within feminism and gender studies, where submission is still, to a large extent, understood one-sidedly as a negative term implying powerlessness, as a violation of one's freedom, or a moral weakness. As Manon Garcia notes, "[t]here is something so taboo in the idea that human beings could submit themselves without being forced to" that there are only two thinkers who pondered submission: Étienne de La Boétie and Sigmund Freud (2). This chapter will reframe the concept of submission and manifest its potential in intersectional analyses concerning social behavior.

To establish the applicability of the concept of submission, it is necessary to provide a clarification of its scope and meaning. Even in zoology, the term "submission" is often used and understood intuitively, denoting the behavior of higher primates, wolves, or dogs. Lorenz (1949, 1953) understands submission as the uncovering of vulnerable parts to the opponent. Later, however, he redefined it as a form of ritualized non-aggression (Lorenz 1963). An animal adopts submissive behavior when conflict could lead to a significant loss or death. Developing Lorenz's ideas, Rudolf Schenkel differentiates between active and passive submission, defining the former as follows: "Active submission is a contact activity in which signs of inferiority are evident [...]. There is no hostility in this attitude" (1967, 323). Passive submission is then understood as Lorenz's original concept of submission defined by the uncovering of neck, belly, and intimate parts. When discussing active submission in wolf packs, Nathan B. Childs understands active submission as "a friendly expression of respect for the privilege of another wolf [...] a respectful bow to the superior." In contrast, passive submission is motivated by fear and helplessness (2004, 24–25). The term "active submission" further appeared in Johannes Renders' monograph *Freedom through Submission: Muslim-talk in Contemporary Denmark* (2021), though the term is directly used only once, in the sense of *aslama*, i.e., "giving oneself entirely to God" (Bravmann 2017, 441).

For the purposes of this essay, active submission will be understood as a type of behavior that is adopted in situations in which an inferior social role of the protagonists is either implied or expected. Faced with dismissal or abuse, the characters neither question nor feel a need to challenge their seemingly subservient role. Focusing on their clearly predefined goals, they conform without feeling hurt (or often even diminished), adjusting to any arising situation. On the one hand, there is no sign of friendliness; nor is there hostility, resistance or (fear) aggression on the other hand. Letting their life situations arise and change, they simply keep a calm attitude even when attacked, manipulated, or abused.

It is in this sense that the concept will be applied to Bloom's novel. The novel's protagonist, Lillian Leyb, is portrayed as a fluid (though not passive) character, offering little to no resistance to the events around her. Unlike Blanche Dubois, the protagonist of *A Streetcar Named Desire* (1947), Lillian is not passively driven by her desires and external forces; instead, she actively shapes her circumstances. She emigrates from Turov (today's Belarus) to America, after a pogrom, in which her husband was killed, daughter was lost, and Lillian herself was severely hurt, believing her whole family to be dead. Starting as one of the thousands of Eastern European immigrants who have no education, cannot speak the language and are willing to accept any job available, Lillian Leyb shows resilience when persuading local theater managers to hire her as a seamstress, although she is no conventional beauty and, what is worse, does not have the necessary skills. Her courage is, however, in stark contrast to her past-induced trauma, which is manifested in recurrent nightmares.

The strong influence of the past resurfaces after she hears from her newly arrived cousin Raisele that her daughter is alive and is moving to Siberia with Lillian's former neighbors; she is determined to leave America and her new life behind, and to return to Russia to reunite with her daughter. Without any savings, Lillian embarks on a journey through the American landscape, facing psychological, physical, and sexual violence, as well as the harshness of the Alaskan climate.

The quest of the protagonist, as well as her name, is inspired by a story of an East European immigrant Lillian Alling, who felt homesick in New York and, in 1926, decided to walk home to Siberia via the Yukon and the Bering Strait. Reaching Dawson in 1928, she bought and old boat and sailed the Yukon River. The end of her journey remains unknown, though there was a report by Soviet officials of a woman accompanied by two Eskimo men, claiming to have arrived from America (Hoyle 2001, 110). Similarly to Alling, the novel's protagonist moves through the American landscape, is imprisoned to survive the winter, and attempts to sail the Yukon River. While Alling was already considered a heroine and a mystery woman, (Hodgins and Hobbs 1985, 133), Leyb remained anonymous and did not receive any protection or support on her journey.

In the sections to follow, the chapter discusses the protagonist's behavior in times of struggle and hardship, focusing predominantly on her mindset and the actively submissive attitude she adopted when faced with various forms of danger. The study is divided into four subsections, focusing on 1) psychological violence which Lillian had to endure after her arrival to America, namely the mental impact of sexual abuse and dismissive or patronizing behavior; 2) past physical violence, ranging from the punishments by her mother to the assault she suffered in the pogrom; moving on to 3) a combination of mental and physical forms of aggression, violence, and maltreatment of an immigrant woman moving alone through the American landscape; and closing with 4) the threats posed by the wilderness and the harsh Alaskan climate.

The Psychological Abuse of an Immigrant Woman

Bloom set her novel in the years 1924 and 1925. At that time, the mistrust towards immigrants in America—which became apparent at the turn of the 20th century—reached its peak, especially in connection with the economic recession after the Great War and the Russian revolution of 1917. As Irving Howe observes, the magnitude of immigration caused a significant sense of discomfort in American society, leading to a pronounced anti-foreign sentiment

(50). In response to the social turmoil of the first decades, two acts imposing limits on immigration were passed, targeting specifically those national and ethnic groups that formed the majority of newcomers before the Great War, namely Eastern Europeans, Southern Europeans and the Japanese. In 1921, the Emergency Quota Act established strict quotas on immigration, followed by the 1924 Johnson-Reed Act, which not only confirmed but also further regulated the number of newcomers. Both acts responded to the widespread fear of Americans that the alien masses would steal jobs from American workers, raise criminality levels, endanger American national identity, and affect American politics. Alvin Johnson, the representative of Washington state, firmly believed that the emergency lay in the fact that America was turning into a "dumping ground" for "the dependents, the human wreckage of the war", as well as communist radicals (Gurock 2009, 148).

One of those wrecked dependents is the novel's protagonist, Lillian Leyb. At the age of twenty-two, she is "an orphan, a widow, and a mother of a dead child, for which there's not even a special word, it's such a terrible thing" (Bloom 2004, 62). Her arrival to America is marked by death and loss, and she starts the new phase of her life (not planning on a new beginning or a fresh start), wearing "a dead man's coat" and "holding a dead man's leather bag" (62). There are no indications of Lillian's visions of America—she never mentions America as the promised land, as many immigrants at the time did, nor does she seek success. She seems resigned to her new location, knowing that in Europe there was nothing left of her former life: no family, no home. Little did she know that, at the time, the country was suspicious of immigrants and American anti-Semitism was on the rise. Even though America still had a reputation of a land open to Jews, the newly passed laws gave rise to a new sense of insecurity and necessity to prove to Americans that Jews, and especially immigrant Jews from Eastern Europe, posed no danger to the political and cultural life in America, and could become valuable and loyal citizens.

The growing textile industry and the flourishing of Yiddish theatres were the staples of American immigrant experience, especially for the Eastern European Jews, as was manifested in Irving

Howe's classic collection of essays, *World of Our Fathers: The Journey of the East European Jews to America and the Life They Found and Made* (1976). Both tropes are employed in Bloom's novel as well. Upon arrival, Lillian spends her first month among other immigrant women, working in the clothing industry, with "her hands [...] dyed blue" (3). The opening of the novel conforms to the traditions of immigrant narrative in the style of Abraham Cahan, Mary Antin and Anzia Yezierska, featuring isolation, as well as harsh living and working conditions. The newcomers usually share one room with two or three other immigrants and spend the whole day working. Their social contact with Americans was thus severely limited. To alter her life situation, Lillian decides to apply for a job in Goldfadn theater as a seamstress. She is not discouraged by the huge crowd of other immigrant women seeking a job, pushing her way to the front in this "all-girl Ellis Island" (3).

From the opening paragraphs, Lillian is presented as an active, resilient woman, who is willing to take her future into her own hands. She does not put herself into a victim position, she does not feel discouraged by competition or unknown surroundings. Instead, she actively seeks out opportunities to improve her life. Nevertheless, she does not protest against the condescending behavior of the theatre owner Reuben Burstein and his son Meyer:

> The two men move through the crowd like gardeners inspecting the flower beds of English estates, like plantation owners on market day. Whatever it is like, Lillian doesn't care. She will be the flower, the slave, the pretty thing or the despised and necessary thing, as long as she is the thing chosen from among the other things. (Bloom 2004, 5)

Lillian is a down-to-earth, realistic woman with acute observation skills. Upon a close examination of Reuben, she hears the carefully suppressed melody of Yiddish. As she is aware that most women waiting for the job can not only sew well but also speak English, she presses close to Reuben Burstein and says, "My name is Lillian Leyb. I speak Yiddish very well, as you can hear, and I also speak Russian very well" (6). Her move is not unnoticed by the others and is met with immediate scorn: "The crowd of women look at her as if she has just hoisted up her skirt to her waist and shown her bare bottom to the world; it is just that vulgar, that embarrassing, that effective" (6). The hostility and disdain culminate after Lillian is selected for the job. Still, neither the patronizing behavior of Reuben, nor the contemptuous attitude of other women, seems to bother Lillian, as long as she achieves her goal. She does not feel any sense of shame, self-loathing, or self-pity.

By accurately analyzing her position as an unskilled immigrant from Eastern Europe, who must compete against other immigrant women, Lillian realizes that the only way she can succeed, is to adopt a submissive stance towards the men in power. This choice of conduct is defined as "attention-seeking behavior" (Miller 2006). Lillian offers behavior which she expects the man to appreciate: physical contact, whispering into his ear, letting him know that she is prepared to do anything she is told without any form of resentment. She is able and willing to adopt this attitude despite her past experience: she has lived through the murder of her family, the loss of her daughter, an "ocean crossing like a death march" (Bloom 2004, 6), sex with strangers, the smell of men, urine, food, and need. Her past, however, did not make her bitter—she knows that to succeed, she must smile and look as a fresh and happy immigrant woman, who is grateful and fulfilled by coming to America.

Scars of Physical Violence

While Lillian seems unaffected by the past, showing no outward signs of fear-aggression or hostility, each night she relives her past-induced trauma, re-witnessing the blood bath in which she lost her family:

> She sees everything now, in all directions. The red floor. Her husband lying in the doorway, covered in blood so thick his night-shirt is black and stiff with it. There are things on the floor between them: her grandmother's teapot in four pieces, the bucket, standing on its mouth, the cloth they hung for privacy. A hand. Her mother is lying on the floor, too, gutted like a chicken through her apron, which falls like a rough curtain on either side of her. Lillian stands naked in the red room and the color recedes, like the tide. (9)

Even though Lillian survived, she was slashed across her chest. What remained was a thin red line. She thus bears scars of political violence both on her body and in her mind. Her current life strategy is therefore to observe the modern world and move with it, as there is no other place for her to be. There is no home, no family to return to. Together with her life in Turov, she has also discarded any sense of her past self. She is aware that even though she might have been special in her hometown, in America she is one of millions, an insignificant, invisible female immigrant: "In English, she is the ugly stepchild; people are not inspired to give her things; they don't even want her to be where they are looking" (15).

This scar across her chest is not the only mark of violence on Lillian's body; there is also a small oval purple scar on her shoulder. Depending on who is asking, Lillian provides multiple stories which would explain the origin of her scars without sounding dramatic or offensive to her listeners. She knows that people often ask questions but are not ready for, or interested in, the truth. The theatre owner, Reuben Burstein, is one of the few people to whom she can relate and with whom she is willing to share her true story, as she knows that they both come from the same geographical and political background. Reuben himself bears many scars from Russia:

> the blue cleft in his shin, long and wide as a butter knife, from the train he jumped out of near Uman; the tip of the finger lost to the ax in Lutsk; two toes gone to frostbite, and his feet ache even now in winter, as if crying for their lost parts; the thick ribbon of white braided skin around his neck, a bad night in Odessa. Czar Alexander II is killed, so what must they do but chase Jewish actors down the street with a wire noose. (44–45)

Reuben understands the underlying, often subconscious, desire to tell the tragic story of the scars. The physical marks are the remains of the memories of violence and loss, the survival of those who bear them. That is why he asks Lillian about her shoulder scar. She feels immense pleasure, as she feels important and seen, but at the same time wants him to repeat the question and show his genuine interest. That is why she only provides a brief answer: "My mother was not a patient woman" (45). She is carefully choosing her words, to prolong the moment and to control the narrative. Eventually, she tells him "the story she can tell" (46). Her narrative is simple, without any judgement. The only correction she uses is to objectivize the story version to refrain from emotional coloring:

> When I was a little girl, I was helping [...]. I thought that I was helping my mother to cook. She was making barley soup. A little chicken, cups of barley. I chop the onions, give her the bowl of onions. I stay standing there, I want to see, I want to stir, I want to help more. I am in her way, she bumps into me when she goes to get the chicken. She picks up the hot spoon from out of the soup, and *ssst,* into my shoulder, to teach me a lesson. That's the story (46).

After their timid lovemaking, Reuben reminds Lillian that nobody really wants to hear about the tragic tales behind the marks of physical violence. Such stories are not found appropriate and attractive in women. When asked, she should refrain from relating the truth and provide a short, comforting, innocent tale, and dismiss her past by praising the men's love-making technique.

The sexual encounter with Reuben's son Meyer has a different quality. Meyer is the one who turns Lillian into his official mistress, buying her silk underwear, renting a flat, and bringing her food. Yet, he is not the one who wants to have sex with her. He is only using her as a cover of his closeted homosexuality. She simply cannot believe that this young and handsome man is not only not attracted to her, but also feels repulsed by her proximity and her naked body. As he does not want to share his secret with her, and does not realize that she senses his discomfort, to avoid any suspicion from her side, he proceeds with the intercourse:

> He spits on his hand and rubs his spit into her, it makes her cringe but it is necessary, she is dry as a summer stream, and then, as if she has some little deformity that he is careful of, some small difficulty he must mind, he tucks a pillow under her stomach, and then another, and then he pats her twice, for warning or for comfort. He pulls her close with one strong arm and enters her so neatly that there may be only three or four inches of them that touch at all, and he bangs against her backside like a heavy wood door in a storm, and then the storm passes and the door swings out and quietly away. (52)

Meyer may be repelled by the female body, yet he can relate to her nightmares. The suppressed desire, guilt and trauma are something that he understands. Moreover, he imagines Lillian's "handsome husband, slim with long dark hair, tragic-looking. He imagines them making love" (53).

Even though Lillian is emotionally and physically closer to Reuben, and her body responds to his undemanding kindness, she does not avoid Meyer's attention. Her body is equally as fluid and non-judgmental as her mind. She actively engages in whatever the present moment requires, accepting the position of a submissive immigrant, not even having any expectations concerning the stability of their contract-based love triangle. Curiously though, when reflecting on her sexual encounters with Meyer, she remembers the bodily sensations she felt when she was giving birth: "coming up to her bare, swollen feet as if they were some new animal. [...] [S]he felt a snake of pain from her back to her groin to her rib cage, circling her body, biting as it went" (54). Yet she does not comment on it further, letting her memories come up and go, without holding on to them. The same strategy is applied to any conscious memories she has of the past.

The scarring does not only affect people, but also places. When recalling the sight of Turov after the massacre, Lillian recalls what it looked and felt like:

> Turov had been like Kishinev after the massacre, like Bessarabia, like Nanking, like Constantinople, humans destroying one another like hurricanes through houses: babies torn to pieces or fed to dogs, streets piled with corpses and people on their way to being corpses, toddlers clinging to the hands of their dead mothers, and police officers looking away, poking a stick through promising debris. Lillian took it in as best she could, her hand over her eyes as if against bright light, looking for Sophie. (58–59)

Walking through the scarred landscape and searching for her lost daughter, Lillian absorbs the sight of utter destruction and desperation, contemplating the false sense of security of local Jews who believed that living in peace with their non-Jewish neighbors would protect them from the pogrom. Instead, they were filling up their small synagogue with dead bodies. Lillian stops the fruitless search after Aunt Mariam tells her that she saw her daughter floating in the river, with her blue ribbons in the weeds.

Abuse on the Move: Handling the Female (Im)migrant

Lillian's life with the Bursteins comes to an end after her cousin Raisele arrives in America and tells Lillian that her daughter is alive and is heading to Siberia together with her former neighbors. Without any hesitation, Lillian is determined to return to Europe and find her child.

Here, the narrative leaves the established format of autobiographical immigrant stories based on the "pursuit of happiness" and search for the American dream and turns into a quest narrative. Because of her lack of financial stability, Lillian realizes that she cannot use any official or legal means of transport and must rely on the kindness of her benefactors. Yet, the power-relations changed, without her noticing. Her departure leads to the rapid physical and mental decline of the elderly Reuben, who loses his sight and, unwilling to use a cane or an assistant, shuts down and dies within a year. Reuben also loses a close friend and a colleague, Yaakov Shimmelman, a tailor, actor and playwright. Yaakov is the only one who understands Lillian's urge to search for her daughter. He is also the one who provides her with a winter coat with inner pockets filled with a small sum of money and a knife. It is he who also arranges for her a journey on a train without her having to pay for a ticket. After her departure, he feels that his life is over. He stops performing, barricades himself in his flat, and commits suicide.

With the limited money she has, Lillian cannot afford a steamboat ticket or any other official means of travel. Unlike the famous traveler, Lillian Alling, who refused any other form of transport and was determined to walk, Lillian Leyb resorts to extra-legal forms of travel, which are, however, often connected with gendered violence. With the help of the ageing actor, Yaakov, Lillian travels in a broom closet of a train, where she can barely fit, in complete darkness. Remembering the soft bed which she shared with Reuben, she feels a slight resentment towards her situation and surroundings. After months of clean clothing and comfortable life, she is standing at another station in a dirty dress, sweating under her heavy winter coat, turning, once again, invisible to the passers-by. She realizes that her thoughts are a pure expression of vanity and dismisses them as soon as they arise. When approached by a porter, she has already accepted her place and can face his contempt: "'Ticket, miss?' a porter says, and the way he says 'miss' would be a lesson to Meyer Burstein, it is so rich in contempt and nuanced surmise and the quick conclusion that the only way this woman will leave Chicago is flat on her back with her panties down" (102). During her next train ride, she meets another conductor, Red McGann, who has a boyish expression and smiles at her: "It is not the worst smile she will ever see, but it has the kind of tenderness you find on the faces of boys who love their dogs and kick them" (103). She asks him if he would be willing to let her stay in the broom closet and bring her a coffee and sandwich for five dollars. Yet Red does not seem to care for her money. Instead, he pushes her into a lavatory, unbuttons his trousers and pushes Lillian's shoulders down:

> She breathes through her mouth so as not to have to take in the scent of Red McGann, so as not to remember any more of this than the cracked black-and-white tile under the navy-blue muffler and his black shoes on either side of her. She pushes her hair back and licks her lips, and Red McGann sighs. You're a pet, you are, he says. She cannot raise him. He is as soft in her mouth as oatmeal. Lillian handles him as if he were a lover, as if he were Reuben after a long day. (103)

Her softness and acceptance of his needs and behavior shift their power relations. Without any further manipulation or requirements, Red wants to persuade Lillian that he is a good man after all and that others would ask for both money and sex. He is there seeking understanding and appreciation rather than sexual release.

Besides contempt and sexual abuse, in Seattle, Lillian loses her focus and is assaulted and robbed. She wakes up on the ground without her belongings, sensing light kicks in her ribs. A young colored girl is urging her to get up if she wants to stay alive. Lillian wakes up, heavily bruised, in the bed of a colored woman who calls herself Gumdrop, who is a professional sex worker. Gumdrop works for her cousin Snooky Salt and she seems content with their arrangement:

> Snooky Salt is Gumdrop's pimp, and he is not the worst pimp a girl could have. He appreciates Gumdrop's specialty, doesn't send over customers who want a big fat woman with breasts they can bury their whole faces in, or older gentlemen who say they want a sweet little babygirl like Gumdrop but really want to be sweet little baby- girls themselves, for which Gumdrop has no patience and no accessories. (115)

Yet, secretly, she is planning to become independent, dreaming of fulfilling her ambitions to become the first colored madam in Seattle, or even better—to be the head of the "whores' union." She introduces Lillian to Snooky, warning her that small men behave like snakes, since they are dangerous and insecure. Lillian once again adopts her attitude of active submission and lets Snooky feed her biscuits: "She's wearing a green dress borrowed from the whore down the hall, she's letting herself be fed, in public, by a colored man in a black-and-white houndstooth suit and a lilac derby with boots to match, and she knows just how bad it looks" (118). She is working for a black sex worker and a black pimp is trying to court her. Though she feels that it is a strange situation to be in, she does not object to it: in comparison to her past experience, there were worse things happening to her. Little does she know that Gumdrop is planning to get back the money which Snooky keeps for himself. Under the pretense of a threesome, both women get Snooky drunk and sleepy. When Gumdrop drops the strongbox, which crashes to the floor, Snooky is suddenly alert and angry and attacks Gumdrop:

> Snooky reaches for Gumdrop's wrists to force her hand open, thinking that he'll fuck her and beat her senseless, and if she's out of commission for a week she'll remember this lesson, and he'll have to do Lillian, too, because it's somehow worse that a white girl to whom he has taken a fancy for no reason is trying to steal from him. (132)

During their struggle, Lillian falls on his back, driving a dagger through Snooky's heart. Watching him bleed to death, both women realize that he could have lived if they had not been driven by fear that their lives have been wasted and that their life goals were getting more and more distant. Gumdrop changes her plans and, instead of becoming the head of the union, she becomes a teacher, marries a Jewish man, converts to Judaism and raises three children (and gets her figure back each time). So far, Gumdrop, alias Clothilde, is the only character in the book who revolts against her life situation and finds happiness.

Another chapter of Lillian's journey through the urban wilderness takes her to Winslow, Alaska, where she falls asleep in a bar and is found by the local constable Arthur Gilpin who takes her home, feeds her and has sex with her. After the dinner, she is determined to continue her journey; however, he handcuffs her to a banister, knowing that she would not be able to survive outside in the Alaskan winter. To prevent her from disappearing into the night, he sends her to the Hazelton Agrarian Work Center for Women for theft. Imprisonment in the all-women environment represents the only option for a woman migrant to survive the Alaskan winter without a map, money or experience.

In the correction center, Lillian meets Chinky, whose whole family has turned immigrant stereotyping into a flourishing business. Lillian and Chinky grow fond of each other and develop a mutual friendship. Similarly to Gumdrop, their ways part in the spring after they are both released and Chinky returns to her family and its flourishing business, which has turned out to be their survival strategy in a land hostile to, or at least suspicious of, immigrants:

> Chinky's number one job, her whole family's bread and butter, is acting like decent Christian people. Chinky plays The Girl, her sister is The Miss and sometimes The Invalid, her mother is The Blind Servant or else The Ladies' Aide (miscarriages that look natural and emergency baby-switching), and Mr. Chang is The Minister or The Medium or The Herbalist. Xiu-mei is especially good at being The Miss, in pert porkpie hat and gray skirt, clutching the white leather Bible in both hands, her eyes always lowered as if Jesus is appearing in the floorboards, but no one is as good at the show as Chinky's father. (171)

Embracing the stereotypes, the Chang family pretend to be law-abiding assimilated citizens, grateful for the conversion to Christianity. Like Gumdrop, Chinky is also determined to step out of the family game. She escapes with a young boy she met on a steamship, and they establish a flourishing business in Alaska, where Chinky passes as an Inuit.

Using the example of Gumdrop and Chinky, Bloom depicts the resilience and the acquired power of both women to escape enslaving patriarchal structures, be those dictated by a cousin or father, and seek their own fulfillment. Both the former sex worker and the thief are inspired by Lillian's determination to find her daughter and her resolve to disregard any social situation or expectation.

Surviving the Wilderness

Lillian's journey leads through the spring Alaskan landscape. Lillian has never encountered such a severe climate and is not prepared for the dangers of untamed natural forces. Depictions of nature are relatively rare in the predominantly urban-based American Jewish literature; Jewish immigrants predominantly settled in cities, where they could form communities and have better chances at employment.[1] Bloom also avoids extensive depictions of natural scenes; instead, she highlights several details and colors to create a recognizable and relatable sense of a landscape:

> Everything white is her enemy. The sun on the Alaskan snow is bright and terrible; she would be blind by now if not for the scarf wrapped around her head and eyes. She needs to keep looking at the clumps of red berries—the red is a small comfort and it rests her eyes. And the knock-kneed brown moose, a tired group of ten, yards ahead of her for the last three days, comfort her, too. (193)

Lillian does not admire nature, nor does she contemplate its potential healing or transformative power. She seems to understand and interpret the landscape purely as another dangerous place on her journey to Siberia. Her struggles with the hostile climate are often framed by cultural and/or mythological projection. The attack of the mosquito swarm is therefore likened to the attack of the Furies, dispensing punishment in the Underworld:

> They rise up in April, awkward and irritable but dogged, like people who have slept too long. Thousands of them swarm, mating in midair. Their

---

[1] For a discussion of the centrality of the urban setting in American Jewish literature see e.g. Michael Hoberman, *A Hundred Acres of America: The Geography of Jewish American Literary History* (2019).

> wings whine in her ears like small Furies (Alecto, Megaera, and Tisiphone, and she would have had their names tattooed on her hip, had she known this was coming) and they burrow into her hair and her scalp, into her ears, in the tender place behind her earlobes, beneath her eyelids. (187)

While pondering the mythical dimension of her plight, Lillian is still capable of covering long distances on foot, and she is even able to hunt, make fire and keep herself warm and fed. While killing and skinning her catch, she feels ashamed and is glad that no one has seen her. She is still judging her own behavior, especially the hunting, by the standards she has learned from books. Her sense of inferiority and insignificance are so deeply ingrained in her that she cannot stop judging herself:

> It is a serious, shaming, and necessary and satisfying business and she is glad that no one sees her kill [porcupines], or wrap her hands in her bloody coat to avoid their quills or cut their skins off in a way that is nothing like the elegant undressing she's seen men do; it is as awkward and uneven as tearing heavy cloth by hand and she must pull bits of singed skin off the cooked creatures before she can eat them. She does it and when it makes her sick she drinks water until it has all passed out of her. (189)

Each day she manages to kill some animal. However, remembering Yaakov, she pays respect to them by recreating their skeletons on both sides of her campfire, as Native Americans did. Her vision of nature is, however, gradually shifting from a rational, culture-imposing concept to a more mythological or transcendentalist understanding of the world. The natural environment seems even more dangerous than the urban one, where Lillian can recognize and follow the rules of a social hierarchy. Yet, nature is not portrayed as a willful adversary, even though it is harsh and largely indifferent. As Northrop Frye observes, Native Americans represent a more authentic, mythological vision of the world, which leads to the "immigrant mentality" being replaced by "indigenous mentality" (Frye 2003, 476). The vastness and untamed character of the wilderness provides her with a different perspective on society and her struggles. She becomes truly aware of not only social and gender inferiority but, on a larger scale, the insignificance and frailty of human life itself. This experience prepares her for giving up on her plans and embracing life and a potential love:

> What Lillian can see clearly is her place in the scale of this country, how easily the entire Lower East Side could drop into the crevasses ahead of her. She is a gnat, and what had been her whole world is no more than a small junk pile, old boots and body parts, an overturned basket in the middle of the world's thoroughfare. (Bloom 2004, 193–4)

Despite her awe of nature, she understands that it is people, and especially men, who are prepared to hurt or kill her without any reason or purpose. When passing a cabin, she sees a shotgun aiming at her from the porch. She remembers wild west movies, puts down her bag, raises her hands and lets her hair fall on her shoulders. Lillian is aware that she must show clear signs of submission and surrender and manifest her femininity and harmlessness.

Like most inhabitants of the frontier, the man is an exile, one of many who is escaping his violent past. He considers shooting her on the spot, as this is the smartest and easiest solution: "There's no reason to keep the shot-gun turned on her except that he can and it puts off the moment he has to speak to her" (205). In the meantime, he is already imagining playing a game of chess with her and taking her to bed. Still, these frontier encounters have their rules and Lillian is determined to follow them: "[S]he ducks her head as she's seen women do in the West. It is the very last trace of a curtsy. The formality strikes them both but there's no smiling at it; people up here have been known to kill each other over a dropped phrase or the failure to return a pie plate" (205). When seeing Lillian's calm and submissive manner and her deteriorated body, he suddenly feels compassion towards her, reading her body as "a map of pain" (207).

The mosquitoes, low temperatures and exhaustive walking have left their marks on Lillian's body; her ankles are heavily bruised, and her feet are covered in soaring, infected blisters, smelling of rotting meat. For the first time, it seems that Lillian has found somebody who did not feel the urge to mistreat her or to manifest his power over her body and mind. An exile himself, John Bishop washes her clothes, prepares dinner and lets her sleep at night. When she leaves early in the morning not to wake him up, she fights the urge to stay with him. For the first time during her journey, she feels the temptation to remain where she is and enjoy the unexpected human connection she managed to establish. Remembering the stories from classical mythology and the Bible, where turning back had fatal consequences — be it the opening of the forbidden box or turning into a pillar of salt — she, nevertheless, turns back to say goodbye to the man who treated her with love and kindness. She appreciates that he perceived her body, the scars, bruises, and blisters, and did not turn away, which makes her return to make love to him:

> But in the morning everything can, and must, be seen. Daylight takes us; it peels us like fruit. Their two bodies are rough and tanned along the arms and neck, shy white everywhere else, and they are marked by travel and trouble all over, like people twice their age. There are signs of misjudgment and misfortune: blackened toes, nails half gone, festering sores, her circle of bug bites, purple with white-pricked centers, his two blackened scabs of frostbite, thick, coal-like ovals cracked with red, winking slits, a barbed-wire scar, still livid, circling his wrist; lilac, mauve, and purple chafings under her arms. (219)

After listening to her story, the man decides to join her quest. As he cannot go back to his home and the women he loved after he accidentally killed a man, he is open to starting a new life with Lillian. They embark on their, now shared, journey, yet their plans are changed by nature. Lillian gets lost during a huge, unexpected snowstorm. After reaching John's old cabin, she finds his note that he went searching for her. She waits for twenty-one days, looking for any sign of his presence and then moves on with her quest. Even though she cannot stop thinking about him and it breaks her heart, the longing to reunite with her daughter is stronger. She reaches Dawson City and finds an old local man, who is willing to prepare and sell her a boat that would take her to Siberia. What she does not know is that John Bishop has survived, was taken care of by the local Han tribe and is determined to follow Lillian anywhere she would go. They reunite at the Yukon River, as Lillian's voyage ends shortly after it has started. Unable to navigate or control her boat, she hits a rock. Exhausted, Lillian crawls to the shore where she collapses. The first thing she sees is John's helping hand. After several attempts to get to Siberia, Lillian and John settle in Skagway, get married and have two children. While she does not reach her primary goal to find her daughter, Lillian's quest turns out to be transformative and, eventually, she manages to not only find peace with the past, but also find romance and continue with her life.

To provide a more satisfying ending for the readers, Bloom briefly outlines the fate of Lillian's daughter Sophie. She was saved by Lillian's former neighbors, who took her in as their own child they did not have. They hoped that Lillian would become a distant memory, an aunt she once knew. After the pogrom, they escaped to Siberia, where the Jews were allowed to stay in Tikhonaia (renamed to Birobidzhan), which was called the Zionist paradise, without drinking water, surrounded by swamps. There was the Kaganovich Jewish Theater and a newspaper, where locals could write in Yiddish and celebrate the greatness of the Soviet. Then the family moved to Vladivostok and Sophie went to university. She became a poet and translator and is happily married.

Concluding Remarks

Amy Bloom's novel combines several established formats, ranging from immigration narratives to the Bildungsroman, while, at the same time, utilizing the story of Lillian Alling. Throughout the novel, the female protagonist faces various forms of gender-based violence, be it physical, sexual, emotional, or verbal. Due to her lack of financial means, she cannot use the official modes of transport and must rely on extra-legal forms, for which she "pays" by physical discomfort, contempt, and sex. Often, she must resort to theft to be able to continue her journey or be incarcerated for a theft she did not commit to have a warm and safe place to survive the winter. Regardless of the nature of violence or harshness, Lillian never seems to oppose or question reality. On the contrary, she always accepts it and consciously presents herself as submissive. She acknowledges her perceived social inferiority based on her gender, ethnicity, and land of origin. She is aware that, as a powerless and unskilled woman immigrant or physically weak woman facing the Alaskan wilderness, she cannot survive if she resents or opposes reality.

As such, the concept of active submission has proven to a be a valuable tool not only for survival, both in urban and natural spaces, but also for reaching mental stability and moral integrity. Recognizing one's position in society and the world, offering no signs of active resistance, or putting them aside once they arise, enabled the protagonist to continue on her journey without resorting to the attitude or behavior of her tormentors. Instead, she is willing to suffer any discomfort or maltreatment if it is necessary for achieving her only goal: finding her child. She is the mistress of both a theatre director and his gay son; she goes to prison and almost freezes to death in Alaska, yet her character is not altered. Her body, as well as her subconscious mind, may be scarred, but her presence and active surrender to reality remains intact. Active submission can thus be applied to literary studies as denoting a behavior which consciously accepts an inferior or weaker role in family, community, or nature, without compromising one's identity or integrity. It further provides an alternative and viable survival strategy for characters that focus on their life goals, considering daily struggles as irrelevant and temporary.

Bibliography

Bloom, Amy. 2007. *Away*. New York: Random House.

Bravman, M. M. 1977. *Studies in Semitic Philology*, edited by G. F. Pijper. Leiden: Brill.

Childs, Nathan B. 2004. *Shaping the Wolf Inside Your Dog*. Victoria: Trafford Publishing.

Frye, Northrop. 2003. *Northrop Frye on Canada*. Vol. 12 of *Collected Works of Northrop Frye*, edited by Jean O'Grady and David Staines. Toronto: U of Toronto P.

Garcia, Manon. 2018. *We Are Not Born Submissive: How Patriarchy Shapes Women's Lives*. Princeton, NJ: Princeton UP.

Gurock, Jeffrey S. 2009. *Orthodox Jews in America*. Bloomington, IN: Indiana UP.

Hoberman, Michael. 2019. *A Hundred Acres of America: The Geography of Jewish American Literary History*. New Brunswick, NJ: Rutgers UP.

Hodgins, Bruce W., and Margaret Hobbs, eds. 1985. *Nastawgan: The Canadian North by Canoe & Snowshoe*. Toronto: Betelgeuse Books.

Hoyle, Gwyneth. 2001. *Flowers in the Snow: The Life of Isobel Wylie Hutchison*. Lincoln, NE: U of Nebraska P.

Howe, Irving. [1976] 2005. *World of Our Fathers: The Journey of the East European Jews to America and the Life They Found and Made*. New York: New York UP.

Lorenz, Konrad. 1949. *Er redete mit dem Vieh, den Vögeln und den Fischen*. Vienna: Borotha.

Lorenz, Konrad. 1953. "Verstandigung unter Tieren." *Forum* 1: 47–48.

———. 1963. *Das sogenannte Böse. Eine Naturgeschichte der Aggression*. Vienna: Borotha.

Miller, Pat. 2006. "Understanding Dog Appeasement Signals." *WholeDog Journal*. March 7,

Renders, Johannes. 2021. *Freedom through Submission: Muslim-talk in Contemporary Denmark*. Boston, MA: Brill.

Schenkel, Rudolf. 1967. "Submission: Its Features and Function in the Wolf and Dog." *American Zoologist* 7: 319–329.

Whole Dog Journal. 2006. https://www.whole-dog-journal.com/behavior/understanding-dog-appeasement-signals/

Williams, Tennessee. 1947. *A Streetcar Named Desire*. Cambridge, MA: New Directions.

Migration and Terrorism

Terrorism and Transnational Identity: Islamic State Recruiting among Second-Generation Migrants and Kamila Shamsie's *Home Fire*

Cassandra Falke

Introduction: Cross-cultural Experience as a Catalyst for Recruiting

In the twenty-first century, more and more of us are migrants. A recent study of global human migration found that 244 million people live outside their country of origin (UN Population Fund 2015). That has more than doubled since 1960 (92 million) and is expected to nearly double again by 2050 (405 million) (Davis, et al. 2013, 1). It would be going too far to say that migrancy is a new norm, but, as Paul Carter (1992) writes, it is becoming more "urgent to develop a framework of thinking that makes the migrant central, not ancillary to the historical process. We need to disarm the genealogical rhetoric of blood, property and frontiers and to substitute for it a lateral account of social relations" (7–8). Such a lateral account will require that we rethink the extent to which identity is within our control. Phenomenological and communitarian accounts of identity development portray selfhood as developing within a given framework of intersubjective relationships. These frameworks include family and community relationships that precede one's birth as well as a whole matrix of relationships that develop because of proximity or personal choice (Zahavi and Overgaard 2020). Constructionist accounts of identity creation similarly assume a matrix of cultural relationships that give individuals the language and symbolic structures needed to performatively define themselves (McWilliams 2018; Gergen 1997). These conceptions of selfhood accept that much of who we are to become is given. We do not decide it. We do not pick our bodies, the location in which we grown up or our families. The ideology of Islamic terrorism says otherwise; it says you can make yourself who you want to be—a hero, a martyr, an individual not defined by circumstance.

The already complex processes of identity formation are even more complex for immigrants. Migrants to a new country must navigate cultural, institutional, and linguistic differences in order to exert control over life choices that are intimately connected with identity—choices about one's occupation, friends, and self-expression. Each of these fields contributes to a migrant's conception of him or herself and shapes the behaviors that constitute meaningful action. How do I have a meaningful life? How do I improve the world of my immediate experience for my own sake and for the sake of other people I care about? Our ability to answer these questions depends on our ability to navigate cultural, institutional, and communicative structures.

My inquiry in this chapter centers on the ways that terrorist organizations use the complexities of cross-cultural experience to catalyze recruits' identification with transnational jihadi goals. I will focus particularly on ISIS and Al-Qaeda, looking at profiles of jihadis claiming Islamic State (IS) and Al-Qaeda linkages in Europe as well as at these organizations' recruiting literature, particularly their English-language online magazines. The chapter then turns to a fictional representation of Islamic State recruiting that brought the organization's methods to public attention. Kamila Shamsie's *Home Fire* explicitly connects IS's recruiting successes in England to intergenerational immigrant anxieties about identifying as, and being accepted as, British. By manipulating the language of community and the belief in a supra-historical place that can serve as a surrogate homeland, Al-Qaeda and IS tap into a conception of home derived from a classical nationalist narrative in which place, community, and shared belief are supposed to provide the grounding for identity (Miscevic 2001, Ch. 2). But they do so by abstracting place, community and shared belief from the actual surroundings in which individuals are raised and projecting them onto the (now-destroyed) caliphate or an imagined transnational, trans-historical idealized community. Al-Qaeda utilized this technique effectively in Europe in the first decade of the 2000s, and it was further refined by the Islamic State in the 2010s. Offering a new community and new opportunity for identity creation seems to have been effective in both organizations' recruiting of terrorist actors and foreign fighters.

In her award-winning 2017 novel *Home Fire*, Kamila Shamsie identifies IS's manipulation of national identities in recruiting, showing how discourses of national belonging in Britain posit an ideal of belonging but systematically undermine individuals' attempts to integrate Britishness and loyalty to Islam. In addition to being an innovative rewriting of *Antigone*, *Home Fire* represents for the English reading public the subtlety of IS's transnational appeal, and the ways IS builds on and modifies earlier strategies used to recruit young Muslims to violent non-state organizations. By highlighting the givenness of our personal pasts and the ways in which cultural expectations precede individual decision making, Shamsie clarifies why IS's rhetoric of making a clean start is so attractive. When her character, Parvaiz, a young, talented British sound artist, leaves his sisters and his country to join the caliphate, Shamsie integrates the mesh of "push" (Pokalova 2019) and "pull" (Venhaus 2010) forces that scholars identify as motivating foreign fighters and "homegrown" terrorist recruits, shaping an individualized character readers can empathize with.

Home Fire centers around two families. The Pasha family consists of three siblings—an older sister, Isma, and a twin brother and sister pair, Parvaiz and Aneeka, who are seven years younger. Abandoned by their jihadi father, they were raised by their mother and grandmother in until both died during Isma's university years. The siblings have taken different paths by the time the novel begins. Isma is starting a PhD in the US. Aneeka is about to begin studying law, and Parvaiz is working as a greengrocer's assistant and refining his talent as a sound engineer. The other family, the Lones, includes an Irish-American mother and Pakistani-British father. One of their two children, a successful daughter called Emily, enters the novel only briefly. The other, a son called Eamonn, who is between Isma and Aneeka in age, becomes a friend to the older sister in the US and then a lover to the younger back in London. The Pasha and Lone families both came to England in the fifties from the Punjab region of Pakistan, and both settled in Wembley, but two generations later, the young people on whom the book is centered live at opposite ends of the London class spectrum.

Narrated side-by-side, the different trajectories of the Pasha and Lone families highlight the socio-cultural expectations faced by British immigrants from Islamic backgrounds. Karamat Lone, who becomes home secretary within the novel's temporal frame, advocates for integration and pronounces himself an atheist, but recites "Ayat al-Kursi as a kind of reflex" (110).[1] According to his son, Eamonn, Karamat credits having succeeded in politics to his embrace of "British values" (53). Eamonn reports that "'It's harder for him'" to make it in politics, "'Because of his background'" (53). Isma, Aneeka and Parvaiz's father, Adil Pasha, abandoned the family when Isma was "too young to remember either his departure or his presence before it" (49), first to fight in "Kashmir, Chechnya, Kosovo" and then starting in October 2001, in Afghanistan (50). He was imprisoned in Bagram in early 2002 and was reported to have died on the way to Guantánamo (51). The siblings know very little about their father's life and death. Demonstrating faithfulness to Britain requires that they reject their association with him, even to the extent that they cannot ask about the circumstances of his death. Consequently, when an ISIS recruiter tells Adil Pasha's story to Parvaiz, he opens up a whole new way for Parvaiz to see himself as Adil Pasha's son, and a crucial part of that new narrative is that Adil "saw beyond the lie of national boundaries" (130).

With an ardent British patriot fathering one family and a transnationally oriented terrorist the other, Shamsie uses the book's first generation born in Britain to chart a spectrum of ways to navigate the conflicting pressures of national and familial identity. Members of the second generation, who are the main focus of her book, must make their choices within the restrictions created by their parents' choices before them. Their differing perspectives become clear after Isma mentions "the British government" and "the benefits of the

---

[1] The 255th verse of the 2nd chapter of the *Quran*, Al-Baqarah, is sometimes recited as a prayer of protection.

welfare state—including state school and the NHS" in a conversation with Eamonn. Eamonn "saw the state as part of himself," but "that had never been possible for anyone in her family" (51). Because of the novel's sophisticated reckoning with transnational identity and ISIS recruiting, I return to Shamsie's novel at the end of my chapter. The first half focuses on Islamic terrorism and transnational identity more generally.

Terrorism and Second-Generation Immigrants

Although it is impossible to create a "terrorist profile" for twenty-first century Europe, most individuals convicted of terror activities are residents of a country to which their parents migrated. In the 90s and early 2000s, many researchers assumed that terrorists must come from a poor background, that they must be poorly educated, or psychologically incapacitated in some way, in order to be fooled into finding terrorism to be a meaningful form of personal and political expression. But time and time again, researchers have proven these assumptions wrong (Kruegar 2018; Sageman 2008). Most European terrorists are lower-middle class, educated, sane. The identity categories that they most often share are that they are male, under 30 years of age, and the sons of migrants; three of the four young men involved in the London underground bombing in July of 2005 (the 7/7 attacks) were second-generation British citizens of Pakistani origins. The fourth convict was born in Jamaica but raised in England. They were between the ages of 18 and 30. Jamal Zougam, one of the men convicted in relation to the 2004 Madrid train bombings, had moved to Spain from Morocco at the age of ten. "Most of the key participants" in the Hofstad group responsible for the murder of Theo van Gogh in the Netherlands were "young Dutch Moroccans" (Bakker 2010, 172). Mohammed Bouyeri, who committed the murder, was the son of Berber-Moroccan immigrants. Abdelhamid Abaaoud, the mastermind behind the November 2015 Paris attacks that killed 130 people, who is suspected of planning seven other attacks, was the Belgian son of a Moroccan immigrant. The national lineage of these terror actors sometimes reflects colonialist legacies. "Second-generation British Muslims of

Pakistani origin are responsible for the majority of terrorist acts by British Muslims outside of Great Britain and in Great Britain itself" (Rabasa and Benard 2014, 58–9). In Spain, "of the total Jihadists arrested (or died) in Spain between 2013 and 2017, 73.4% are of Moroccan origin" (Reinares and García-Calvo 2018).

According to the UN Security Council's Resolutions 2178 (2014) and 2396 (2017), foreign fighters leaving Europe to fight for groups performing terrorism are now legally defined as "foreign terrorist fighters," meaning that the term "terrorist" now applies legally to people known to have committed terror attacks and people who immigrated with the intent to join recognized terrorist organizations. According to the International Center for the Study of Radicalization, 41,490 people from 80 countries had migrated to be part of the caliphate or been born in its territory (Cook and Vale 2018, 3). Estimates for what percentage of these were second-generation immigrants before immigrating to the caliphate vary, but perhaps 60% (Benmelech and Klor 2020, 1481). Fewer than 20% of these are from Western Europe, with the majority coming from the former Soviet Republics, followed by the Middle East (Barrett 2017, 11).

It is worth pausing over the fact that first- and second-generation immigrants to and from Europe constitute a tiny percentage of terrorist actors in the world. The data on second-generation immigrants in Europe should not be misinterpreted as reflective of terrorist activity globally. As Alex Schmid points out, "the countries of the democratic West (North America, Australia and the European countries) themselves have, with the exception of the attacks of 11 September 2001, suffered only 0.5 per cent of all fatalities from terrorism in the last 15 years" (2016, 12). He also raises the question of terrorism by state actors, which he suggests threatens up to 36% of the global population (18–9). State-sponsored violence drives national and international displacement, so if states are considered terror actors, there are hundreds of thousands of multi-generational terror victims for every single non-state terrorist with an immigrant background. If, as Derek Summerfield argues, torture is a form of terrorism, then Parvaiz, Isma and Aneeka are victims of terrorism through their father's torture. Summarizing his exploration of migration and terrorism, Schmid makes a crucial point: "The blind eye of many governments to state terrorism of allied regimes, combined with the general state fixation on non-state terrorist actors, has contributed to overlooking one of the most powerful drivers of forced migration—regime or state terrorism" (2003, 20).

Bearing this in mind, it is still the case that, measured against other non-state actors, IS and al-Qaeda have been remarkably effective in recruiting internationally, and in terms of their efforts to recruit Europeans, they have succeeded most among Western Europe's sons of immigrants, so the phenomenon of second-generation recruitment remains crucial to understand. The predominance of second-generation immigrants among terrorist leaders in some European countries has given rise to the "failed integration hypothesis" (Precht 2007, 45–6), which suggests that the failure to integrate into a host-culture makes individuals particularly vulnerable to radicalization. Failed integration has also been used as a lens through which to view the foreign fighter phenomenon (Benmelech and Klor 2020, 1459). I do not want to dispute the failed integration thesis as much as to shift the focus from failed integration in the host country toward the successful integration of these individuals into a transnational extremist jihadi culture. Second-generation residents of a country are in a unique situation regarding their vulnerability toward radicalization. They may face real or imagined bias based on their heritage, appearance, religious practices or accent (Aleksynska and Algan 2010). As mediators between a private, household culture derived from one national milieu and the public culture of another, they see the opportunities the host country may offer as well as the barriers that frequently prevent access to them.

They may experience what Georg Lukacs (1917) calls transcendental homelessness. This is the term Lukacs uses to describe the novel in a secular and migratory age. He juxtaposes the experience of transcendental homelessness to the profound at-homeness that characters manifest in Greek tragedy. Each character in classical tragedy, he says, "is related at his deepest roots to every other figure; all understand one another because all speak the same language, all trust one another, be it as mortal enemies, for all are striving in the same way towards the same center" (44). This network of mutual trust and understanding that persists even in the midst of conflict exemplifies a stable framework for developing an identity that is at home in a culture. In contrast, the modern, transcendentally homeless figure discovers an "essence" and purpose for life only through a philosophical quest for something that means more than life. When no unified framework is given through which one can make decisions about living a purposeful life, individuals may live contentedly as philosophical travelers, moving from one set of beliefs and norms to another as the situation dictates. Many contemporary Europeans are at home in their transcendental homelessness. Their lives appear secure, appear enough. But individuals raised in migrant families, who live with a simultaneous awareness of contradictory ways of being at home in the world, may find this dissatisfying and seek a more stable structure for meaning-making. Imagining that their parents or grandparents had a chance to be at home in a culture in the way Lukacs describes, imagining that residents of their host-country who are part of the ethnic majority also live culturally "at home," second-generation migrants may experience contemporary transcendental homelessness as a tragic loss.

Constructing a Homeland

Using theological language, IS and Al-Qaeda promote a view of identity that transfers feelings of loyalty to a land to the idea of an eternal kingdom of blessed martyrs. The structure of conflicts involved in mobilizing people's loyalty to this eternal kingdom and transnational community is not so different from the structure operative in a regionally based minority whose land is threatened. In the case of regionally based ethnic minorities, radical communities that arise based on a threat to minority land frame the violence they endorse as defensive. These radical communities continue to exist after the threat to their area has ceased, but they lose power as the emotional energy derived from an imminent threat dies away (Waldmann, et al. 2009, 52). This mirrors closely the four-step pattern that counter-terror scholar Marc Sageman has identified as repeatedly manifesting itself in the radicalization of Islamic terrorists. Sageman writes that terror recruits: 1) feel moral outrage at a perceived threat, 2) interpret this threat as part of an us/them battle, 3) find energy for action through some personal, emotional connection to the conflict, and then 4) mobilize through connections with a terrorist network (Sageman 2008, 3–4). In the process of recruitment, future terrorists begin to feel that their home is in a transnational radical community of Salafi Muslims and that their community of fellow Muslims is threatened by "crusader" nations. The language of crusades reinforces the geo-political structure of this perceived conflict, and the language of family reinforces, across differences of national culture, the existence of a community under threat. In place of loyalty to a local community, they promote loyalty to a transnational "brotherhood" of radical Islam. The terms "brotherhood" and "sisterhood" fill IS and Al-Qaeda propaganda. In a videotaped speech, the leader of the London Underground bombers, Sidique Khan (2015), reported that he was "directly responsible for protecting and avenging [his] Muslim brothers and sisters."

Some researchers interested in second-generation migratory identity and terrorism have assumed that "it would make no sense" for these residents "to launch a frontal attack against state and societal constructions producing" the "prosperity" that they and their parents frequently enjoy (Waldmann, et al. 2009, 63) unless a "conflict with the political power holders of the country of origin also spills over to the host country" (63). Logical though this presumption is, it is a logic based on national identity as a central category of one´s self-conception and sense of purpose. Violent Islamic extremism rejects nationality as an identity category compatible with the practice of Islam, and in doing so it draws on a time-tested practice. As David Malet (2010) points out in his historical overview of foreign fighters, "In conflicts from the Spanish Civil War to the Afghanistan War, insurgencies consistently recruited foreigners by framing the local war as one that threatened a shared transnational identity group and necessitated a defensive mobilization" (97), and the same logic has been used by jihadi terrorist groups in their recruiting. A document produced by the now-banned UK group Al Ghurabaa, or "the strangers," exemplifies this. Identity, they say:

> composes the mentality of the person, composes of the emotions and the feelings of the person and it is related to his physical [...] character and behavior [...] Furthermore, the identity of the individual is different from the identity of the society, because it could be that you have an Islamic identity and yet you are living between the man-made identities of the Kufr society. (cited in Huband 2010, 129)

The document eventually begins to invoke the language of nationhood, but this language is detached from politically existent nations. "We are a nation that has its own Islamic belief, its own Islamic concepts, culture, behavior, history, its own identity. So the fact that they are living in Europe, in UK, France or Italy etc. that does not mean that they have a British identity or French identity" (cited in Huband 2010, 129, 131). Here, the conglomeration of concepts associated with nationhood—culture, beliefs, history—is derived from European nationalism, but projected onto an abstract ideal of Islamic nationhood. This was written nine years before the declaration of the IS caliphate, so the nation to which this author refers has no geographical referent, but identity is still configured in relation to nationality. As Reem Ahmed and Daniela Pisoiu have recognized "jihadi subculture is driven by the need to resist [...] Western mainstream norms and values" (2017, 161). For a subculture that takes a transnational "umma" as its ideological base, nationalism itself is another unwelcome national norm. Indeed, IS calls nationalism an apostasy (*Rumiyah* 5, 4), but the concept of the nation as a cultural homeland continues to haunt the discourse of identity in radical Islam.

This can clearly be seen in the Al-Qaeda and IS recruiting magazines. In 2010, Al-Qaeda began the web-publication of a color magazine called *Inspire*, designed to give aspiring terrorists in Europe and North America the practical knowledge and personal motivation they need to commit spectacular violence. Although initially mocked—*Wired* magazine called it "a lifestyle rag for conspiracy-minded *takfiri*" (Ackerman 2010) — *Inspire* has subsequently received more serious attention from counter-terror researchers. The Tsarnaev brothers who carried out the Boston Marathon bombings in 2013 learned to make their homemade weapons by reading the magazine. Peter Neumann, Director of the International Center for the Study of Radicalization, commented at the time of their arrest that he was not surprised; *Inspire* had been on the hard drives of terrorists in "almost all the home-grown cases [...] over the past three years in Britain and in America" (Romdhani 2013). Between 2014 and 2017, IS produced 28 issues of a similar magazine. The magazine contains more original material than *Inspire* and features more variety of materials, including extended theological and political arguments with novel foci as well as practical information about how to carry out attacks at various levels of severity. For its first two years, the magazine was called *Dabiq*, after a town in Northern Syria associated with the hopes for a universal Islamic caliphate. However, in September of 2016, the title was changed from *Dabiq*, to *Rumiyah*, or Rome. The immediate cause of the name change seems to be the imminent loss of IS control over the city (it fell to the Free Syrian Army in October 2016), but the change also signals the magazine's increasing international focus.

These magazines exhort young Muslims to become jihadis either by migrating to IS controlled areas or by embracing the battle for a new, transnational "umma" where they are. They use concepts that Muslims are, or feel like they should be, familiar with to promote loyalty to a Salafi jihad abstracted from any particular geopolitical situation. I will just mention three concepts to illustrate this practice. The first is jihad itself. The word means "struggle." The concept of jihad can be divided into an internal practice of struggle against impurities, and an external practice of denouncing or committing violence against threats to Islam. IS has defined jihad as a defensive war in which the "crusader nations" have attacked Islam in the Middle East and in individual acts of discrimination all over the world. Individuals who belong to the voting population of these nations are held responsible for the acts of their elected governments and thereby become legitimate targets of violence. The language of the nation-state pervades IS's pronouncements about jihad, with jihadis calling themselves "soldiers" and individual attacks by knife or truck defined as part of a "war."

A second concept that has been manipulated to support the goals of a transnational jihadi "community" is the concept of hegira. The hegira, or migration on behalf of Islam, is commended in the Qur'an and associated with Mohammed's transition from a religious to a religious *and* political leader as he moved from Mecca to Medina. The Qur'an states "if anyone leaves home toward God and his Messenger and is then overtaken by death, his reward from God is sure. God is most forgiving and most merciful" ("An-Nisa" Surah 4: 100). Whereas this verse has sometimes been viewed as consolation for Muslims persecuted in areas where they are minorities, ISIS has embellished the concept to make it primarily a call to battle. In *Rumiyah*, hegira is presented as an abiding obligation to wage war: "Yes, hijrah will not cease as long as the enemy—the kuffar and the murtaddin (one who abandons Islam)—are fought, whether that means the fight is in Iraq or Sham, or whether the fight is somewhere else. For there will be an armed group of this ummah fighting for the cause of Allah until the Messiah descends to lead them in the last of the epic battles" (4, 2).

A final concept worth mentioning is *jahili*. *Jahiliyyah*, or "ignorance," refers to the tribal practices Mohamed asked his followers to overcome. ISIS used the concept to define an "unholy" loyalty to a nation, tribe, ethnicity or theological school (*Rumiyah* 5, 11). Although the ISIS position on these concepts has become more codified since the creation of their magazine, the use of similar ideas to build up a transnational community committed to violence has been around at least since the 90s, when Osama bin Laden issued his "Declaration of War" against the United States. The same commitment to a transnational jihad via a transnational construction of Muslim identity can be seen in several of the terror events that have occurred in Europe since 9/11.

The relevance for my inquiry today into the concepts of *jihad*, *hegira* and *jahili* and the European terrorists' embrace of them is that they are part of an ongoing development of a transnational framework for identity construction, one that uses ways of homemaking and meaning-making that Europe's population of first- and second-generation Muslim immigrants is likely to be sensitive to. On the one hand, as Benedict Anderson has argued, the ideological building blocks of nationalistic loyalty are "capable of being transplanted, with varying degrees of self-consciousness, to a great variety of social terrains" (4). Growing up in societies where national identity serves as a collection of behaviors and perspectives to define oneself within or against, second-generation immigrants know what their host country is not giving them in terms of their identity. On the other hand, even if their relationship to Islam is limited to a kind of historical-cultural inheritance, they are aware of it as a means through which people are able to construct meaningful identities. Mobilizing the ideological machinery normally at work in nationalism for a "community" that does not require geo-spatial stability, contemporary jihadi networks convince recruits that they can provide a home. This home, in contrast to the homeland their families have left and the home they have been raised in, is one that they can choose. It is one that appears to give them the freedom to choose their identity.

The international maintenance of an ideology flexible enough to suit different political environments and identity types is only possible because of the roles local leaders play in recruiting. Petter Nesser identified four roles in his case studies of multiple European terror networks. The spokespeople for these cells tend to be what he calls "entrepreneurs" and their "protégés." Their articulation of why they have turned to violence is logical, albeit based on the very flawed assumption that other human beings can be killed as symbolic representations of their nation or religion. Entrepreneurs "proactively connect with jihadi networks, and they proactively recruit, socialize and train their cadre" (92). They are "charismatic religious and political activists possessing a strong sense of justice" (92). Mohammed Siddique Khan, for example, was the "entrepreneur" of the group who carried out the London bombings. "Sid," as he was called, was a graduate of Leeds Metropolitan University. He worked as a teacher's assistant at a primary school and was a committed social activist, running an Islamic bookshop and working with the Kashmiri Welfare Association. In his videotaped speech explaining his motivation for bombing the underground, he critiques the media and the government of Britain as symbolic of the broadly "power and wealth obsessed" culture and expresses his longing for the "gardens of paradise" where he will form a new community with other "martyrs, messengers, and [...] heroes."

Second in command of these cells are figures Nasser calls protégés. These individuals are typically "intelligent, well-educated, and well-mannered." They "excel in what they do professionally, academically and socially" (93). Shehzed Tanweer was the protégé within the London cell. Like Khan, he was the son of Pakistani immigrants. Although he seems to have been well-integrated into British society for most of his life, around the time he turned 20 he began spending more and more time with Khan and the two became more and more radical. Both felt a conviction that Muslims in Britain and around the world were systematically persecuted, and both justified killing the civilians of "crusader" nations as a defensive action in a global attempt to repulse Western violence. Both traveled to Pakistan for indoctrination and training within their new chosen community, successfully deceiving the family and local community back in Yorkshire, the community they had not chosen.

National Identity and Terrorist Recruiting in *Home Fire*

Kamala Shamsie's *Home Fire* makes visible for anglophone novel readers the ways in which IS operatives manipulate terrorist and foreign fighter recruits with the language of belonging. Farooq, if we use Nesser's schema for analysis, is the entrepreneur, and Parvaiz becomes his protégé. Nesser describes how "Entrepreneurs reach out to what we refer to as misfits and drifters among their social networks, with a view to recruiting them for violent jihad [...] The entrepreneurs socialize, politicize and manipulate the misfits and drifters that commonly involve criminals and socially deprived people, and turn them into tools for terrorist groups" (Nesser et al. 2016, 7). Parvaiz is no criminal, but he and his sisters keep a low social profile because of who their father was. They are socially deprived in that they cannot engage others who do not know their family without fear of Adil Pasha's terrorist associations being discovered. Parvaiz has interiorized his sister's caution and shame:

> He'd grown up knowing that his father was a shameful secret, one that must be kept from the world outside or else posters would appear around Preston Road with the line DO YOU KNOW WHO YOUR NEIGHBORS ARE? and rocks would be thrown through windows and he and his sisters wouldn't receive invitations to the homes of their classmates and no girl would ever say yes to him. (128)

Not only his social life, but also his imagination of a social life is permeated by fear that others will learn the "shameful secret" of his father's terrorist activity. In typologies like Nasser's, "misfits," "criminals and socially-deprived people" belong in the same category because of the roles they go on to play in terrorist networks, but Parvaiz's social deprivation reads like a tragic outcome of his father's story as much as the beginning of the story of his radicalization.

In keeping with Nesser's characterization of entrepreneurs, Farooq is "resourceful, politicized and activist-minded" (7). He greets Parvaiz before Parvaiz sees him, and based on his accent, Parvaiz initially perceives him as "a non-Arab Muslim who is trying too hard" (125). But that initial impression is quickly replaced with an image of "glamor," "flourish" and "simply masculine" confidence (125). Although he is pictured as resourceful in many ways, Farooq's most adept move is identifying Parvaiz's insecurities as a fatherless son. He shames Parvaiz for respecting his sisters' guidance, introducing an unequal gender dichotomy that Parvaiz has never used to interpret himself or his sisters before (132). Farooq is battle-hardened; he is eleven years older than Parvaiz and therefore just the right age to step in as a surrogate big brother without being old enough to oust Adil Pasha from his paternal position. Farooq presents himself as able to help Parvaiz find a purpose-filled future. Painting Adil Pasha as a hero, Farooq offers Parvaiz a source of pride (128). The talented but directionless Parvaiz lets the promise of a new identity through which he could find both direction and a sense of acceptance as his father's son pull him away from his sisters. Rather than describing the torture Ali Pasha endured at

Bagram, Farooq has two of his cousins torture Parvaiz in the apartment the three of them share, shaming him for not trying to find out more about what his father went through (138–141). Farooq leads Parvaiz to see his father's torture, the imperialist history of the West, and the Christian fear of Islam (131) as "part of an us/them battle" in Sageman's words. It takes little persuasion for Parvaiz to feel a "personal, emotional connection to the conflict" (3–4) since he now experiences the shame he has always felt at being Adil Pasha's son as shame in himself.

The final step in radicalizing Parvaiz is to connect him with a terrorist network (Nesser, et al. 2016, 7), a step Farooq takes a few days later by showing Parvaiz an online IS recruiting brochure. Farooq presents the caliphate as an idealized nation-state with a unified, pro-immigrant culture and a successful welfare system: "a place where migrants coming in to join are treated like kings, given more in benefits than the locals to acknowledge all they've given up to reach there. A place where skin color doesn't matter. Where schools and hospitals are free, and rich and poor have the same facilities" (147). Narrating Parvaiz's encounter with ISIS printed propaganda serves at least three functions in the novel. First, it shows the final step in a radicalization process that scholars recognize as common, and yet one that is rarely portrayed in a way that makes the steps comprehensible as choices that a virtuous, intelligent and beloved human being would make. Second, it highlights the role the Islamic State's media production played in presenting the caliphate as an alternative homeland recruits could choose to belong to. Finally, it hints at the gap between any nation's projection of itself and the lived experience of growing up in that nation as a first-, second-, or even third-generation immigrant. Shamsie portrays Isma and Aneeka as both having succeeded in the competitive UK educational system. Karamat Lone, as already mentioned, becomes home secretary. If Home Secretary Lone, Isma and Aneeka showed up in statistics, they would contribute to a picture that "skin color doesn't matter" in London either, but their success requires careful everyday navigation of bias.

In the novel's first scene, Isma is being interrogated at Heathrow Airport, trying to fly to Massachusetts where she will begin her PhD in sociology.

> "Do you consider yourself British?" the man asked.
> "I am British."
> "But do you consider yourself British?"
> "I've lived here all my life." She meant there was no other country of which she could feel herself a part, but the words came out sounding evasive (5).

The question of what it means to be British, or how someone from a Pakistani family can perform being British enough, recurs in all five main characters' narratives. The novel emphasizes the gap between Isma's performance of belonging and experience of belonging by pointing out the difference between what she means and what she imagines the interviewer will have heard. The following paragraph recounts her practicing with Aneeka beforehand for such an interrogation. The sisters had anticipated questions about the Queen, about suicide bombings, about *The Great British Bake-Off*, and Shia/Sunni violence (5–6). The list reveals the concoction of mundane knowledge and political perspective that Aneeka and Isma think equals performing Britishness, and the Heathrow interrogator's pursuit of many of the questions they practiced beforehand implies that they are right. They know how to prove their Britishness when required to do so, but experience being British as a default category ("no other country of which she could feel herself a part") more than a generative part of their identity.

From the very first scene, the novel suggests that the concept of national identity always obscures a gap between performing and living a particular way of being. These two elements of national identity are triangulated with legal citizenship, the element that secures rights-bearing status for an individual. Throughout the novel, passports symbolize characters' rights. Isma's passport is held during her interrogation in Heathrow, and Aneeka's passport is casually taken away when she tries to fly to Istanbul to meet Parvaiz and help him approach the consulate (188). Parvaiz is deprived of his passport twice, first by IS officials when he arrives in Raqqa and second through a law introduced by Karamat Lone, revoking the citizenship of dual-nationals or British citizens who also have foreign national identity cards when they are perceived to act against UK interests. The parallel portrayal of all three siblings having their passports taken away highlights the contingency of citizenship and the rights-bearing status that comes with it or should come with it.

While recognizing that performativity of social norms and legal citizenship confer nationality on individuals through external and sometimes insubstantial processes, the novel ultimately suggests that national culture does shape us in ways we can neither perceive nor prevent. An analepsis later in the "Isma" section of the novel contrasts Isma's performance of Britishness in Heathrow with a much less guarded perspective on second-generation immigrants' Britishness. In a sociology course at university, her professor (and future PhD supervisor), sees her roll her eyes during a lecture on the way control orders within the UK Prevention of Terrorism Act of 2005 pose an unprecedented threat to civil liberties. Professor Shah calls on her. Isma points out that the civil liberties revoked in those acts might technically belong to British citizens, but that the 7/7 terrorists were "rhetorically being made un-British." Even though three of the four had been born in England, the media referred to them as "British of Pakistani descent" or "British Muslim" (40). The scene foreshadows Parvaiz being rhetorically and legally made un-British, but it also shows Isma revealing her defensive, complicated, publicly threatened Britishness almost against her will; she gets caught rolling her eyes.

In a cruel inversion of Isma's test of Britishness, Parvaiz must perform in a way that proves his loyalty to ISIS, and here Shamsie develops further the idea that upbringing, including our experience of belonging or not belonging to externally determined national categories, marks us in ways we cannot control. At the moments the caliphate makes its most terrible demands on Parvaiz, Shamsie portrays the performance of "Mohammed bin Bagram," the ISIS operative Parvaiz has supposedly become, as insubstantial compared to the complexity of the character we have come to know. She hints at the body's capacity to rebel against decisions that do not fit with behavior sedimented into hands and face through years of other actions — how we look at others, hold their gaze, hear the modification in their voice. When asked to record the soundscape of a beheading, Parvaiz "bent over, stomach emptying" (171). Parvaiz hears his grandmother's prayer out of the victim's mouth; he dares to look the man in the eyes (172). He shakes too much to hold the microphone and is sent to wait in an SUV (172-3). In contrast, when he sends Aneeka the text to say he is approaching the consulate alone, he "pressed send, his hands steady" (181). In addition to highlighting ways the body binds us to our past selves, Shamsie emphasizes the ways home reaches for us through accents, cooking smells, manners of greeting. In another scene set in the caliphate, when Parvaiz hears a woman calling for help, trapped in rubble after a Syrian airstrike, it is her London accent that undoes him and prompts him to call Aneeka (178-9). That call begins his attempt to escape IS (178-9).

Home Fire suggests that "failed integration" theories need to incorporate more complex understandings of identity. In volunteering for the local library, holding a job, finishing school, commemorating the jubilee with his "aunty" (183), Parvaiz would have appeared as successfully integrated in most statistical measures. However, his and his sisters' lived experience of Britishness was of something they always had to prove, something always sullied by the presence of Pakistaniness and their father's blood within them. The last thing Parvaiz sees is the British Consulate in Istanbul with "the brick wall with black spikes rising from it that allowed only a partial glimpse of the façade" but with "the red, white, and blue flag that fluttered from the roof, cheerful in all its colors" unobstructed (183). He is shot by Farooq trying to reach that façade.

Like Polynices in Sophocles´s *Antigone*, Parvaiz is killed while officially an enemy of the state although in Shamsie's retelling, readers know that he continued to see himself as British and was seeking the legal protection extended to UK citizens abroad at the moment of his death. The final sections of *Home Fire* develop a Sophoclean irony between the public treatment of Parvaiz's death as a terrorist and readers' perception of him as a beloved brother and self-identified Brit trying to come home. Although most of the novel's chapters are focalized through one of the siblings or Karamat Lone, some, especially in the "Aneeka" section, appear as news releases, closed caption dialogue from televised news or Twitter feeds. It is in one such chapter that readers learn Lone has revoked the citizenship of foreign fighters with dual nationality (192-3) and that based on this rule he will not allow Parvaiz's body to be repatriated to England. In successive British news feeds, we see Parvaiz labeled a terrorist (210), see him dubbed "Pervy Pasha" (194) and see Aneeka become "Knickers" Pasha (214). In Pakistani news, Parvais is portrayed as "a greater enemy of Islam than even America or Israel, and so he should never be described as a 'jihadi'" (232). Aneeka is "a sinner, a fornicator, and should be flogged" (232). Only Aneeka, the Antigone figure, sees Parvaiz as a complex individual who deserves to be mourned. In contrast to Antigone, she fights not primarily for an honorable burial (she sits with the corpse above ground in a park in Karachi), but for recognition of his Britishness.

By making Britishness so central, Shamsie hints at the modern reliance of basic human rights on having the right nationality and having that nationality recognized. She also shows the extent to which legal national belonging lies outside of individual control, dependent on accidents of birth. More than that, however, the novel emphasizes the way in which nationality is allowed to conceal humanity. The novel condemns frameworks that drive people like Pervaiz to seek belonging according to the us/them categorization proffered by both Karamat Lone and Farooq and portrays the Islamic State's promise to offer its recruits a new identity as hopeless and tragic. Terry Lone, Karamat's wife, gets the last extended speech in the book. She does not talk about Britain, Pakistan or the caliphate. She does not talk about citizenship or passports. She presents Aneeka—the sinner, "Knickers"—to Karamat and to readers as a "sad child," an "orphaned student, who wants for her brother what she never had for her father: a grave beside which she can sit and weep for the awful pitiable mess of her family life" (267).

Conclusion

Cyberspace creates sites of belonging that do not depend on passports or extradition status. Traits like accent and skin color, which may lead to exclusion in face-to-face encounters, often remain invisible in online community-building. It remains to be seen how the "virtual caliphate" will develop. Although English-language media releases from IS have become irregular, they continue. Following the collapse of the caliphate, foreign fighters from 80 nations remain in limbo, "tens of thousands of captured ISIS members whom no nation wants to repatriate," and as many more wives and children, a crisis, not of transcendental, but actual homelessness (Wright 2019). Now that IS has lost physical territory, the role online community-building plays in the organization will only become more essential. In April 2019, when Abu Bakr al-Baghdadi released his final video message, he stressed the organization's global ambitions over local, territorial ones, proclaiming that "The soldiers of the Caliphate's guerrilla units spread in various countries are capable, God permitting, of repeating the lesson of the 'conquest of Mosul' once more, and planting that blessed experience in any land" (cited in Carafella, Wallace and Zhou 2019, 45). Online recruiting and coordination remain central to realizing these ambitions (Carafella, Wallace and Zhou 2019, 44). Although it is not clear whether the distribution of online information in English and French will continue under IS control, there is no doubt that what Harleen Gambhir (2016) has called "the virtual caliphate" will continue.

Shamsie herself was born in Pakistan like Karamat Lone, lived in Amherst like Isma, now resides in London where much of the action unfolds, and is a dual citizen of the UK and Pakistan, a trait she shares with four of the novel's five focalizers. Consequently, "the novel is particularly susceptible to anthropologically inflected readings that seek the 'truth' about British Muslims and radicalization" (Ahmed 2020). This is a problematic expectation for a work of art since it risks obscuring the novel's form and artistry. However, Shamsie's novel does do important work in representing IS's recruiting techniques for a wider audience, and she does not back away from that. She said in a 2017 interview that "there's often not enough awareness of the really significant difference between ISIS and other terrorist groups: ISIS really wanted a state. They didn't just want fighters; they wanted doctors, engineers. And they were very much trading on people's sense of isolation and unbelonging [...] Looking at the propaganda, they were appealing to lost boys" (Felsenthal 2017). It is worth noting that Shamsie's portrayal of IS recruiting is accurate, but what is more interesting is that she sustains readers' investment in Parvaiz's character in spite of his recruitment without departing from a realistic recruitment pattern. The empathy readers experience for Parvaiz is thereby made relevant to and transferrable to some of the foreign fighters now awaiting adjudication. Shamsie does not back away from the cruelty of the Islamic State, but in melding the story of an IS recruit with *Antigone*, she shifts the question of justice away from what traitors like Polynices have done to ask how the Creons and Antigones of the world will respond.

Bibliography

Ackerman, Spencer. 2010. "Watch Out, Condé Nast: Al-Qaida Launches English-Language Lifestyle Mag." *Wired*. July 1, 2010. https://www.wired.com/2010/07/al-Qaeda-goes-conde-nast-with-new-lifestyle-mag-in-english/.

Ahmed, Rehana. 2020. "Towards an Ethics of Reading Muslims: Encountering Difference in Kamila Shamsie's *Home Fire*." *Textual Practice* 35 (7): 1145–61. doi:10.1080/0950236X.2020.1731582.

Ahmed, Reem, and Daniela Pisoiu. 2017. "Beyond Borders: The Transnational Identity of the Jihadi Subculture in Europe." In *Border Politics: Defining Spaces of Governance and Forms of Transgressions*, edited by Cengiz Günay and Nina Witjes, 161–173. Cham: Springer.

Aleksynska, Mariya, and Yann Algan. 2010. "Assimilation and Integration of Immigrants in Europe." IZA Discussion Paper No. 5185. September 27, 2010. https://ssrn.com/abstract=1682706.

Bakker, Edwin. 2010. "Islamism, Radicalisation and Jihadism in the Netherlands: Main Developments and Countermeasures." In *Understanding Violent Radicalisation: Terrorist and Jihadist Movements in Europe*, edited by Magnus Ranstorp, 168–190. New York: Routledge.

Barrett, Richard. 2017. "Beyond the Caliphate: Foreign Fighters and the Threat of Returnees." *The Soufan Center*. October 24, 2017. https://thesoufancenter.org/research/beyond-caliphate/.

Benmelech, Efraim, and Esteban F. Klor. 2020. "What Explains the Flow of Foreign Fighters to ISIS?" *Terrorism and Political Violence* 32 (7): 1458–1481.

Carafella, Jennifer, Brandon Wallace, and Jason Zhou. 2019. *ISIS's Second Comeback: Assessing the Next ISIS Insurgency*. Washington: Institute for the Study of War.

Carter, Paul. 1992. *Living in a New Country: History, Traveling and Language*. London: Faber & Faber.

Cook, Joana, and Gina Vale. 2018. "From Daesh to 'Diaspora': Tracing the Women and Minors of Islamic State." *International Center for the Study of Radicalisation*. Report 2018. https://icsr.info/wp-content/uploads/2018/07/Women-in-ISIS-report_20180719_web.pdf.

Dabiq. Issues 1–15. Al Hayat Media Center. https://clarionproject.org/isis-issues-dabiq-magazine-13-gitmo-trump-not-mentioned/.

Davis, Kyle F., Paolo D'Odorico, Francesco Laio, and Luca Ridolfi. 2013. "Global Spatio-Temporal Patterns in Human Migration: A Complex Network Perspective." *PLoS ONE* 8 (1): 1–8.

Felsenthal, Julie. 2017. "Kamila Shamsie's Brilliant Home Fire Is a Greek Tragedy for the Age of ISIS." *Vogue*. August 16, 2017. https://www.vogue.com/article/kamila-shamsie-home-fire#:~:text=I%20think%20there's%20often%20not,sense%20of%20isolation%20and%20unbelonging.

Gambhir, Harleen. 2016. *The Virtual Caliphate: ISIS's Information Warfare*. Washington: Institute for the Study of War.

Gergen, Kenneth J. 1997. *Realities and Relationships: Soundings in Social Constructions*. Cambridge, MA: Harvard UP.

Huband, Mark. 2010. "Radicalisation and Recruitment in Europe: the UK Case." In *Understanding Violent Radicalisation: Terrorist and Jihadist Movements in Europe*, edited by Magnus Ranstorp, 117–143. New York: Routledge.

Khan, Mohammed Sidique. 2015. "Our Words Are Dead until We Give Them Life with Our Blood." *MEMRI*. September 1, 2005. http://www.memritv.org/clip/en/835.htm.

Kruegar, Alan B. 2018. *What Makes a Terrorist? Economics and the Roots of Terrorism*. Princeton, NJ: Princeton UP.

Lukacs, Georg. 1917. *The Theory of the Novel: A Historico-philosophical Essay on the Forms of Great Epic Literature*. Translated by Anna Bostok. Cambridge, MA: MIT Press.

Malet, David. 2010. "Why Foreign Fighters? Historical Perspectives and Solutions" *Orbis* 54 (1): 97–114.

McWilliams, Spencer A. 2018. "Who Do You Think You Are? Evolving Ethical Meaning Making." *Journal of Constructivist Psychology* 31 (4): 376-387.

Miscevic, Nenad. 2001. *Nationalism and Beyond: Introducing Moral Debate about Values*. Budapest: Central European UP.

Nesser, Petter, Anne Stenersen, and Emilie Oftedal. 2016. "Jihadi Terrorism in Europe." *Perspectives on Terrorism* 10 (6): 3-24.

Pokalova, Elena. 2019. "Driving Factors behind Foreign Fighters in Syria and Iraq." *Studies in Conflict & Terrorism* 42 (9): 798-818.

Precht, Tomas. 2007. *Home Grown Terrorism and Islamist Radicalization in Europe: From Conversion to Terrorism*. Copenhagen: Danish Ministry of Defense.

Haleem, M.A.S. Abdel, trans. *The Qu'ran*. Oxford: Oxford UP, 2008.

Rabasa, Angel, and Benard, Cheryl. 2014. *Eurojihad*. Cambridge: Cambridge UP.

Reinares, Fernando, and Carola Garcia-Calvo. 2018. *Moroccans and the Second Generation among Jihadists in Spain*. Madrid: Elcano Royal Institute.

Romdhani, Oussama. 2013. "Lone Wolves' Strike in London and Paris." *Al-Arabiya in English*, May 26, 2013. https://english.alarabiya.net/views/news/world/2013/05/26/-Lone-Wolves-strike-in-London-and-Paris-.

Rumiyah. Issues 1-13. Al Hayat Media Center. https://clarionproject.org/latest-issue-isis-rumiyah-magazine-released/.

Sageman, Marc. 2008. *Leaderless Jihad: Terror Networks in the Twenty-First Century*. Philadelphia, PA: U of Pennsylvania P.

Schmid, Alex P. 2016. *Links between Terrorism and Migration: An Exploration*. The Hague: International Centre for Counter-Terrorism.

Shamsie, Kamila. 2017. *Home Fire*. New York: Riverhead.

Summerfield, Derek. 2003. "Fighting 'Terrorism' with Torture." *BMJ (Clinical Research Ed.)* 326 (7393): 773-4.

UN Population Fund. 2015. "Migration." Last modified December 23, 2015. https://www.unfpa.org/migration#:~:text=In%202015%2C%20244%20million%20people,better%20economic%20and%20social%20opportunities.

Venhaus, John M. 2010. *Looking for a Fight: Why Youth Join al-Qaeda and How to Prevent It*. Carlisle, PA: US Army War College.

Waldmann, Peter, Matenia Sirseloudi, and Stefan Malthaner. 2009. "Where Does the Radicalization Process Lead? Radical Community, Radical Networks and Radical Subcultures." In *Understanding Violent Radicalisation: Terrorist and Jihadist Movements in Europe*, edited by Magnus Ranstorp, 50–67. London: Routledge.

Wright, Robin. 2019. "The Dangerous Dregs of ISIS." *The New Yorker*, April 16, 2019. https://www.newyorker.com/news/dispatch/the-dangerous-dregs-of-isis.

Zahavi, Dan, and Søren Overgaard. 2020. "Intersubjectivity." Vol. 6 of *International Encyclopedia of Ethics*, edited by Hugh LaFollette. Oxford: Wiley.

Terrorism as Communication in Arthur Koestler's *Thieves in the Night*

Zénó Vernyik and Sándor Klapcsik

Introduction: Koestler's Novel on the Terrorist's Journey

This chapter intends to reinterpret the literary critical consensus on the representation of terrorist acts committed by the early Zionist Jewish immigrants of the 1930s in Arthur Koestler's *Thieves in the Night* (1946). Based on our close reading of the novel and 21st-century theoretical discussions on terrorism, and especially observations in John Horgan's *The Psychology of Terrorism* (2005), an alternative explanation to violence committed by immigrants is offered. This interpretation emphasizes that terrorism is rarely triggered by a single traumatic event. On the contrary, it is usually caused by progressive "communal identification" (88) with (other) victims of oppression and should be interpreted as a "form of communication" (2) between minorities and other members of the society. Furthermore, with the novel focusing especially on the moral, social and psychological development of Joseph, its protagonist-focalizer, who embraces terrorism on his journey of becoming a fully integrated member of Palestinian society, the controversial nature of terrorism notwithstanding, it is also argued that Koestler's novel can be categorized as a *Bildungsroman*.

Although *Thieves in the Night* for decades belonged amongst Koestler's most casually dismissed novels,[1] and, in English, for more than 35 years, also amongst his least frequently discussed ones, it has recently seen a strong resurgence of academic interest.[2]

---

[1] Such assessments occurred already at the novel's publication (cf. e.g. Fitzsimons 1947, 110; Hillbrook 1946, 512) and continued throughout its reception (Pearson 1978, 32, 149; Cesarani 1998, 246–47; Márton 2006, 206; Scammell 2009, 282).

[2] The last monograph published in English offering a complex analysis of the novel before the publication of *Arthur Koestler's Fiction and the Genre of the Novel:*

Back in the 1970s and 1980s Mark Levene certainly belonged to a minority with his opinion that "time has conspired with narrative skill to give Koestler's novel a continuing value" (Levene 1984, 97), as the majority of commentators rather sided with Sidney A. Pearson, Jr, who decried the book as his "least successful novel from any perspective" (Pearson 1978, 12). *Thieves in the Night* has since been arguably established as one of Koestler's major works, with continuing relevance (Stähler 2015, 243; Vernyik 2016b, 25; Calder 2021, 180, 195; Inbari 2021, 216–17).

Yet, even given this newly found interest, the novel's motif of the making of a terrorist has most typically been merely acknowledged (Gordon 1994, 15; Holt 2021, 7–8; Stähler 2015, 239; 2017, 202–3; 2018, 31; Vernyik 2016a, 74; 2016b, 27; Weßel 2014, 48), at times tiptoed around or overlooked (Salt 2021; Vernyik 2019), and only rarely discussed in considerable detail (Calder 2021, 189–97; Gordon 1991, 161–63; Inbari 2021, 209–11).[3] Nevertheless, it is arguably the central motif and driving force of the story, as identified by multiple commentators (cf. e.g. Holme 1946, 3; MacDonagh 1946, 6; Calder 1968, 200; Levene 1984, 96, 98; Gordon 1991, 161; Scammell 2009, 279), given that this conversion from pacifist to terrorist concerns the novel's focalizer-protagonist, Joseph. It is thus, at the very least, puzzling that this intriguing metamorphosis has not attracted more attention.

Accordingly, this chapter contests the rather widespread view that Joseph's embracing of terrorism is a sudden decision, an emotional reaction to a single tragic event (cf. e.g. Chamberlain 1946, 1163; Holme 1946, 3; J. M. D. P. 1946, 3; Mortimer 1946, 134; Conner 1947, 59; Fremantle 1947, 494; Glazer 1947, 56; Gordon 1994, 15; Buckard 2004, 228; Laval 2005, 388, 392; Scammell 2009, 280; Saun-

---

Rubashov and Beyond (Vernyik 2021) appeared in 1984 (Levene 1984). This recent volume offers two chapters on *Thieves in the Night* (Calder 2021; Inbari 2021). The situation with academic articles is even worse, with the first ones devoted solely, or at least primarily, to the novel in English appearing only in the second half of the 2010s (Stähler 2017; 2018; Vernyik 2016a; 2016b; 2019) and the early 2020s (Holt 2021; Salt 2021).

3   Here, we have only listed recent sources. Earlier texts with discussions of this motif are cited below when relevant.

ders 2017, 82). In our view, Koestler's novel presents Joseph's transformation as a slow, gradual, and continuous process, in which Dina's murder, the most frequently mentioned reason for his *volte-face* alleged by the critical consensus, is just one of many factors. In fact, as it is shown below, while Joseph's transformation certainly has a personal, emotional component, which includes not only his reaction to the fate of Dina, but also to that of the refugee Wilhelm Brodetsky, its primary cause is Johan Galtung's (1969) concept of structural violence exerted by the British administration against both the Jewish settlers in Palestine and against the refugees arriving in massive numbers from Europe. In addition, we further assert that since Joseph's transformation is effectively *the story* of the novel, *Thieves in the Night* can thus be seen as a *Bildungsroman*.

Beating Around the Bush: Reasons to Avoid Discussing the Terrorist Motif

The first explanation for the meagre and inadequate critical response to the terrorism portrayed in the novel might be found in the historical period and geographical location in which the story is set. Albeit published in 1946, *Thieves in the Night* portrays life on a kibbutz in Mandatory Palestine between 1937 and 1939, through the eyes of Joseph, a member of the English gentry, with a Russian Jewish father, who decides to join the Zionist settlers. This information is of considerable importance, since these three specific years arguably form a crucial turning point both in the project of the area's Jewish resettlement and of the history of Mandatory Palestine in general.

The novel's wider historical context, the 1930s, could probably best be characterized, both in terms of immigration and infrastructural projects, as a Zionist success story: "immigration [...] increase[d], land was being purchased and cultivated and industrial developments continued apace. Oil refinery in Haifa, potash extraction at the Dead Sea, cement manufacture and tobacco and cigarette production continued to grow while agricultural exports rose" (Turnberg 2021, 158). In fact, in terms of immigration, this decade, with the exception of 1939 and 1940, seems an even more marked success: "some 250,000 Jews arrived between 1929 and 1939; that is, about twice as many as in the previous ten years" (159).

Yet, it is important to emphasize that this hardly means a reversal of the demographic composition of Palestine. Jewish inhabitants remain a minority in the period, albeit one with an increasing weight:

> By 1938 there were over 400,000 Jews, 990,000 Muslim Arabs and 110,000 Christian Arabs living there. Although the proportion of Jews had risen remarkably from the 58,000 of 1919, the total number of Arab had risen to a greater extent, a 461,000 increase against 342,000 for the Jews. But while 90 per cent of the rise in numbers of Jews was due to immigration and only 10 per cent due to natural increases from child-birth, the reverse was true of the Arabs; 90 per cent of their increase followed natural causes, including a reduced death rate. (191)

These major demographic changes, understandably, do not pass without conflicts. In fact, attacks, protests, terrorism, vandalism and many other forms of unrest and violence are regular in the 1930s. Yet, their severity and frequency are markedly lower in most of the decade than in the specific period chosen by Koestler: the years 1937–39. In this brief interval, events change for the worse for the settlers, first slowly, and then in 1939 suddenly and radically:

> In 1937, the Royal [Peel] Commission [...] admitted that the British could not concede both the Arab claim to self-government *and* secure the establishment of the Jewish National Home. At that point (1937), Britain's attempt to resolve the contradiction between its obligations to the Arabs and the Jews was seen as involving a choice between two courses of action: either terminating the Mandate and establishing a Jewish state in part of Palestine (while annexing the Arab part to Trans-Jordan), or putting a "political high limit" on the volume of Jewish immigration. (Halamish 2020, 174; emphasis original)

This admission partially coincides with, and is partially the result of, three significant developments: (1) the successes of Hitler, Mussolini and Franco, and the looming of the Second World War on the horizon (Turnberg 2021, 177–78); (2) challenges to British colonial rule on the Indian subcontinent (178); and (3) the change of Arab tactics within Palestine itself, and especially the 1936–39 Revolt (Kochavi 1998, 146).

Even more disappointingly for the settlers, in the end, the British ultimately decide to reject, or at least indefinitely postpone, the idea of partition:

> In July 1937, [the British government] published a White Paper setting the number of Jewish immigrants at 1,000 a month, pending an adoption of an alternative solution to the conflict. In its White Paper of May 1939, on the eve of World War Two, Britain officially abandoned the first option raised by the Peel Commission — partition — and announced its intention to establish within ten years an independent Palestine State, in which Arabs and Jews would share government in a way that safeguarded the essential interests of each community. (Halamish 2020, 174–75)

What is more, the White Paper stipulates a limit to immigration that is both much humbler than customary during most of the 1930s, and, just as crucially, one that would be guaranteed only for a very limited time:

> Now an arbitrary limit was to be enforced of 10,000 immigrants a year for the following five years plus 25,000 over that period at the discretion of the Jewish Agency, a total of up to 75,000 in five years. Any illegal immigration was to be taken from the total. […] After a period of five years […] the Arabs […] would determine all future Jewish immigration. (Turnberg 2021, 196)

This, of course, is not observed passively by the settlers either. Amongst others, "the Zionists tried to undermine Britain's immigration policy by sending to Palestine tens of thousands of illegal immigrants, as the British called them, from different ports of Europe and by mobilizing American pressure to force London to open the gates of Palestine to the Jewish DPs [=displaced persons]" (Kochavi 1998, 146). As Koestler's novel itself makes it clear, these tactics are far from all the Jewish settlers use. It is in this increasingly explosive period of three years that *Thieves in the Night* is set, and the portrayal of a controversial period rarely if ever leads to an uncontroversial novel.

The second, probably even more crucial, reason for *Thieves in the Night*'s continuing controversy, and scholars' aversion to discussing its main motif of Joseph's conversion to terrorism, might just as well be the fact that our retrospect of more than eighty years certainly has not rendered the project of the Zionist settlement of

Palestine, and the resulting Palestinian-Israeli conflict, any less controversial. Historically speaking:

> What the Arabs most desired was national independence, and they were concerned lest they become a minority under Jewish domination in their own country. They complained that Jewish immigration not only threatened their status as the majority in the country but also harmed them economically. From the very beginning of the Mandate, the Arabs consistently called for the immediate cessation of Jewish immigration. [...] In their eyes, the Jews were not refugees seeking shelter, but settlers, intent on taking possession of their land, with the goal of achieving sovereignty. (Halamish 2020, 173)

The partitioning of the territory, first seriously suggested by the Peel Report in 1937, and subsequently turned into reality roughly a decade later, did little to ease this fundamental opposition in opinion, and arguably may have even worsened it. In the decision's immediate aftermath,

> on 29 November, 1947, the General Assembly of the United Nations voted to divide Palestine into Jewish and Arab states. The Jews enthusiastically approved the plan while the Arabs firmly rejected it. Riots against the United States broke out in several Arab countries while in Palestine armed fighting began between Arabs and Jewish residents. The Arab League threatened to use force in order to block the division of Palestine. (Kochavi 1998, 162)

With such obviously incompatible starting points, let it suffice to establish its continuing relevance and unresolved status as "the most globally diffused and intractable" conflict, one "whose metamorphosing recurrence and growing chain of links to global terrorism has intensified security surveillance and restrictions on civil liberty all over the world" (Ozohu-Suleiman and Ishak 2014, 285). This conflict has been, "[f]or decades[,] the source of explosive debates" and also "a stage for recurring outbreaks of violence and human rights violations on both conflict sides" that has thus continuously "demanded a large material and psychological investment of the societies involved" (Stahel and Cohrs 2015, 1). At present, just as much as back in the late 1930s, when the plot of *Thieves in the Night* takes place, and in 1946, when it was published, the following equally holds:

There are two contrasting ways of representing and interpreting the conflict. The pro-Israeli perspective emphasizes the return to the ancient homeland and the heroic effort as pioneers in harsh conditions and in an inhospitable territory. As such, Zionism is a legitimate expression of Jewish nationalism, especially after the struggle for survival after WWII. The pro-Palestinian perspective sees the Jewish national revival as an example of European colonist expansion into the Middle East, as a foreign intrusion and an attempt to overpower the indigenous population. (Hildebrandt-Wypych 2022)

This very incommensurability and the conflict's unique persistence "has raised the question of whether the Israel-Palestinian conflict is beyond resolution" (Pratiwi, Syarafi, and Nauvarian 2022, 168).

Thirdly, terrorism, in itself, frequently invites strategies of silence, avoidance, or euphemism over those of speech, confrontation, and preciseness. In W. J. T. Mitchell's words: "Terrorists speak the language of the unspeakable. They perform and stage the unimaginable" since "terror […] fuses the divine and the demonic in a single unspeakable and unimaginable compound" (Mitchell 2005, 298). This might be one of the reasons why, discussing the terrorist attacks of 9/11, Elaine Martin stresses:

> In the immediate aftermath of the terrorist attacks, […] [understanding their causes] was not an acceptable thought. Any effort to understand, explain, or investigate the cause of the attacks was perceived as an attempt at justification. Providing a reason for the attacks transformed them into the acts of rational people, and it was preferable to view the perpetrators as madmen operating in an irrational world. (Martin 2007)

One of Mitchell's two suggested meanings of "cloning terror", namely "an image of terrorism as a virulent, destructive life-form that is being 'propagated' […] by the very means that is supposed to destroy it" (Mitchell 2005, 300) is pertinent here. Terrorism is not only, and not even primarily, a battle of arms, but of narratives, of signification:

> The terrorist and the counter-terrorist are engaged in the same essentially aesthetic and literary endeavor; to describe a picture, to craft a narrative of events, and in so doing elevate impression to the status of reality, even truth. The terrorist presents a story of heroism and necessary sacrifice. The counter-terrorist presents a counter-narrative of defiance and vengeance, replacing the image of the martyr with that of inhumanity, even bestiality. The rhetorical struggle is a slippery one, engaged in a linguistic environment, to borrow Derrida's phrase, of "semantic instability." (Ward 2008, 254)

This explains why viewing "the perpetrators as madmen operating in an irrational world" (Martin 2007) is typically preferred over trying to explain and especially rationalize the behavior of terrorists (Ward 2008, 254).

Fictional texts, however, are frequently opposed to this politically preferred isolationism; there is a long and significant literary tradition of literary texts breaching this taboo:

> In any number of authors from Schiller, Kleist, and Dostoevsky through Mary McCarthy, Doris Lessing, and Friedrich Dürrenmatt, to Salman Rushdie, Don DeLillo, and J. M. Coetzee [...] there seems to be a single project: to contextualize terrorists and terrorism temporally, causally, and historically. In its opposition to the officially promulgated "ideological and cultural battle against terrorism" cited by Said, literature and films thus play a revolutionary role seemingly aiding and abetting terrorism by explaining/rationalizing/legitimizing it and by "humanizing" terrorist figures. (Martin 2007)

Thieves in the Night, as illustrated below, arguably fits into this very tradition with its description of the protagonist's conversion to terrorism.

Controversial Then, Controversial Now: The Critical Reception

It is thus logical to surmise that Koestler's novel, taking an unambiguously pro-Israeli stance in the Israeli-Palestinian conflict, which has remained controversial to this day, portraying one of its most heated pre-partition periods, and doing so by the politically contentious artistic strategy of humanizing the terrorist, is likely to have remained controversial. That it *has*, indeed, remained controversial can be clearly illustrated by one of the most recent articles discussing, amongst others, *Thieves in the Night*:

> Kanafani's 1969 novel *'A'id ila Haifa* (*Returning to Haifa*), [...] [a] fictional elaboration of Kanafani's critical writing on the Zionist use of the "weapon of literature" (*silah al-adab*) and the potential for a Palestinian literature of resistance, the novel makes explicit the role of Zionist propaganda fiction in the colonization of Palestine when it directly names Koestler's novel *Thieves in the Night* as the book that leads Kanafani's Iphrat and Miriam Koshen to Haifa. (Holt 2021, 4)

While Elizabeth M. Holt here arguably merely summarizes Ghassan Kanafani's view of Koestler's text, later on in the same article, it is her own authorial voice that claims that "Khalidi's article, like Kanafani's fiction and literary criticism, gave the lie to everything Koestler's long novel, *Thieves in the Night*, stood for—idylls of Zion, the settlers of Ezra's Tower, the desert blooming under the careful watch of the Haganah" (7). It is also Holt, the author of the 2021 article, and not one of the Palestinian writers and editors whose texts provide the opportunity for her critical engagement with Koestler's novel, who apostrophizes *Thieves in the Night* as "a calculated novel, invested in optics, surveillance, and the Zionist cause" (7), adding that "[t]he racism in Koestler's Zionist propaganda fiction that Kanafani had decried, in his 1965 lecture and articles and in *Fi al-adab al-sahyuni*, is here unmistakable (as is the misogyny)" (8). In a similar vein, another article published in 2021, this time by Jeremy Salt, has this much to say:

> While perpetuating the propaganda of a neglected land, Koestler introduces a new element in *Thieves in the Night*, the sexual depravity that resurfaces in *Promise and Fulfilment* and the later novels of Leon Uris. At the subliminal level of author and reader, it might be said that this line of sexual attack and moral invalidation of the native Palestinian population fed off centuries of anti-Muslim Christian polemics in which sexual lust and violence were complementary themes.[...] The technique of denigration is the same as in *Promise and Fulfilment*. Koestler puts repressed sexuality into the minds of his Arab characters so it is they and not the author or one of his Zionist settlers who expose themselves to the reader's disgust. (Salt 2021, 47)

Elsewhere in the same article, still in reference to *Thieves in the Night*, he talks of a "stream of racist abuse" (49), and apostrophizes the establishment of the State of Israel as the "ethnic cleansing of Palestinians from their homeland" (46). Whether or not Holt's and Salt's claims are objective, well-substantiated, or if all their arguments and selection of secondary sources are beyond criticism is beside the point here.[4] What is of relevance, is that these two articles

---

4   We most certainly have no intention here to contest Jeremy Salt's and Elizabeth Holt's claims about the novel's clear political activism, and active support of the Jewish settlers' cause. Nor is Koestler's book without a whole range of issues in terms of its characterization, ranging from the potentially misogynistic to the stereotypical, and controversial opinions are also explicitly voiced by basically

clearly show that Koestler's novel is just as likely to strike a raw nerve in the 2020s, as it did in the 1940s.

Turning now to a discussion of the novel, it was a frequent charge at its publication, and one that has been occasionally recurring ever since, that Joseph's conversion to terrorism is the result of little else than blind revenge, in reaction to the single, violent event of Dina's brutal murder. "Joseph loves peace, he loves the amenities of the Western way of life. But when the Arabs rape and kill the girl Dina, who had already been raped by Nazis in the central [sic] European 'night of the long knives,' he decides that the concept of 'collective guilt' must be applied to the Arabs as a whole," as one contemporary reviewer claims (Chamberlain 1946, 1163). Similarly, another reader stresses: "we are equally unconvinced (and unmoved) by his jump to the terrorists (when the girl he loves is raped and killed by the Arabs); and not knowing what he believes, we don't know what he has to give up to become a terrorist" (Glazer 1947, 56).[5] Strikingly, more than sixty years later, Michael Scammell does

---

all of its characters. This much is already admitted above, and is also voiced by sources both closer in time to its publications and more recent ones (cf. e.g. Calder 1968, 277; 2021, 184–86; Gordon 1991, 163; 2021, 241–43; Inbari 2021, 201–4; Stähler 2017, 200, 203). The book certainly is partisan at the very least and biased at most. At the same time, this still does not make certain specific practices and decisions admissible from a strictly academic point of view. Salt's reference to the "irony that a man who fantasised about the rape of a child should himself be repeatedly accused of sexual violence, including rape" (2021, 46), which serves to undermine the claims and the portrayal of characters in Koestler's texts, is both a textbook case of an *ad hominem* attack, and that of failing to distinguish not only between the biological author and the implied author, but also between the position of the latter and the variety of positions represented by the perspectives of individual characters in the novel. The other article, Elizabeth Holt's, certainly steers far, by a wide margin, of errors of argumentation, yet it nevertheless shares a common blind spot with Salt's paper: neither of these two texts refers to, much less critically tackles, the arguments of Vernyik (2016b), an article that analyzes Koestler's portrayal of Palestinians in detail, and claims that, albeit frequently based in stereotypes, these characters more often than not belie, break free of, or undermine those very stereotypes. This is either striking oversight or potentially a case (or rather two cases) of cherry-picking the sources to be included in the papers' literature review.

5   While Dina was, indeed, arguably raped by her interrogators back in Europe, there is no textual evidence of the Palestinians committing sexual violence against her, albeit this unfounded claim is surprisingly frequent and stubborn in the reception. For more on this, see Vernyik (2016b, 31–32, 37–38). In addition, in should not remain unnoticed that this is the only review of *Thieves in the*

little else but reiterate the same view: "A similar motivational weakness attends Joseph's embrace of terrorism. The rape and murder of Dina are acts with even more powerful sexual overtones, and although Joseph explicitly denies that her death is the cause of his conversion, its placement in the section of the novel called 'Days of Wrath' contradicts that assertion" (Scammell 2009, 282). Far from being the last such interpretation, it is for this alleged brisk turn of events that the novel is criticized by Ranen Omer-Sherman:

> In the third section of the novel, after Dina is raped and murdered, Joseph seeks revenge from an old comrade who has left the kibbutz to establish a militia closely resembling the Stern Gang. Eventually, Joseph also departs to join the Jewish terrorist movement as well, and we are meant to regard his repudiation of the moderate kibbutz as a laudable, even evolutionary act marking the authentic maturation of both a cause and the individual. (Omer-Sherman 2015, 44)

In fact, even Axel Stähler, although much more nuanced, careful and detailed in his treatment of Joseph's conversion to terrorism, discussing other factors as well, ultimately decides to emphasize that Dina's "fate proves crucial to Joseph's radicalization" and talks of the scene's ability to "invest the reader with a sense of emotional involvement, conveying the desire for revenge" (Stähler 2017, 203) rather than the fact that the conversion is a complex and slower process, aspects he otherwise acknowledges in passing (202).

Yet, as some commentators have noticed, *Thieves in the Night* is arguably a complex and multivocal novel, even if its sympathies are clearly on the side of the Zionist settlers. It has been noted that "[i]n

---

Night that we know of that uses the first person plural to make its claims. While some might see this as no more than a mere idiosyncrasy, it could likewise be argued that instead of using the third person singular, which would implicitly draw attention to either the writer or the book, or the first person singular, implicitly signifying that what is communicated is the critic's own assessment, this choice broadens the position of assessment to an interpretive community (possibly of educated readers or critics in general) thereby strengthening its status as a voice of authority. Likewise, this "we" might also imply the inclusion of reader himself or herself, thus arguably lowering the distance (or the possibility of distancing) between the critical position of the reviewer and the reader. Whether it was a conscious decision of the critic, a stylistic quirk of his, or an accident is not of prime importance, since the change may be effective on the reader, whether intended or not.

its diversity of viewpoint and immediacy of visual detail, the novel processes a breadth that is uncharacteristic not only of Koestler's work, but of political fiction in general" (Levene 1984, 98). Koestler, in this novel, "provides a full and intelligently analyzed account of the opinions of all factions of the three parties: the Arabs, the English and the Jews. In the course of the unfolding of the plot, he develops an almost encyclopedic knowledge, expressed in part through the portrayal of the characters, in part through dialogs, and in part through the author-narrator's commentary"[6] (Strelka 2006, 66; my translation). Similarly, a recent account finds the novel hardly black and white and oversimplified in its portrayal:

> The Jewish settlers are determined to make the land productive, the Arabs to co-exist with it as they have always done. [...] particularly through Joseph, the novel's central character, who responds to both the beauty of the land and the imperative to ensure its dynamic future as homeland, both aspects are sympathetically explored. In contrast, the British presence in Palestine is expressed by Koestler as that of a colonialist power with a romanticized perception of Palestine as Holy Land occupied by a colorful tribal people. These tensions are heightened by the metaphorical resonance of Koestler's narrative. (Calder 2021, 177)

These three quotes, covering more than forty years, may serve to illustrate that the opinion that *Thieves in the Night* is not short of complexity has arguably prevailed throughout the decades.

As already mentioned above, the process of Joseph's transformation is gradual. In fact, it is so gradual that his first encounter with the idea of terrorism occurs as early as his first night in Ezra's Tower, the kibbutz in which most of the story unfolds. At this point, only the bare minimum of the infrastructure is ready, and the discussion takes place in a dining-hall which has no electric light just yet (Koestler 1946, 54). Joseph mostly plays the role of an observant by-stander in this discussion, with the topic emerging in a dialog

---

[6] "er eine ebenso vollständige wie klug analysierte Darstellung sämtlicher Meinungen aller Fraktionen der drei Parteien, Araber, Engländer und Juden gibt. Er entwickelt dabei im Verlauf der Entfaltung der Handlung ein geradezu enzyklopädisches Wissen, das teils in der Charakteristik der Figuren, teils in deren Gesprächen, teils in den Kommentaren des auktorialen Erzählers zum Ausdruck gebracht wird."

between Reuben and Simeon (57). At this point, Joseph's significant distance from the topic ensures that his reactions are based primarily on how Dina, the girl he is in love with, reacts, and not on the topic of discussion itself: "The barometer rose: if Dina supported Simeon, then her previous praise of Bauman had also to be seen in a purely objective light" (57).

In this phase, while the attention of the other participants of the discussion is focused on the ethics of using terror to achieve their desired goals, Joseph's is mostly attuned to the atmosphere of the debate, rather than its contents. Effectively, he is "following the argument with one half of his mind" (58), yet he grows pale (59) realizing the severity of some of Simeon's suggestions, and shortly after he sees the suffering of the European refugees in a vivid, almost hallucinatory flash of imagination:

> He closed his eyes for a moment. Something extraordinary was happening to him, something which he had never experienced before. He saw the drowning people before his eyes. It was a sharp, short flash which lasted only a split second but was fantastically clear. There were hundreds of them, with arms and legs sticking out of the water, but there was no sound and the whole scene was laid out on a calm and peaceful sea basking in the hot sun. (59–60)

Eventually, the emotional strain gets too intense for Joseph to linger any longer, and he leaves the dining-hall unnoticed (61). Yet, his ability to observe even the minutest changes to the emotional barometer, to borrow Joseph's own phrase, remains. When Dina is feeling too disturbed by the discussion, he hurries to calm her down (58). And, most importantly, he registers the respect Simeon's endorsement of terrorism brings him:

> It had become quiet around them. There was now quite a crowd round their table. Joseph [...] observed [...] how Simeon grew in stature when he had an audience. Practically everybody here was opposed to the views he held, but they listened to him with a reluctant admiration, and the longer they listened the stronger became his spell over them. (58)

In short, while Joseph does occasionally participate in the discussion through token questions aimed primarily at the elucidation of key points, his role, at this point, is that of an unusually emotionally attuned observer who is already aware that the endorsement of terrorism may bring social visibility and even admiration, even if not necessarily approval.

Readers do not have to wait long to encounter the next step on Joseph's way to conversion. Soon, Ezra's Tower is attacked by locals dissatisfied with the foundation of yet another Jewish communal settlement. Joseph, one of the men "firing for the first time in their lives at human targets" (66), rapidly acquires a taste for killing:

> His heart drummed, he felt an annoying pressure in the bladder, and after the second volley of the attackers he lost a few drops of his water. At the same time *he was in a way enjoying himself*. "That happens to everybody the first time in battle," he told himself serenely. A bullet whined past, quite close so it seemed. "A hail of bullets round my bloody head," he explained to himself. [...] He pulled the trigger and was deafened by the crash. "At night it sounds louder," he thought. "Now we must wait for a gun-flash and fire at it immediately." He did so, and would have given a lot to know whether he had hit something. "Ha," he told himself, "that's *the hunting passion awakening*." He began to *positively enjoy himself*. (66; our emphasis)

Joseph, who originally embraces the values which his upper-middle class upbringing in the English countryside and his Oxford education gave him (75), and then switches those for "the lure of an exotic country, the fascination of a romantic revival and the appeal of a social utopia" (77), makes a notable step towards his final and definitive change of allegiance while acquiring a taste for blood.

This step on his journey towards terrorism is followed in rapid succession by one just as crucial: his ability to find comfort in surrendering his own will, as well as his critical facilities, to the biddings of a higher authority.[7] Already during the aforementioned

---

[7] That Joseph's embracing of terrorism as a solution is possibly in outright contradiction to the message of *Darkness at Noon* (1940) has been a matter of discussion since the publication of *Thieves in the Night* in 1946. Without going too much into details, one of the central themes of Koestler's political novels is the dilemma whether achieving desirable/moral/correct ends can justify the use of undesirable/immoral/incorrect means. For a comprehensive discussion of this topic in Koestler's oeuvre see above else Ingle (1999; 2021). What makes *Thieves in the Night* special in this respect is that, at least at first sight, this novel seemingly advocates the opposite of what the other novels might seem to stand for. Scholars have discussed this contradiction for decades now, and have reached various conclusions on this issue (Cf. e.g. Mortimer 1946, 136; Fitzsimons 1947, 109; Glazer 1947, 57–58; Atkins 1956, 185–203; Calder 1968, 211–17;

night attack, in response to Reuben's command, Joseph makes the following mental note: "In all his anxiety he thought that Reuben was a brick, and that *it was a great comfort to obey blindly* instead of having to decide what to do" (69; our emphasis). This allows him not only to avoid, at least momentarily, struggling with ethical dilemmas, but to effectively empty his mind of all thought: "Joseph aimed and fired in quick succession at target-flashes which now seemed only a few yards away; he felt his head swim and yet his *fingers worked with smooth precision*; somewhere at the back of his mind a last spark of self-consciousness marveled at the *nimble automaton* which his body had become" (69; our emphasis).

Not long after that, Joseph also realizes that fighting actively for the change the community craves, not even shying away from killing for the sake of the community, can bring the approval of that very community:

> He closed his eyes and after a while opened them again and saw that she was looking at him with a kind of approval." Reuben looked in before you came," she said. "He mentioned that you had done quite well." So Dina had specially inquired after him, Joseph thought happily. And Reuben had approved of him. He suddenly felt the tears shoot into his eyes. Oh, it was good to be approved of. There was nothing better than to be approved of — to like and be liked. In that moment he was so full of a warm, simple certainty about everything that he felt no shame and no need to pose. (73)

This is not unlike Joseph's earlier recognition that Simeon's support for terrorism brought the kibbutzniks' silent admiration. Yet, while that admiration was mixed with disapproval, Joseph's willingness, and ability, to kill for them is received with no such mixed feelings: his behavior is unambiguously approved by those closest to him, including the woman he loves.

Of course, Joseph realizes that fighting for a cause might just as easily involve dying for it, yet he finds solace in Naphtali's fate. Naphtali is a young boy not even Dina likes (73), although she is

---

Pearson 1978, 149–50; Levene 1984, 100–103; Gordon 1991, 161–65; Cesarani 1998, 249–50; Saunders 2017, 73–75, 83–84; Calder 2021, 183–84; Gordon 2021, 240–43; Inbari 2021, 209–11). This discussion lies outside the focus of this chapter, however interesting it is.

positive about most if not all. Joseph sees Naphtali as a "poor, squinting little fool" (82). An avid pacifist, Naphtali declares:

> "I don't believe in violence," he cried. "I hate violence. We have to come to an understanding with the Arabs…"
> "But if they don't wish to come to an understanding with you?" said Simeon, who had regained his calm and his caustic tone.
> "We have to educate them. We must get them to join our trade unions. We have to emancipate the fellaheen and break the influence of their priests and replace their chauvinism by class-consciousness." (60)

During the fateful night when Joseph acquires a taste for blood and a strong liking for following orders, something radically different happens to the pacifist youth:

> The youngster by the name of Naphtali had kept some hold on himself until the light went out. From that moment he had been a shaking, teeth-chattering bundle of horror. […] When Reuben started throwing his hand grenades, Naphtali finally went off his head. He jumped up and down on one spot, gurgling inarticulate sounds and biting his clenched fists. His neighbours were too busy to pay any attention to him. He went on leaping into the air like a joyful child, gurgling and whimpering, until something hit him massively in the eye. […] He saw great coloured circles spinning and crossing each other like flaming hoops that jugglers throw into the air, and everything became rather quiet; only one last fiery wheel kept turning and expanding, until it too faded and only darkness and peace remained. (71)

Yet, regardless of his strong opposition to violence, his mental breakdown and self-induced death during the night attack, and even belying his not being a favorite of the settlers, Naphtali ends up as an icon: "He has since become a hero and our local patron saint. Particularly as the poor, squinting little fool did not believe in violence and had so much set his heart on educating our Neighbours. However, heroes should be looked at through the telescope, not through the microscope" (82). From this perspective, even dying in the process of fighting for the community is a victory: one is bound to be revered as a hero, even despite oneself, and even if one's death is truly unheroic.

One might understandably interject that accepting such nonsensical, paradoxical and dogmatic hero-creation is not much different from blindly obeying the nonsensical rules of a higher authority, itself a controversial maxim, as mentioned above. It is important to recognize that in both cases, i.e. both in the case of describing Naphtali's canonization as a hero despite his views and his actions, and in the case of Joseph's frank admission that he enjoys a total surrender to the commands of a superior and the total suspension of moral and ethical considerations, these claims are made by Joseph, the character who is on his way of actually becoming a terrorist. That is, these are the views of the terrorist-to-be, whose transformation is portrayed by the novel, and not those of the implied author, much less the biological author. Also, at least in the case of Naphtali becoming a hero, not even Joseph's, the terrorist's, position is one of approval, much rather of sarcasm, as both the sentence "heroes should be looked at through the telescope, not through the microscope" and calling Naphtali a "poor, squinting little fool" illustrate (Koestler 1946, 82). In addition, while Joseph, as shown above, clearly recognizes that terrorism offers the benefit of becoming an admired hero in the community, he neither sees terrorists as heroes, nor does he consider himself a hero, not even after joining the terrorist organization. He directly discusses this with Bauman, the terrorist leader, moments before agreeing to join:

> "Oh, I know," said Joseph. "It was a world of pink mirages and now we have entered the age of the New Realism. But it startles me that its up-to-date, stream-lined power logics should be accompanied by all this maudlin opera stuff –Wotan and Blood and Soil and Roman Fasces. And it's the same among your arm-lifting terror-scouts. They think they are the heirs to young David and the Maccabeans. Between you and me, Bauman—if the Maccabeans hadn't been such bloody heroes, our ancestors would have become Hellenised and would probably have escaped the ghetto..." (Koestler 1946, 300)

In fact, Joseph categorically denies that blindly following orders can be considered an act of heroism, early on in the novel: "I thought it must take some guts to act as a decoy, but since our heroic period is over, playing at war has lost its attraction for me. And even while it lasted and we had two to three raids every week and random sniping almost every night, it had soon all become a tedious routine and the main worry was lack of sleep" (106). And while he uses the term "heroic period" here, it is in reference to the early, pioneering stage of founding a kibbutz, with its nomadic conditions and the adventure of creatively overcoming hardships, not in reference to the fighting, which he sees as rather a tiring and exhausting routine. In short, while Joseph himself is fully aware that others might see him as a hero whether he wants it or not, he himself "has no pretensions to being a revolutionary hero" (Calder 1968, 217).

Returning now to Joseph's path of conversion, one certainly must admit that no embracing of terrorism could happen without some ideological change. Accordingly, Joseph finds himself on the same platform as Simeon early in the story. At first, this is more of an allegation made by the other settlers, not something Joseph himself embraces, or even recognizes: "'Joseph's got under the influence of the Bauman-people,' said Max. 'He wants to throw bombs first on the Arabs, then on the English'" (156). Yet, shortly afterwards, in fact, during the same debate, he actively embraces this political position:

> "But *I don't want to be reasonable*," I shouted. "I have had enough of being reasonable for two thousand years while the others were not. I was the reasonable fly running in zigzags over the window-pane because there was light on the other side and I had my legs torn out and my wings burnt off with matches. I am through with your reasonableness."
> "So what do you propose to do?" Reuben asked coolly. Despite his calm voice I heard the warning undertone.
> "I don't know," I said, feeling my rage change into impotence. "I only know that we have been offered one per cent of our country as a reasonable compromise. And *I know that* on that first night here *when we* were attacked in the open and *could shoot back with a clean conscience and the blessing of God, I felt happy to kill…*" (157–58; our emphasis)

At this point, Joseph has already openly accepted the necessity of violence and has also realized that killing for a cause is a position he himself is able and willing to take. At the same time, he does not make any active effort to join the terrorists just yet.

The common understanding of what pushes Joseph towards terrorism is, as already mentioned above, that "Joseph vacillates until Dina is brutally raped and killed one night […] after secretly visiting a cave containing the bones of 'Joshua the Ancestor'"

(Scammell 2009, 280).[8] Yet, as argued above, Joseph's conversion has several steps predating Dina's murder. At the same time, there is certainly no reason to reject this event as a crucial one. After all, Joseph visits Simeon after the murder and asks him in clear terms for retaliatory action: "'The only question for me is,' he said vehemently, 'whether your crowd is willing and able to settle this, or not. Everything else doesn't matter'" (Koestler 1946, 264).

However, there is similarly no reason to accept Dina's murder as a single and unique event, much less as one solely responsible for his embracing of terrorist methods. On the contrary, even if one insists on the idea that such conversions are the results of dramatic events (as I show below, this position is in itself also far from uncontroversial), there is at least one more similar tragedy that might deserve the label of the final straw: the fate of Wilhelm Brodetsky. Brodetsky is described as a "thin little man with an ear-trumpet" whose "neck was long and thin like a scrofulous child's," walking with "quick, jerky steps" (237) and who is at an unspecified old age. Joseph meets him at the Magistrate's Court in Haifa, where he goes to see his trial, since he overheard people in the Co-Operative Office discussing "a case of illegal immigration" (235). Behind this formal and bureaucratic label, however, seeing Brodetsky for the first time in the courthouse, Joseph finds a crushing, yet heroic fate:

> Mr. Wilmot proceeded to read out the charge, according to which the accused person had, on the date specified, arrived in territorial waters on board the Rumanian cattle ship *Assimi* carrying two hundred and fifty-one persons without immigration permits. The vessel had been intercepted by coastal patrol and ordered to return with its passengers to its Rumanian port of origin, but permitted to take food, drinking water and medical supplies, as epidemics had broken out on board. Under cover of night, while the detained vessel was riding at anchor in Haifa port, the accused person had jumped overboard and swum ashore, thereby entering the country without permission contrary to the Immigration Ordinance of 1933. He had been found lying unconscious on the beach by an Arab watchman and handed over to the Police. (237–38)

---

[8] It is also worth mentioning here once more that, however widespread the belief, *there is no textual evidence* of Dina being also raped by her assailants rather than "merely" brutally murdered. For more on this, see Vernyik (2016b, 37–38).

While the magistrate judge somewhat sympathizes with Brodetsky's situation, and lowers the old man's prison sentence from six months to three months, he nevertheless is clear that following this period of incarceration, he "shall recommend to His Excellency the High Commissioner that he be deported" (242). The judge, Mr. Wilmot, arrives at this decision although he makes it known in unambiguous terms that he does not doubt the truthfulness of the claims made by Mr. Weinstein, Brodetsky's lawyer, namely that Brodetsky and innumerable other illegal immigrants are "escaping from danger of life" (239) and, just as importantly, "[h]unted by the Police, without passports or legal residence, it was materially impossible for them to [...] apply for an immigration permit and wait for probably a year or two until their turn on the quota came" (240). In Mr. Wilmot's own words, he is "sensitive to the truth of what Mr. Weinstein said" and that "the conditions in certain countries in Europe have caused what one may call a stampede of the mass of the persecuted out of those territories" and not only of that, but also that under "these circumstances deterrent punishment can have little effect" (241). In fact, he even goes as far as to openly admit that it is perfectly "possible that [he is] wrong and that such cases should be dealt with differently," yet, even with all that in mind, he still sentences Brodetsky to a prison sentence and subsequent deportation, leading to a scene where the old man is "half dragged, half carried out by two Arab policemen, trying to hang on to his lawyer's sleeve and yelling in a shrill, sobbing voice" (242).

What makes it clear that Wilhelm Brodetsky's case might also be of enough emotional importance to Joseph for it to be seen as an alternative, or at least additional, catalyst, besides Dina's fate, however, is not only the disturbing nature of the case itself. Crucially, leaving the courthouse, Joseph welcomes his numerous duties for the day, since this way he finds "no time for brooding" (243). Yet, he cannot escape the ambiguous verdict's influence: when he falls asleep in the room he shares with several others in Haifa, he is "woken again after a few hours by the wailing of the *Assimi's* siren," interrupting a dream in which he is "on the point of making his voice heard and catching at last the white-wigged Speaker's eye," directly recalling the parliamentary discussions of migration quotas mentioned earlier by Joseph, but also arguably alluding to the trial he has recently witnessed, only to be drawn to the window shortly after by the ship's siren wailing yet another time (244). With Joseph observing the events unfolding below, it is unclear whether it is the narrator or Joseph himself who notes: "Through the window, down in the harbour, the mast-tops of the *Assimi* could be seen slowly moving past the long breakwater towards the open sea, followed by a swarm of circling seagulls; carrying its passengers towards the sunny Mediterranean and the various forms of death awaiting them" (244). What is clear, however, is that slightly earlier that day, back at the courthouse, during his brief dialog with Weinstein, the issue of terrorism, or at least armed resistance, directly emerges:

> "Are you going to appeal?" Joseph asked.
> "What?" said Weinstein. "Oh yes, as usual." His eyes, which again reminded Joseph of Simeon's, focused on Joseph's dispatch-case.
> "Are you a clerk?" he asked.
> "No—I am from a Settlement."
> "Settlement," Weinstein repeated. His cigarette was still twitching up and down. "And what are you carrying there?"
> "Papers," said Joseph.
> "…Papers," Weinstein repeated. "We are all carrying papers. Perhaps we should be carrying revolvers." (242)

Joseph shares the sentiment, and, as it emerges shortly, albeit not immediately, after this scene, he even joins a group carrying guns rather than papers. Thus, Wilhelm Brodetsky's unfortunate fate, and Joseph's witnessing of some of its events, might be also considered as events that provide him the final push towards actively engaging in terrorism.

However this might be, it is even questionable if such a fixation on one or more key traumatic event(s) is entirely warranted. As John Horgan (2005) explains, "[i]t can be misleading to attempt to identify the presence of unifying catalyst events as unambiguous 'push' factors" (88) for multiple reasons. First of all, while some terrorists might have, indeed, experienced such traumatic events, "for others that victimization may not necessarily be proximal or real"

(88) at all. In fact, for many, there is no such event, and their decision to engage in terrorism might simply stem from "a sense of communal identification with those victimized" (88). Besides, it is unlikely that a single catalyst event or even a set of such events could, in themselves, account for such a radical change: "it may well be the case that their true significance is likely to be more potent to those already progressing through some already existing 'borderline' activity, such as expressing support via peaceful protest or something else" (90). What he proposes instead is a model where "involvement in terrorism" is understood "as a process that is susceptible to, and limited by, among other things, strategic and psychological factors at whatever stage or degree of involvement we are examining" (85). As shown above, Joseph's conversion is exactly this kind of slow and continuous process, and while Dina's brutal murder and Wilhelm Brodetsky's court case might indeed be interpreted as potential catalysts, they can certainly only play this role because of Joseph's preexisting history of gradual attraction to terrorism.

Brodetsky's and Dina's stories have a common feature of crucial importance: both are disenfranchised victims of violence, more specifically, violence perpetrated by the more powerful against the disenfranchised, the dominant against the frustrated and marginalized groups. For Dina, this means violence perpetrated by men against a woman, but also, at the same time, by the Arabic speaking majority on a member of the Jewish minority. For Brodetsky, it is violence perpetrated by the state against a refugee, or as the state apparatus sees him, an illegal immigrant. The reason it is crucial to notice this is because terrorism is a tool typically used by the weak against the strong (Waisová 2009, 141; Mooney and Young 2005, 116). While "terrorists are motivated by political goals that they believe are furthered by their actions" (Krueger 2007, 4), it is not just any kind of politics, but one emerging from "the (often legitimate) grievance of a group of people over resources denied or identity and its expression thwarted;" it is politics as practiced by "the frustrated and the denigrated" (Mooney and Young 2005, 122).

This also explains why, albeit different groups are perpetrating the violence in these two cases (the British administration in the case of Brodetsky, and the Arabs in the case of Dina), acts of terrorism in the novel are mostly directed at the British, and not the Arabs, at least in terms of the ultimate addressee of that violence: "there is a distinction to be made between the immediate target of *violence and terror* and the overall target of *terror*: between the terrorist's immediate victim (such as the person who has died from a bombing or a shooting) and the terrorist's *opponent* (which for many terrorist movements represents a government)" (Horgan 2005, 2; emphasis original). It is the British Administration that embodies the government here, the one who is likely to be seen as the oppressor, not the Arabs. Even more so, if one takes into consideration that "countries that occupy other countries are more likely to be targets of terrorism" (Krueger 2007, 81). While there is no *occupation* per se, it is undeniable that, in the period in question, Britain is a third party, exercising the ultimate political power in a territory where it is much more of an outsider than the other two players.

This position is made clear in the novel as well. As early as the settlers' first day on the kibbutz, it becomes evident whom several of them truly blame for their hardships and for what they perceive as preferential treatment for the Arabs, whether rightfully or not:

> "There was no need for Bauman to be polite to that Police officer," he said.
> "Nor for you, Reuben."
> "We were correct to them, that's all," said Reuben.
> "Precisely," said Simeon. He put his fork down. "We keep on being correct and the Arabs keep on shooting. Result: the Arabs are appeased and we pay the bill." (Koestler 1946, 57)

Shortly afterwards, Simeon formulates his position even more concisely: "I assume that the British won't change their policy unless we force them to. I have studied their history, their traditions, their methods" (59). Joseph's recurrent dream is a particularly poignant and poetic indictment of the British:

> At night, when he tried to settle down to sleep, the stream began its turgid flow. At first it was only a trickle of phrases, of arguments to convince an invisible, impersonal, dumb and almighty opponent. Sometimes this opponent appeared as the copper-faced Police Major who had visited them on the first day; sometimes it was the whole House of Commons whose stilted antics had once enchanted him from the Visitors' Gallery; sometimes the

bear-skinned automaton banging his stiff legs down on the gravel in front of Buckingham Palace. But he could never catch the Speaker's eye nor stop the leg-throwing six-footer marching past; and as his plea remained choked in his throat, its pressure increased and the trickle swelled to a torrent, which expanded through his whole body until his stomach contracted in a spasm and he spat green bile into his handkerchief. I shall either get a stomach ulcer, he thought, or join Bauman's terror gang. This is the real alternative. One can reach a point of humiliation where violence is the only outlet. (Koestler 1946, 229)

Joseph's thoughts thoroughly mirror the 21st-century theoretical discussion: he talks about humiliation, he experiences frustration, and so his, at this point merely purported, violence and his already very real anger both target his *opponents*, even using the same word that Horgan (2005) does, who are clearly identified as the British, not the Arabs.

Terrorism as a Means of Communication

This distinction between the victims and the opponents leads many scholars to conclude that terrorism is essentially a "form of communication" (Horgan 2005, 2; cf. also Schinkel 2009, 190–94), since "immediate victims are not as important as the broader message sent to the public" (Krueger 2007, 15). Some, as Ian Ward (2008), already quoted above, even see it as a form of "essentially aesthetic and literary endeavor" in which the terrorist primarily tries "to describe a picture, to craft a narrative of events, and in so doing elevate impression to the status of reality, even truth," or, in other words, while the terrorist's struggle is very real, and so is the damage caused, it is nevertheless a "rhetorical struggle" with an "audience [...] try[ing] to make some sense of all this, pick[ing] [its] way through the heroes and anti-heroes, the mythologies and the realities" (254).

That terrorism is an essentially communicative act is perfectly clear to Bauman, the leader of Joseph's terrorist group. He describes the reason for the necessity of violence as follows:

"It follows that we have to do two things if we want to avoid drowning altogether. One is persuasion [...] Two is making a hell of a nuisance of ourselves. Driving each argument home with a bang. Otherwise they won't listen. [...] We have to force them to take us seriously, then they'll do business with us. But to achieve that we have to speak the only language they understand…" He patted with his fist the gun under his leather jacket. "That's the new Esperanto," he concluded. "Surprising how easy it is to learn. Everybody understands it from Shanghai to Madrid." (Koestler 1946, 299)

Just as crucially, the settlers-turned-terrorists in *Thieves in the Night* are not only aware that the violent deeds of terrorism constitute a communicative act, but also that they would not work without other, less aggressive forms of communication providing the onlookers with the preferred key to interpreting the events. Among those forms are radio broadcasts:

> During the last week, however, it had succeeded in establishing a secret short-wave transmitter operating on wavelength 37.3 for about two hours a day. […] The contents of the broadcasts were divided about equally between attacks on the Mandatory Power's alleged anti-Zionist policy and attacks on the passivity of the *Haganah*, the leftist Defence Organisation controlled by the official Zionist bodies. The broadcasts began and closed with a recorded chorus of the Hebrew national anthem and were interspersed with the slogan "Your kin is murdered in Europe. What are you doing about it?" monotonously repeated every five minutes. The switch in emphasis from anti-Arab to anti-British propaganda was marked, and seemed to point to intended terroristic action against the Administration. (202)

But communication is not limited to the media; a similar message is sent by the priests of the Yeshurun Central Synagogue in Jerusalem:

> There was a silence while the congregation waited for the next canonical prayer, as laid down in the rigid rules of the service. But instead of intoning it the priest suddenly swerved round to face the crowd, and, lifting both arms above his head, in a thundering voice cried out the words of David's psalm […] Facing the audience with his arms lifted up and tears running down his face, he stood in the poise of the ancient High Priests of Israel. Two attendants moved up to him from the right and the left, one holding the five-armed Maccabean candlestick with the candles aflame, the other a printed copy of the White Paper. He took the paper first and with a wrathful gesture of his narrow hands tore it up; then held the candles to it and let it go up in flames. (324)

As further communicative acts serving the proliferation of the message that not only the Jewish settlers, but all of the Jews in Europe are wronged by the British Administration, and that they have no options remaining but to resist, one should mention "groups of boys and girls march[ing] in military formation through Jerusalem" (321), "smashing shop windows, among them those of a German restaurant and a British department store in Jaffa Road" (326), vandalizing phone booths and street lamps (328), "posters bearing slogans like 'We were here before the British and shall be here when they are gone' and 'For Zion's sake will I not hold my peace and for Jerusalem's sake will I not rest'" or strikes, processions and protests (321).

Johan Galtung, in his seminal text on violence, "Violence, Peace and Peace Research", divides violence into two basic types: personal (or direct) and structural. He defines the former as "the type of violence where there is an actor that commits the violence" (Galtung 1969, 170), and the latter as a form where "violence is built into the structure and shows up as unequal power and consequently as unequal life chances" (171), albeit typically "[t]here may not be any person who directly harms another person" (171) present at all. A further relevant parameter is his distinction between the latent and manifest form of violence, whether personal or structural (172). Seen in the light of these two dichotomies, the form of violence exclusively utilized by the Arab inhabitants of Palestine in the late 1930s, as represented in Koestler's novel, is manifest personal violence: attacking and brutally killing Dina or trying to destroy the newly, and stealthily built Ezra's Tower at the beginning of the novel. The Jewish actors, both those within and outside the terrorist group portrayed, arguably also exclusively resort to personal violence; however, their repertoire also includes its latent form. Examples of their use of manifest personal violence include them fighting back when the Arabs attack their kibbutzim, their assassination of the mukhtar in reaction to Dina's murder, their physical attacks on the buildings of the British administration's institutions, and them tackling policemen and in some cases even stealing their guns. Forms of latent personal violence include the poster campaign mentioned above, the sermon in the synagogue, and especially the temporary hijacking of the frequency of the official radio to transmit the recruiting ad of the terrorists instead of the scheduled program, which would highlight the new rules for immigration introduced by the British administration. While the British authorities also do not refrain from personal forms of violence, both latent (in the form of police patrols and identity checks) and manifest (the police beating the protesters and guards torturing some prisoners), they are the only ones able to operate structural forms of violence: most importantly restrictions on immigration and, to a lesser extent, temporarily, also on the free movement of people. Just as crucially, it operates in the form of the distribution of resources (one may recall the Jewish settlers' complaints about their tax payments being used for building roads and infrastructure for the Arab settlements). This is, of course, in line with the political situation at the time: it is the British administration that exercises the powers of the government, thus enjoying exclusive access to structural forms of violence, while the other two players, the Jewish and Arab, must use the only form of violence available to them: direct personal violence. It is worth noting, however, that the Jewish settlers' ability to consistently, and persistently, operate also latent forms of personal violence shows them as better organized, and much more institutionalized than their Arab counterparts.

Conclusion: From Pacifist Youth to Terrorist Adult — *Thieves in the Night* as a *Bildungsroman*

Leaving behind the specific functions of terrorism and its relation to, and various functions in, the lives of various members of the community, as well as the types of violence appearing in the context of terrorism, let us now return to the character of Joseph, the novel's focalizer-protagonist. Joseph, as mentioned above, appears at the beginning of this novel as an idealistic pacifist youth, hurt and lost, in search of his place in the world. In contrast, at the end of the novel, he is an adult, firmly rooted both in the community of the kibbutz and the terrorist organization he joins, no longer a passive observer, but participating actively in forming not only his own fate, but also that of his community. In other words, *Thieves in the Night* is arguably a *Bildungsroman*, and more specifically, its British variety:

> Very simply, the Germans tended to focus attention on the individual's cultivation, while neglecting responsibility for the national culture. The English tried, with marked success, to be attentive toward both: one's development as an *I* depended not only on the richness of one's inner life, but on the affiliations one had with the people—family, friends, acquaintances, and strangers—who constituted and shared one's social environment. (Jeffers 2005, 35; emphasis original)

Joseph, just like numerous other protagonists of this genre, "is decidedly part of his social milieu, and his social milieu is part of him. Intersubjectivity—life with, for, and through other people—is an inextinguishable determinant of his identity, and the question of his responsibility to them isn't sidestepped" (36).

In fact, one of the novel's central metaphors, barren land, and the radically different attitude the local Arabs and the Jewish settlers have towards it, ties into this specifically British variety of the novel of development rather well. Reuben, one of Joseph's fellow kibutzniks, criticizes the Arabs in the following manner: "You have neglected the land. You let the terraces fall to ruin, and the rain carried the earth away. We shall clean the hill of the stones and bring tractors and fertilisers" (Koestler 1946, 36). The elderly, Turkish-looking Arab rejects this attitude: "'What the valley bears is enough for us,' said the old man. 'Where God put stones, man should not carry them away. We shall live as our fathers lived and we do not want your money and your tractors and your fertilisers'" (36). It is a perfectly understandable position, and probably also more in harmony with our 21st-century visions of ecological agriculture, and in fact one that even Joseph in the novel acknowledges is a valid position (38). Yet, in the terrorist-leader, Bauman's, words, they "cannot afford to see the other man's point" (38). While this arguably is in harmony with the terrorists' need to communicate their own narrative clearly, unambiguously, and forcefully, this is also a result of the specific ideology informing the British *Bildungsroman*:

> the specific British version of self-cultivation [is] [...] composed of liberal education, utilitarianism, an emphasis on physical training and fitness, a robust work ethic and the ideology of self-help, aimed at a practical concept of *Bildung* which was more narrowly focused on individual biography and personal achievement. Samuel Smiles's popular work *Self-Help* (1859) epito-

mizes this mid-Victorian bourgeois ideology, insisting that "man can triumph over circumstances, and subject them to his will" (10). (Zwierlein 2012, 337)

It is exactly this belief in the settler's right to "triumph over circumstances, and subject them to his will" that the kibbutzniks and the terrorists share, allowing Joseph to seamlessly fit into both communities at the same time.

This is especially so since "Britain's specific brand of liberalism" understands the "'self-governing' liberties of individuals and local communities" alike (Goodlad 2003, viii, x quoted in Zwierlien 2012, 338), extending this license of the individual to his or her immediate social environment. As John Horgan emphasizes, at least in one of the two major types of terrorist groups, terrorists are "not estranged from their families or communities," but rather the opposite: active participation in terrorist activities might be seen as "a right of passage, a movement towards consolidation of one's identity within the broader community" (Horgan 2005, 91), similarly to how the protagonist of the *Bildungsroman* "is decidedly part of his social milieu, and his social milieu is part of him" (Jeffers 2005, 36), with the individual's development happening in the interplay of the opposing forces of "a self-expressive ego confronted with the community's demands for self-repression" (51), likewise leading to a range of "initiatory tests that every inwardly developing *Bildungsheld* must at least try to pass" constituting "the rite-of-passage peripeties" of the genre's "archetypal plot" (52).

Thus, while, for some, Joseph's story, showcasing and dissecting the trajectory leading from idealist youth to a terrorist adult, might seem too disturbing and immoral to merit the label of *Bildungsroman*, it is important to stress that this genre, by definition, does not portray an uncontroversial path to an abstract, universal morality. On the contrary, it shows "a deep interest in the mechanisms which make maturing individuals develop their own capacities while at the same time integrating into society" (Zwierlein 2012, 336). That is to say, it always portrays integration into a specific society at a specific time and place. It is "an example of the social embedding of literary genres: offering case studies of individuals negotiating the dynamic interplay between active self-formation and passive subjection to external influences" (336). In the genre's classic era of the 18th and 19th centuries, this typically means "the massively influential Puritan vision of life as a 'vocation' […] and the Goethean and Humboldtian versions of *Bildung*" (337), but it entails something completely different in late 1930s Palestine: "In the logic of the ice age tolerance became a luxury and purity a vice. There was no way to escape the dilemma. To wash one's hands and let others do the dirty job was a hypocrisy, not a solution. To expose oneself was the only redeeming factor" (Koestler 1946, 304). In this sense, Joseph's story is quite arguably indeed that of development and maturation, growing into the civic ideal of late 1930s Palestine: the terrorist.

To sum up, this chapter interprets terrorist crimes committed by the newly settled Zionist immigrants as one form of communicative acts on their side to express their message of frustration with the British Administration in Koestler's *Thieves in the Night*. More broadly, it is a reaction to structural violence, a form of violence which is the result of recurring deliberate attempts to maintain and intensify unequal power structures in a multiethnic society, including the strategy of limiting, or even eliminating immigration.

Addendum: Reading Koestler's *Thieves in the Night* Following October 7, 2023

The idea of writing this chapter emerged back in September 2012, during Zénó Vernyik's first visit to the Koestler Archives held at the Center for Research Collections at the University of Edinburgh, yet with other projects taking priority, it first gained structured form almost five years later, in February 2017, while visiting the Border Poetics / Border Culture Research Group of the University of Tromsø. It then went through further stages of development following its presentation at the Interpreting Migration Conference organized in April of the same year by the Borders and Migration Research Group of the Technical University of Liberec. Just during these same five years, Europe has encountered the 2015 refugee crisis, the Charlie Hebdo shooting, the 2016 attacks and bombings in France and Germany, and the Manchester Arena bombing, and major terrorist attacks struck the continent in the following years as well. Certain elements of the Ukraine–Russia conflicts have also shown elements of terrorism at least since 2014.

The Israeli-Palestinian conflict, the novel's more direct concern than terrorism in general, as conceded in the introductory parts of this chapter, with various intensities throughout the decades has also led to a whole range of forms of violence in the same period. This included both terrorism and military attacks, with periodically inflaming conflicts. It is probably enough to recall the 2014 Gaza War, the 2014 Jerusalem unrest, or the 2015–2016 Habba/Intifada of the Individuals as examples, to realize this, not to mention the whole range of violent incidents during 2023, eventually culminating in the 2023 Israel–Hamas War.

The continuous presence of terrorism both in Europe and elsewhere in the world in general, and the persistently unresolved status of the Israeli–Palestinian conflict in particular, with the lasting presence of not only terrorism, but also of other forms of violence, including its state sanctioned form, in the region rather directly explains the continuing relevance of Koestler's text. Sadly, the most recent events only further increased its contemporary relevance, with questions such as what leads to terrorism, what makes an individual embrace the calling of a terrorist, what roles do governments have in the emergence and worsening of terrorism, having become all the more pressing.

At the same time, as we have discussed above, *Thieves in the Night* is certainly a partisan text, clearly supporting the Jewish settlers' decision to resort to terrorist means to achieve their goals. The book provocatively and unashamedly supports the Zionist cause. It is thus very important to realize that the book makes this choice in the context of the Palestine of 1937–1939. Those in power in the period were the British and the majority population was formed by the Palestinian inhabitants. This specific period, the colonialist project of Zionism (on Zionism's ties to colonialism see e.g. Mor 2023;

Pycińska 2023) also coincided with anti-Jewish violence in Germany and German-occupied territories, pogroms and deportation, and the establishment of ghettos. Thus, a large number of Jewish refugees either themselves naturally saw Mandatory Palestine as a viable alternative or were being forced to do so by the Nazi government (on Germany's role in the Zionist project see e.g. Abed-Rabbo 2023). In this situation, massive numbers were willing to take the risk of illegal immigration, even after the British Administration's introduction of stricter settlement limits and immigration policies, as discussed above. In such a situation, representing the Zionist settlers as a disenfranchised minority pushed by a double bind consisting of the measures of the British administration and of the political situation in Europe to take desperate measures is understandable, even if controversial and debatable.

Today, however, the geopolitical, historical and social context is radically different. What is more, it arguably has been radically different since Israel's 1948 declaration of independence from Mandatory Palestine, and especially since the 1967 Six-day War. The novel's 1946 endorsement of Jewish violence cannot and should not be understood universally and should not be applied to the present situation: a situation where Israel is an internationally (albeit certainly not universally) recognized country with its own army, secret service and police force, with roughly twice the population of the Palestinian State. In contrast, at the very least the sovereignty and territorial autonomy of Palestine is severely limited by Israel in a whole range of ways, including the de facto occupation of most of its territory (cf. e.g. Aral 2023; Singha and Rahman 2022; Baconi 2021). *If* in 1937–1939, or even in 1946, at the time of the book's publication, it *was* feasible to see the Jewish settlers as the underdog, basically using terrorist tactics as their last resort "to avoid drowning altogether" (Koestler 1946, 299), in 2024 it is equally as feasible to see Palestinians as the underdog who are threatened by the Jewish majority and Israel's various policies with "drowning altogether".

In fact, if there is *any* universal message to be found in *Thieves in the Night* besides its revelatory description of the individual's journey from peaceful existence to active terrorism, it may be that there are certain conditions under which the use of force, even terrorism, in self-defense, could be acceptable:

> Not only is [Koestler] concerned to show that there are situations in which violence is justifiable, if not necessary. The terrorists are not *ipso facto* "fascist" because they throw bombs into […] administrative offices. It is the fact that a concern with the world of politics means a concern with the modes of action, and that such a concern amounts to a commitment to choice, that Koestler emphasizes. […] Here we are only too aware of the dangerous ground he is treading on. By what standards, in what perspective, is the justification for terroristic action assessed? The very nature of this kind of justification invites attack from the shocked liberal conscience. But Koestler does not base his appeal on an emotional plea for the ending of the persecution of his race. It is closer to a pragmatic defense of the action of a desperate people in their fight for existence. (Calder 1968, 202)

This is, of course, a controversial message, and as discussed above, potentially in contradiction with the message of *Darkness at Noon*. Whether it truly is, or the biographical Koestler's position was always different from Rubashov's, or even if Rubashov's own realization was truly that the end does not justify the means, or something else altogether, would lead far from the present discussion.

The authors of this chapter certainly do not endorse terrorism on either side of this conflict, much less in general. This, however, should not mean that we should refrain from discussing terrorism's function as a means of communication as postulated by Horgan (2005) and illustrated by Koestler's *Thieves in the Night*, much less should it mean refraining from discussing terrorism, its socio-political, historical and geographic complexities, or its cultural representations. Major challenges to a peaceful existence cannot be successfully tackled by strategies of simplistic refusal, categorical condemnation or avoidance, only through analysis, critical thinking and public discussion.

Bibliography

Abed-Rabbo, Samir. 2023. "Germany's Never-Ending Guilt Trip." *Arab Studies Quarterly* 45 (1): 8–33.

Aral, Berdal. 2023. "Israel's Fateful March: From Settler Colonialism to Genocidal State." *Insight Turkey* 25 (4): 181–96. https://doi.org/10.25253/99.2023254.11.

Atkins, John. 1956. *Arthur Koestler*. London: Neville Spearman.

Baconi, Tareq. 2021. "The Gaza Strip: Humanitarian Crisis and Lost Statehood." In *Rethinking Statehood in Palestine*, edited by Leila H. Farsakh, 54–79. Oakland, CA: U of California P. https://www.jstor.org/stable/j.ctv2rb768k.8.

Buckard, Christian. 2004. *Arthur Koestler: Ein extremes Leben 1905–1983*. Munich: C. H. Beck.

Calder, Jenni. 1968. *Chronicles of Conscience: A Study of George Orwell and Arthur Koestler*. London: Secker & Warburg.

— — —. 2021. "*Thieves in the Night*: Land and Identity." In *Arthur Koestler's Fiction and the Genre of the Novel: Rubashov and Beyond*, edited by Zénó Vernyik, 177–98. Lanham, MD: Lexington.

Cesarani, David. 1998. *Arthur Koestler: The Homeless Mind*. London: Heinemann.

Chamberlain, John. 1946. "The New Books." *Harper's Magazine* 193 (12): 1159–66.

Conner, John. 1947. "Thieves in the Night. By Arthur Koestler. The MacMillan Company." *Leatherneck* 30 (4): 59.

Fitzsimons, Matthew Anthony. 1947. "The Modern Crisis." *The Review of Politics* 9 (1): 107–10.

Fremantle, Anne. 1947. "What Comes Naturally." *Commonweal*, February 28, 1947.

Galtung, Johan. 1969. "Violence, Peace and Peace Research." *Journal of Peace Research* 6 (3): 167–91.

Glazer, Nathan. 1947. "The Parlor Terrorists: Koestler's Fellow Travelers and Their Politics." *Commentary*, January 1, 1947.

Goodlad, Lauren M. E. 2003. *Victorian Literature and the Victorian State: Character and Governance in a Liberal Society*. Baltimore, MD: Johns Hopkins UP.

Gordon, Louis A. 1991. "Arthur Koestler and His Ties to Zionism and Jabotinsky." *Studies in Zionism* 12 (2): 149–68.

— — —. 1994. "Koestler Revisited." *Midstream*, March 1994.

— — —. 2021. "*The Call-Girls*: A Valedictory Novel." In *Arthur Koestler's Fiction and the Genre of the Novel: Rubashov and Beyond*, edited by Zénó Vernyik, 223–46. Lanham, MD: Lexington.

Halamish, Aviva. 2020. "Jewish Immigration: The Base of the Palestine Triangle." In *The British Mandate in Palestine: A Centenary Volume, 1920–2020*, edited by Michael J. Cohen, 172–88. Abingdon: Routledge.

Hildebrandt-Wypych, Dobrochna. 2022. "Contrasting Narratives of the Israeli-Palestinian Conflict in Polish History Textbooks." *Frontiers in Education* 7. https://www.frontiersin.org/articles/10.3389/feduc.2022.815830.

Hillbrook, Roy. 1946. "Notes on Current Books." *Current History* 11 (64): 509-12.

Holme, Christopher. 1946. "Zion." *The Observer*, November 3, 1946.

Holt, Elizabeth M. 2021. "Resistance Literature and Occupied Palestine in Cold War Beirut." *Journal of Palestine Studies* 50 (1): 3-18.

Horgan, John. 2005. *The Psychology of Terrorism*. London: Routledge.

Inbari, Motti. 2021. "Arthur Koestler and the Jewish Race According to *Thieves in the Night*." In *Arthur Koestler's Fiction and the Genre of the Novel: Rubashov and Beyond*, edited by Zénó Vernyik, 199-219. Lanham, MD: Lexington.

Ingle, Stephen. 1999. "Politics and Literature: Means and Ends in Koestler." *Political Studies* 47 (2): 329-44.

— — —. 2021. "Images of Revolution: Orwell's *Animal Farm* and Koestler's *The Gladiators*." In *Arthur Koestler's Fiction and the Genre of the Novel: Rubashov and Beyond*, edited by Zénó Vernyik, 61-83. Lanham, MD: Lexington.

J. M. D. P. 1946. "Mr. Koestler." *Manchester Guardian*, October 25, 1946.

Jeffers, Thomas L. 2005. *Apprenticeships: The Bildungsroman from Goethe to Santayana*. New York: Palgrave Macmillan.

Kochavi, Arieh J. 1998. "The Struggle against Jewish Immigration to Palestine." *Middle Eastern Studies* 34 (3): 146-67.

Koestler, Arthur. 1940. *Darkness at Noon*. Translated by Daphne Hardy. London: Jonathan Cape.

— — —. 1946. *Thieves in the Night: Chronicle of an Experiment*. London: Macmillan.

Krueger, Alan B. 2007. *What Makes a Terrorist: Economics and the Roots of Terrorism*. Princeton, NJ: Princeton UP.

Laval, Michel. 2005. *L'homme sans Concessions: Arthur Koestler et Son Siècle*. Paris: Calmann-Lévy.

Levene, Mark. 1984. *Arthur Koestler*. New York: Frederick Ungar.

MacDonagh, Donagh. 1946. "Evolution of a Terrorist." *The Irish Times*, November 23, 1946.

Martin, Elaine. 2007. "The Global Phenomenon of 'Humanizing' Terrorism in Literature and Cinema." *CLCWeb: Comparative Literature and Culture* 9 (1): 12-21.

Márton, László. 2006. *Koestler, a lázadó*. Budapest: Pallas.

Mitchell, William John Thomas. 2005. "The Unspeakable and the Unimaginable: Word and Image in a Time of Terror." *English Literary History* 72 (2): 291–308.

Mooney, Jane, and Jock Young. 2005. "Imagining Terrorism: Terrorism and Anti-Terrorism Terrorism, Two Ways of Doing Evil." *Social Justice* 32 (1): 113–25.

Mor, Liron. 2023. "Zionist Speculation: Colonial Vision and Its Sublime Turn." *Theory & Event* 26 (1): 154–85. https://doi.org/10.1353/tae.2023.0007.

Mortimer, Raymond. 1946. "Arthur Koestler." *Atlantic* 178 (5): 132–36.

Omer-Sherman, Ranen. 2015. *Imagining the Kibbutz: Visions of Utopia in Literature and Film*. University Park, PA: Pennsylvania State UP.

Ozohu-Suleiman, Yakubu, and Sidin Ahmad Ishak. 2014. "Local Media in Global Conflict: Southeast Asian Newspapers and the Politics of Peace in Israel/Palestine." *International Journal of Conflict and Violence* 8 (2): 284–95.

Pearson, Sidney A. 1978. *Arthur Koestler*. Boston, MA: Twayne.

Pratiwi, Fadhila Inas, M. Aryo Rasil Syarafi, and Demas Nauvarian. 2022. "Israeli-Palestinian Conflict Beyond Resolution: A Critical Assessment." *Jurnal Ilmu Sosial Dan Ilmu Politik* 26 (2): 168–82. https://doi.org/10.22146/jsp.66935.

Pycińska, Magdalena. 2023. "Israeli and Palestinian Settler Colonialism in New Media: The Case of Roots." *Humanities* 12 (5): 124–136. https://doi.org/10.3390/h12050124.

Salt, Jeremy. 2021. "'Hebrew Tarzans' from Arthur Koestler's *Thieves in the Night* to Netflix and *Fauda*." *Journal of Holy Land and Palestine Studies* 20 (1): 45–61.

Saunders, Edward. 2017. *Arthur Koestler*. London: Reaktion Books.

Scammell, Michael. 2009. *Koestler: The Literary and Political Odyssey of a Twentieth-Century Skeptic*. New York: Random House.

Schinkel, Willem. 2009. "On the Concept of Terrorism." *Contemporary Political Theory* 8 (2): 176–98.

Singha, Arpita, and Uzma Anam Rahman. 2022. "Israel's Ambitions and Motives: Towards an Apprehensive State of Affairs for the Minorities." *World Affairs: The Journal of International Issues* 26 (3): 100–119.

Stahel, Lea, and Cristopher Cohrs. 2015. "Socially Shared Representations of the Israel Palestine Conflict: An Exploration among Conflict Outsiders." *Conflict and Communication Online* 14 (1): 1–19.

Stähler, Axel. 2015. "'Almost Too Good to Be True': Israel in British Jewish Fiction, Pre-Lebanon." In *The Edinburgh Companion to Modern Jewish Fiction*, edited by David Brauner and Axel Stähler, 237–52. Edinburgh: Edinburgh UP.

— — —. 2017. "'Historical Argument' or 'Cowboys and Indian'? Arnold Wesker's TV Screenplay of Arthur Koestler's *Thieves in the Night*." *Jewish Film & New Media* 5 (2): 199–226.

— — —. 2018. "Making Peace or Piecemeal? Arnold Wesker's Screenplay and Wolfgang Storch's TV Adaptation of Arthur Koestler's *Thieves in the Night*." *Jewish Film & New Media* 6 (1): 28–66.

Strelka, Joseph Peter. 2006. *Arthur Koestler: Autor – Kämpfer – Visionär*. Tübingen: Francke.

Turnberg, Leslie. 2021. *Mandate: The Palestine Crucible, 1919–1939*. Elstree: Vallentine Mitchell.

Vernyik, Zénó. 2016a. "'He Is Not English, He Is Not a Novelist; And How Far Is He Even Likeable?' On the Critical Reception of Arthur Koestler's *Thieves in the Night*." *Atlantis. Journal of the Spanish Association for Anglo-American Studies* 38 (1): 71–88.

— — —. 2016b. "'Straight out of the Button-Molder's Own Ladle': On the Complexity of Characters in Arthur Koestler's *Thieves in the Night*." *International Journal of English Studies* 16 (2): 25–43.

— — —. 2019. "'Exceptionally Feeble'? The Role of Circumcision in Arthur Koestler's *Thieves in the Night*." *Ostrava Journal of English Philology* 11 (2): 25–41.

— — —, ed. 2021. *Arthur Koestler's Fiction and the Genre of the Novel: Rubashov and Beyond*. Lanham, MD: Lexington Books.

Waisová, Šárka. 2009. *Současné otázky mezinárodní bezpečnosti*. 2nd ed. Plzeň: Aleš Čeněk.

Ward, Ian. 2008. "Towards a Poethics of Terror." *Law, Culture and the Humanities* 4 (2): 248–79.

Weßel, Matthias. 2014. "'Becoming Anglicized'? The Increasing Importance of English Characters in the Exile Novels of Robert Neumann and Arthur Koestler." *Moravian Journal of Literature and Film* 5 (2): 41–50.

Zwierlein, Anne-Julia. 2012. "The Biology of Social Class: Habit Formation and Social Stratification in Nineteenth-Century British *Bildungsromane* and Scientific Discourse." *Partial Answers* 10 (2): 335–60.

Contributors

Cornel Borit works as a senior academic librarian at the University Library of UiT — The Arctic University of Norway, having as main tasks research, teaching, and course development within Information Literacy and Open Science. He received a joint doctorate in migration literature from Charles University and the Free University of Berlin in 2023. His research focus has mainly been on mythicized representations of migrants and migration in nativist populist discourses in reception societies, as well as on the negotiation of cosmopolitan identities and spaces in literary texts. He has also authored articles and book chapters on migrants' and ethnic minorities' identity (re)configuration, representations of colonial relations in board games, and cultural expressions on AI and data imaginaries.

Vedran Ćatović is a comparative literature scholar. He specializes in humor in literature, especially satire and dark humor. He earned his PhD at the University of Michigan, dedicating his dissertation to satire as a form of social critique and philosophical wisdom in East and West Europe from the 18th to the 20th centuries. He works in English, French, Russian, and Bosnian, and has published articles on various authors in these languages. Vedran also taught language and literature in these languages at the University of Michigan. His current projects include publishing his study of satire as a book and writing about the state of comparative literature as a discipline within the humanities.

Rebecca Deluce is an independent scholar in Stockport, UK, with a degree in English Literature from the University of Huddersfield. She was a member of the editorial team of the 2017 Grist anthology of fiction by emerging artists, *I You He She It: Experiments in Viewpoint* and participated in the organization of the Huddersfield Literature Festival.

Cassandra Falke is professor of English literature at UiT — The Arctic University of Norway, where she also leads the Interdisciplinary Phenomenology Research Group. She has published around forty articles and book chapters and edited or authored six books. Her monographs include *Literature by the Working Classes: English Autobiography, 1820–1848* (2013) and *The Phenomenology of Love and Reading* (2017). *Global Human Rights Fiction*, her newest monograph, is forthcoming from Routledge (open access). Falke has received fellowships from the Fulbright Foundation (2013/2014) and Cornell University's Society for the Humanities (2024/2025).

Ana Belén Martínez García is associate professor of English at the University of Navarra (Pamplona, Spain), and collaborates with the Bonds, Creativity and Culture Group (VCC) at the Institute for Culture and Society (ICS). Her research focuses on human rights life narratives by young migrant activists. Her publications have been featured in journals such as *a/b: Auto/Biography Studies*, *Life Writing*, *Prose Studies*, and *Narrative*. She is the author of *New Forms of Self-Narration: Young Women, Life Writing and Human Rights* (Palgrave, 2020) and has co-edited *Representing 21st-Century Migration in Europe: Performing Borders, Identities and Texts* (Berghahn, 2022).

Sándor Klapcsik is assistant professor at the Technical University of Liberec, in the Czech Republic. He is a cross-border commuter who lives in Poland. His recent articles discuss liminality and acculturation in migrant and ethnic cinema. Before earning his PhD at the Cultural Studies Department of the University of Jyväskylä, Finland, he was a Fulbright-Zoltai Fellow at the University of Minnesota in the US and did long-term research at the University of Liverpool in the UK. His book *Liminality in Fantastic Fiction: A Poststructuralist Approach* was published in 2012.

Irene Alcubilla Troughton is a PhD candidate at Utrecht University within the NWO-funded project *Acting Like a Robot*, where she researches phenomenological and embodied cognition perspectives on movement in theatre and dance as a way to approach the design of human-robot interactions. She holds two RMA degrees in

Media, Art and Performance (Utrecht University), and Theory and Critique of Culture (Carlos III University, Madrid). Her previous work has been featured in robotic conferences and IEEE proceedings, such as *HRI (Human-Robot Interaction)* and *RO-MAN (Robot and Human Interactive Communication)*, as well as in *Performance Research, Journal of Applied Arts and Health, inVisible Culture, Etudes,* and *Body Space and Technology.*

Zénó Vernyik is assistant professor and head of the English Department at the Technical University of Liberec. He is the author of *Cities of Saviors: Urban Space in E. E. Cummings' Complete Poems, 1904–1962 and Peter Ackroyd's Hawksmoor* (Americana eBooks, 2015), the editor of *Arthur Koestler's Fiction and the Genre of the Novel: Rubashov and Beyond* (Lexington Books, 2021), and co-editor of *Crime and Detection in Contemporary Culture* (Americana eBooks, 2018) and *Words into Pictures: E. E. Cummings' Art across Borders* (Cambridge Scholars Publishing, 2007). At present, he is working on a monograph on Arthur Koestler's activist fiction.

Michaela Weiss is associate professor at the Department of English and American Studies at the Institute of Foreign Languages at the Silesian University in Opava, Czech Republic. She teaches courses on English and American literature, literary theory and criticism, and creative reading and writing. Her main areas of interest include American Jewish literature, graphic novels, and women's studies. She has published the monographs *Jewishness as Humanism in Bernard Malamud's Fiction* (2010) and *Tradice a Experiment: Americká židovská próza v období modernismu* (Tradition and Experiment: American Jewish Prose in the Modernist Era, 2020). She co-edited a series of conference proceedings *SILSE: Silesian Studies in English* (2010–2023) and a monograph series *Modern Approaches to Text Analysis* (2017), and *Text Analysis and Interpretation* (2019). She is currently working on the book *Community, Geography, and Language in the Works of Irena Klepfisz.*